Achieving Cultural Change in Networked Libraries

ACHIEVING CULTURAL CHANGE IN NETWORKED LIBRARIES

Edited by
Bruce J. Reid and William Foster

Gower

© Bruce J. Reid and William Foster 2000

Published by
Gower Publishing Limited
Gower House
Croft Road
Aldershot
Hampshire GU11 3HR
England

Gower
Old Post Road
Brookfield
Vermont 05036
USA

British Library Cataloguing in Publication Data
Reid, Bruce J.
    Achieving cultural change in networked libraries
    1. Library information networks
    I. Title II. Foster, William
    021.6'5

ISBN 0 566 08200 4

Typeset in 10 point Century Old Style by Bournemouth Colour Press, Parkstone and printed in Great Britain at the University Press, Cambridge.

Contents

List of figures		vii
List of tables		ix
Notes on contributors		xi
Acknowledgements		xvii
Introduction		
Bruce Reid		

1	Professionalism and the cultural legacy	1
	Bruce Reid	
2	Organizational models for managing academic information	15
	Bruce Reid	
3	Developments in technical services: cultural change and organizational management	27
	William Foster	
4	The Electronic Libraries Programme: a vehicle for academic cultural change	45
	William Foster	
5	Convergence: a review of the literature	63
	Alison Sutton	
6	Technical convergence and the response of the academic institution	77
	Alison Sutton	
7	The change agent	105
	Matt Holland	
8	Identifying and working with stakeholder perspectives	119
	Rob Lloyd-Owen	
9	Organizational culture: assessment, audit and change	137
	Bruce Reid and Helen Williams	

10 The special library environment   153
    Sharon Penfold
11 The TAPin model   173
    Kay Flatten
12 The impact of the TAPin project on LIS staff   191
    Helen Williams and Bruce Reid
13 Learning organization theory in the networked environment   207
    Linda Newall
14 Out of our past: understanding our communication environment   225
    Matt Holland
15 Change, research approaches and the future   243
    Bruce Reid, William Foster and Matt Holland

Glossary   249
Index   277

List of figures

8.1	Sample hexagon clusters of focus group participants' comments	124
11.1	The Venn diagram of the Boolean operator AND	175
11.2	Information skills for dealing with increasing information and complex technology	176
11.3	Factors affecting the take-up and use of IT-assisted information systems	177
11.4	A simplified version of the model for librarian use of the Internet	178
11.5	The TAPin model for networked information support by librarians	180
12.1	TAPin LIS impact questionnaire	192
13.1	Percentage responses reporting the importance and effectiveness of collaborative learning across [all] boundaries	212
13.2	Percentage responses reporting the importance and effectiveness of gaining a competitive edge by applying new technologies quickly and effectively	214
13.3	Percentage responses reporting the importance and effectiveness of converting management data into useful knowledge quickly and appropriately	216
13.4	Percentage responses reporting the importance and effectiveness of enabling every employee to feel that every experience provides him or her with a chance to learn something potentially useful	217
13.5	Changes to mission statements since 1995 by percentage	220
13.6	Changes in IT strategies since 1995 by percentage	221
14.1	The cultural response matrix	230
14.2	The communication matrix	234
14.3	The levels of use matrix	236
14.4	The communication strength matrix	238
14.5	The perceived value matrix	240

List of tables

1.1   Former presidents of the Library Association by sectoral
affiliation   6

2.1   Comparative scope of the information profession in *c.*1950
and *c.*2000   16

6.1   Coding and profiles of the convergence case studies   78

7.1   Comparison of change agent role versus emerging role   109

12.1   Responses from LIS staff to questions about TAPin's effect on
LIS   198

12.2   Frequency of use of networked resources by TAPin librarians   202

13.1   The overall importance and effective application of all
statements by organization   219

Notes on contributors

THE EDITORS

Bruce Reid is Senior Lecturer in the School of Information Studies Management at the University of Central England in Birmingham and Course Director of the Research Entry Masters in Information and Library Management. Following a practitioner career in university libraries in Britain and Australia, he was Academic Adviser (1995–98) to TAPin, one of the eLib projects on training and awareness in networks. He is a former Chair of the West Midlands Online User Group, as well as a former member of SCONUL Advisory Committee on Information Services and has taught numerous short courses on online information retrieval. He has published widely, mainly on service aspects of academic information.

William Foster is Senior Lecturer in the School of Information Studies at the University of Central England in Birmingham and School Head of Teaching, Learning and Quality Assurance of the MA/MSc Information and Library Studies. He is a former Academic Adviser to TAPin, one of the eLib projects on training and awareness in networks. He has previous experience of implementing library management systems and OPAC design, and currently teaches in the area of information retrieval, technical services and web design.

THE CONTRIBUTORS

Kay Flatten was formerly an Associate Professor in the United States where she taught in the Faculty of Education at Iowa State University. She has published two books and researched in the field of exercise and gerontology. She received her Masters in Library Science from the University of Indiana in 1992 and moved to the UK where she is a Chartered Librarian. She was Project Manager for the Electronic Libraries Project TAPin, and researched networked information support in six West Midlands academic libraries. She currently works as Information Technology Librarian, Monmouthshire County Council.

Matt Holland is an expert in the field of subject support within academic libraries. He has postgraduate qualifications in librarianship from Newcastle Polytechnic (now the University of Northumbria at Newcastle) and the University of Central England, and in Management Studies at Bournemouth University. He has worked at Bristol Polytechnic (now the University of the West of England) and Bournemouth University and is currently Subject Librarian for the School of Media Arts and Communication at the latter. His areas of interest are the impact of computers and networks on both students and academic staff.

Rob Lloyd-Owen lectures in information systems at the University of Huddersfield (half-time), and also works as an organizational development consultant. He had previously worked as an analyst and analyst programmer. In 1985 he was seconded from Huddersfield Polytechnic to manage, for the DES, a project to facilitate the integration of IT into the FE curriculum through staff and courseware development. Having then worked for BT as an IT Business Development Consultant and obtained a Masters in Innovation Studies (1995–96) from the University of Huddersfield, he was appointed, at the same University, as Project Manager for Phoenix, an eLib On Demand Publishing Project. There he was responsible for the evaluation of stakeholder reaction to prototypes developed by the Phoenix consortium. He maintains an interest in all aspects of innovation – the initiation and implementation of change – particularly, the human factors.

Linda Newall manages a project partnered with the City Council and the European Development Regional Fund at the University of Central England. This role, in part, follows on from the work of TAPin and as Faculty Web Coordinator and seeks to provide low-cost, focused consultancy and support in the area of ICT to small and medium-sized businesses in Birmingham. Linda also works with the Hysterectomy Association which aims to support a woman's choice through the provision of clear, impartial information.

Sharon Penfold is the Head of Computer Services and Internet Coordinator at the Society of Motor Manufacturers and Traders, having previously been SMMT's Technical Information Manager. Her career has mostly been spent in the special libraries sector, concentrating on the fields of engineering and business. She completed a part-time MBA in 1997, has a strong interest in the application of technology and is currently Editor of *Inform*, the Institute of Information Scientists' newsletter.

Alison Sutton is Librarian in the Department of Meteorology at the University of Reading. She has also worked in university libraries, most recently at the University of Wolverhampton. Her chapters in this book have been developed from research carried out for an MA dissertation at the University of Central England in Birmingham.

Helen Williams was a research assistant in the School of Information Studies at the University of Central England in Birmingham, working for TAPin during the exit phase of the project. She previously worked for the British Library and has undertaken a number of research projects. She is now working at Napier University.

Acknowledgements

We should like to acknowledge the professional support of the staff of the Library of the University of Central England and of Humanities Reading Room 2 of the British Library and the financial support of the Research Committee of the Faculty of Computing, Information, and English, UCE.

Thanks also to Kay Flatten for her confidence that TAPin had still more to deliver after the formal reports had been completed, and to Stephen Rawlinson for reading the manuscript and making many very helpful suggestions. Acknowledgement and thanks to Christine Barry and Bowker-Saur for permission to reproduce Figure 11.2, Christine Barry and Ablex Corporation for Figure 11.3.

Introduction

Bruce Reid

The first aim of this book is to explore the human aspects (individual and social) of using electronically networked academic and research information, with the intention of identifying the pre-existing cultural dispositions which inhibit optimum interaction between users and such electronic resources. The further purpose is to offer, through chapters on the historical inheritance of institutional culture, technological change, qualitative case studies, and theories of communication, dissemination of innovation, and learning organizations, some approaches, concepts, models and tools which will facilitate cultural and organizational change in this area.

The book has its origins partly in the TAPin project which was coordinated and managed from the Centre for Information Research and Training (CIRT) at the University of Central England in Birmingham (UCE) and partly in the research interests of academic staff in the School of Information Studies (UCE) and the work of two Masters research students supervised there contemporaneously with TAPin.

TAPin

TAPin (Training and Awareness Programme in Networks) was part of the Electronic Libraries Programme (eLib) funded by the Joint Information Systems Committee (JISC) of the Higher Education Funding Councils of England, Scotland, and Wales and the Department of Education, Northern Ireland. It sought to improve the quality of teaching and research staff output by identifying staff information needs and developing their information skills. It also aimed to emphasize to end-user academics, and thus ultimately to students, the benefits that can be gained by an understanding and awareness of networked information resources appropriate to specific disciplines. TAPin was a collaborative project based on a consortium of six West Midlands universities: a major traditional research university (Birmingham), a 'Robbins' or 'plate-glass' university with a high research rating (Warwick), a single-site technological university (Aston), and three 'new' universities – the multi-sited universities of Central England, Wolverhampton, and Coventry. The profiles of the universities and their internal structures vary enormously and, together, they represent much of the diversity to be found in the UK higher education sector. The project was coordinated by a steering group consisting of one key link drawn from library senior management in each participating institution, the research team, an eLib representative, and the editors acting as academic consultants.

TAPin focused on three particular disciplines: Life Sciences, Education and Law, with Business as a control group; it worked primarily through subject and systems librarians; and it was conducted in three stages:

1. **A skills and awareness audit**. This consisted of an IT infrastructure audit, an IT strategy survey, and an academic staff survey of all six institutions.
2. **Development of network awareness and skills**. This comprised a training needs assessment of subject and systems librarians, an audit of existing relevant training resources, a tailored training programme for TAPin librarians, development of a model for delivery of training by librarians to academic staff, and delivery of that model.
3. **An impact study**. After an interval of two years, this study repeated the audits of IT infrastructure, IT strategy, and academic staff at all six institutions, and added a survey of TAPin librarians. The aim was to assess the impact of the project.

The TAPin project has been formally reported in a First Annual Report (Flatten, 1996), an Interim Report (Flatten *et al.*, 1996), a Second Annual Report (Newall *et al.*, 1997), and the Impact Study (Flatten *et al.*, 1998). Some of the most significant findings, particularly on changed behaviour in academics and TAPin librarians have been presented in Reid *et al.* (1998). Three chapters in this book (Chapters 11, 12 and 13) draw directly on the TAPin project, but much of the rest has been greatly influenced by the TAPin experience.

MASTERS RESEARCH

In parallel with the two years of TAPin activity, two students on the Research Entry Masters in Information and Library Studies were pursuing research topics closely related both to TAPin and to what has emerged as the central theme of this book. Matt Holland (1997), investigating the abundant literature on the diffusion of innovation and the role of change agents and evaluating its suitability for improving our understanding of the librarian's role in introducing academics to networked information, found that TAPin provided some real-world data to illuminate his reflections. Alison Sutton (1997) carried out a set of qualitative case studies in universities in the Midlands and the South-east in order to elucidate the theory and practice of merger of libraries and computer centres as a response to technical convergence. Her subjects comprised representatives of most points of significance along the degree of merger continuum.

CULTURE CHANGE

Notwithstanding the difficulties involved in establishing and maintaining a user-friendly, up-to-date, reliable, and high-capacity network infrastructure, it is the cultural aspect of ubiquitous networked information that most of us, both as managers and individuals, find more difficult to cope with. This book quite deliberately takes a multiperspective approach to the issue. The cultural change demanded for the optimum exploitation of networked information is being sought in multifarious institutional micro-cultures. Chapter 1, therefore, sets out to trace how the varied history of educational, commercial, research, trade and voluntary institutions, and their differing responses to the gradual professionalization of information work, have shaped their individual cultures. Chapter 2 pursues this analysis in an attempt to identify how these differences in culture have been articulated in preferred structures for managing academic and research information in a range of environments.

Changes in organizational management have also been forced, however, by external pressures from technological change and by the nature and development of the library management and information systems marketplace. The nature of these changes and their effects are characterized by William Foster in Chapter 3. The eLib Programme, of which TAPin was a part, may be viewed as the principal UK institutional change agency in the field of networked library culture and it is from this perspective that the same author, in Chapter 4, considers the scene into which it emerged, follows the strands of its implementation and assesses its early cultural impacts.

One particularly important organizational change that has been a feature of the 1980s and 1990s is the merging of computing and library/information functions in organizations as a response to the technical convergence of their creation, storage, transmission and retrieval technology. In Chapters 5 and 6 Alison Sutton first reviews the very substantial US and UK literature on this phenomenon and draws out some of the main points of debate, as well as the principal theoretical constructs and models. She then proceeds to consider a number of case-study institutions of varied lineage in the Midlands and the South-east, sets them against the theoretical literature, and draws some conclusions about good practice in the light of real-world experience.

There is a longstanding and influential sociological literature on the subject of diffusion of innovation from the 1940s onwards. In Chapter 7 Matt Holland adapts the pre-existing theoretical models to fit the situation in academic library environments and develops an enhanced understanding of networked information use *as* innovation and insights into successful behaviours of academic librarians *as* change agents. In Chapter 8 Rob Lloyd-Owen, former Project Manager of the eLib Project Phoenix, examines the problem of change management in situations where there is a range of stakeholders involved. Drawing on his Phoenix experience, he emphasizes the role of reconciliation of these interest groups and resolution of their variant perspectives in creating a desired future. He also considers and recommends a number of practical ways of achieving this.

In a book about cultural change, it would be remiss not to review the relevant management and LIS professional literature for tools and approaches likely to be of practical help in networked libraries. Accordingly, in Chapter 9 Bruce Reid and Helen Williams consider this area with particular emphasis on culture audit and, drawing on TAPin experience, suggest some ways in which it might be used to facilitate reorientation to networked information.

Non-trivial networked information is used extensively outside the academic sector and therefore the special sector, given some attention in Chapters 1 and 2, is covered extensively in Chapter 10 by Sharon Penfold. She emphasizes the need for a proactive approach in the fast-changing special environment and the need to place the library and information services (LIS) at the heart of corporate objectives, winning battles of ownership for information-related initiatives by close attention to, among other things, change management, strategic planning and creating a physical environment consonant with networks and new ways of working.

The TAPin project sought to achieve its main objectives of training and awareness through a model collaboratively developed and used by project participants. In Chapter 11 Kay Flatten explains the theoretical basis of the model and describes its development and use. She goes on to suggest how it might be adapted to other situations and offers some comments on how it was received in the TAPin context. In Chapter 12 Helen Williams and Bruce Reid review the impact of the planned support provided by TAPin on the LIS and LIS staff of the participating institutions – in particular, on the relationship between them and their academic clients, on how they were perceived and on their own use of networked resources.

Learning organization theory has a special importance to all organizations in times of rapid change and, in Chapter 13, Linda Newall assesses its importance in the networked environment. The theory is set against real-world examples drawn from the strategic level audit carried out at the end of the TAPin project.

Responses to networked information by individual LIS differ considerably and, in Chapter 14, Matt Holland attempts a systematic typology of organizational responses, using an analysis of the communication environment and modes and levels of network use and resulting in a quadrant matrix of the adaptive library, the transforming library, the learning library, and the unresponsive library.

That change is currently inevitable is indisputable, and it must be managed if it is to lead to a desirable future, yet it is the range of cultural issues which are both most intangible and most intractable for information managers and users alike. This book will have succeeded in its main purpose if it increases understanding of some of the problems, provides a range of alternative, practical approaches to moving towards solutions, emphasizes the importance of research in underpinning soundly-based developments, and suggests some desirable topics and modes for future research.

REFERENCES

Flatten, K. (1996), *TAPin First Annual Report*, Birmingham: University of Central England.

Flatten, K. *et al.* (1996), *TAPin: Training & Awareness Programme in Networks: Interim Report*, Birmingham: University of Central England, Centre for Information Research and Training.

Flatten, K. *et al.* (1998), *TAPin: Training & Awareness Programme in Networks: The Impact Study*, Birmingham: University of Central England, Centre for Information Research & Training. http://www.uce.ac.uk/tapin/publications/impact.htm

Holland, M. (1997), 'An exploration of the relevance of theories concerning change agents in the published literature in providing an understanding of the process by which librarians introduce networked information to academics working in higher education', MA dissertation, Birmingham: University of Central England.

Newall, L. *et al.* (1997), *TAPin: Training & Awareness Programme in Networks: Second Annual Report*, Birmingham: University of Central England, Centre for Information Research and Training. http://www.uce.ac.uk/tapin/publications/2annual.htm

Reid, B.J. *et al.* (1998), 'Mapping the academic cultural response to networks: the TAPin experience', *New Review of Academic Librarianship*, **4**, 87–107.

Sutton, A. (1997), 'Convergence: the merger of libraries and computer centres in UK universities', MA dissertation, Birmingham: University of Central England.

1 Professionalism and the cultural legacy

Bruce Reid

INTRODUCTION

The library and information services (LIS) into which networked information is being steadily introduced are not all the same. Their variety has arisen out of their different histories from their creation to the present day, and the key to understanding this variation lies in appreciating the different paths that their development has followed. These can best be illuminated in terms of identifiable events, pressures, and imperatives shaping groups of cognate institutions. Library and information workers, moreover, are not all the same nor have their characteristics remained static through time: steady professionalization has brought about considerable changes in knowledge, skills, status and role.

Accordingly, this chapter pursues an analysis of the themes of the development of the information profession, the organizational history of LIS in groups of similar institutions and the interaction of the two in creating cultural difference. Its intention is to set out the landscape and to determine how it came to be as it is, with particular reference to culture.

ENVIRONMENTS AND USERS

Academic and research information is used most intensively in academic, industrial, commercial and government environments. However, the varying nature of the needs and resulting modes of information management in these different environments over time has given rise to a variety of organizational models. These need to be understood and appreciated since they help define the environments into which networked electronic information has been introduced.

Academic LIS comprise those of universities, polytechnics, colleges, research institutes and some learned and scholarly institutions, including national libraries. The subject range of their information interests is, as a group, unlimited, although, individually, their emphases have varied due to the rise and fall in favour of certain disciplines and the diversity of missions adopted or laid down by government. The principal user groups have remained constant in nature but have increased greatly in size in recent years – academic staff and researchers requiring everything from ancient manuscripts to the latest statistics and students needing course materials for study and project work.

The special LIS environment is, by its nature, more varied and more subject to the vagaries of market preferences, technological change and economic circumstances. Moreover, special LIS will vary in size and role depending on the nature of the organization they serve, as will their subject focus, which will be narrower but frequently deeper than LIS in the academic sector. For the purposes of this discussion, the UNESCO (1971) definition should suffice:

> … those [LIS] maintained by an association, government service, parliament, research institution (excluding university institute), learned society, professional association, museum, business firm, industrial enterprise, chamber of commerce etc or other organised group, the greater part of their collections covering a special field or subject.

PROFESSIONALISM

In an influential book Goode (1969) gave librarianship a place among the 'semi-professions' – occupations such as nursing, teaching and social work that aspire to professional status but do not possess the essential characteristics to achieve it. In an earlier, more detailed analysis of the profession in the US context Goode also provides a useful snapshot of a point in the continuing process of professionalization which may help us appreciate the timescale and nature of their changing role.

> Librarians, nurses, and social workers have spent much energy in trying to professionalize their occupations during the past several decades, but nursing will not become a profession, the other two have not yet become professions, and I am doubtful that the librarians will become full-fledged professionals. (Goode, 1961: 307)

Apart from the characteristics of a profession widely noted in the literature such as being autonomous, organized in professional associations, well paid, and occupying governing posts in society, Goode argues that two traits are sociologically central because they determine all the others:

● prolonged specialized training in a body of abstract knowledge
● a collectivity or service orientation.

Moreover, he argues, the principles of abstract knowledge must be applicable to concrete problems, and clients must believe this to be the case, and the service orientation must entail decisions based not on the professional's self-interest but on the client's need. Measured against these requirements in 1961, librarians were seen to fall short in the former trait rather than the latter.

> The librarian must organize and order the flow of information...must help others to locate it. ... The central gap is of course the failure to develop a general body of scientific knowledge bearing precisely on this problem ... (Goode, 1961: 312)

> Moreover, little if any of the current research in librarianship attempts to develop such general principles. ... even if in fact librarians had such a body of knowledge, the public does not know it, but rather views the librarian as a gatekeeper and the custodian of the 'stock room.' (Ibid.: 313)

> The fully fledged profession can claim the right to be final arbiter in problems under its jurisdiction by referring to its codified knowledge, over which its mastery is greater than that of any other group. (Ibid.: 315)

One final remark on future development, however, has resonances for us now that were not audible in 1961:

> The increasing flow of knowledge and the greater dependence of a technological society on our accumulation of knowledge will augment the economic bargaining power of librarians. (Ibid.: 319)

However Goode's analysis is regarded, it is certainly true that the professionalization of library and information work has taken a long time – longer in the UK than in some other countries and longer in some sectors of the activity than in others, as we shall see below. For the moment let us consider the beginnings of modern librarianship.

THE SCHOLAR-LIBRARIAN

The transitional figure of the scholar-librarian, precursor of professionalism, is an important one for understanding the cultural fault lines between type of library, type of activity and even type of knowledge that create and maintain variant subcultures into the electronic era. At the beginning of the twentieth century a certain Dr Leeper (1900) delivered a paper entitled *A Scholar-Librarian* about Henry Bradshaw, 'the late Librarian of Cambridge University ... who was as great a scholar as he was a librarian'. In the course of his presentation to the Library Association of Australasia he recommends the desirability of scholarship in the librarian but also foreshadows the need for improvements in the status quo.

> I would still contend that the more learning of all kinds the librarian has, so far is he better fitted for his office. ... In these days there are steadily increasing demands being made upon the librarian and they all necessitate a higher educational standard. ... Technical skill in all that relates to library administration is also essential. ... In Harvard University the librarian has the rank and status of a professor; and so he ought to have in every University. (Leeper, 1900)

It is interesting that Bradshaw, the subject of this encomium, vividly

3

demonstrated that 'reluctance to get too seriously organized' characteristic of the scholar-librarian in his reply to Edward Nicholson's invitation to the 1877 meeting of British librarians to establish an 'organisation for mutual exchange of ideas': 'I shall be very glad to take part in your Conference, and do what I can, and learn what I can, but I had very much rather not be a Vice-President, or anything of that kind' (Munford, 1976: 19). A much more recent use of the term 'scholar-librarian' occurs significantly in an obituary on Dietrich Borchardt; although Borchardt's professionalism is unquestioned the writer identifies the trends that make the dual role unlikely to survive: 'The growing professionalism of librarianship, particularly in relation to the explosion in information technology and the emphasis on modern theories of management, renders progressively unlikely the continuing existence of the so called scholar-librarian' (Bryan, 1998: 6).

PROFESSIONAL ASSOCIATIONS

The American Library Association (ALA) was set up in 1876 and, from the outset, published an official (if independent) periodical in the form of the *Library Journal*. The founding conference set up a committee structure to ensure continuity and set a precedent of the presentation of papers of a practical nature to encourage professional discussion. The first issue of the *Library Journal* carried a statement by Justin Winsor on the need for professional training, and the first library school, the School of Library Economy of Columbia College, opened in 1887 soon moving (with Dewey, its progenitor) to the State Library of New York at Albany. In 1890 library classes had begun at Pratt Institute in Brooklyn, in 1892 at Drexel Institute in Philadelphia, and in 1893 at the Armour Institute in Chicago (Thomison, 1978).

The UK Library Association (LA) was established in 1877 but relied at least initially on the (American) *Library Journal* as its official organ until 1882, after which it was followed in succession by *Monthly Notes of the Library Association of the United Kingdom, Library Chronicle, The Library* and, finally in 1899, by the *Library Association Record*. Officers and a committee including academic, public and special librarians were elected and a range of papers was presented over four days (Munford, 1976). The establishment and progress of professional education was not quite so straightforward as it had been in the United States. Examinations for three levels of professional certification (preliminary, second class and first class) were first held under the auspices of the Library Association in 1885. A revised syllabus in 1904 covered six subjects assessed by examination and essay, successful completion of which, along with three years' approved library experience, entitled the candidate to the Diploma of the Library Association. Despite the efforts of the Library Association to organize summer schools, classes and correspondence courses, most candidates had to work largely on their own. However, from 1902, courses in librarianship were offered in collaboration with the London School of Economics and in 1919, with financial support from the Carnegie Trust, the first full-time School of Librarianship was established at University College, London (Thompson, 1977: 115–16).

The Library and Information Association of Australia (LIAA) began in 1937 as the Australian Institute of Librarians and was incorporated by Royal Charter in 1963. Although the first library school was set up in 1960 at the University of New South Wales (Rayward, 1989: 126) and was recognized for the purposes of professional membership by the (then) Library Association of Australia (LAA) the following year (Library Association of Australia, 1961), examinations were still being set and marked by the Association itself until 1980 by which time accredited courses had become accessible in most parts of the country.

It can be seen from the examples above that institutionalized professionalism has been achieved only relatively recently. Moreover, the process and product have differed in the three countries discussed so far. In the United States, despite continuing tensions between TOL (type of library) and TOA (type of activity) interests represented by different divisions and associations (Brichford, 1991), the ALA has represented and drawn its officers from all walks of the profession. In Australia the relatively late institutionalization, coupled with the unusually well organized strength of the special sector led by the nationwide resources of the CSIRO (Commonweath Scientific and Industrial Research Organization) meant that all sectors were closely involved in the LIAA from the outset.

In the UK the Library Association was at least perceived to have had a strong public library bias until 1950 and perhaps later:

A substantial revision of the examination syllabus was brought into operation in 1950, the most significant changes being made in the new Final examination which ... made it possible at last to argue convincingly that the old public library bias had been substantially eliminated. (Munford, 1976: 267)

This perception resulted in less than total support from the academic and special sectors and indirectly to the setting up of Aslib (Association of Special Libraries and Information Bureaux) (1926) and the Institute of Information Scientists (IIS) (1958). An analysis of the affiliations of former presidents of the Library Association provides a rough indicator of orientation and core interests, which is good enough for trend analysis if we compare the first 100 years with the last 20 (see Table 1.1).

The decreasing role of non-professionals and increased participation of the Library Schools is a confirmation of increased professionalization. It can also be readily seen from the breakdown in Table 1.1 that special librarians, in particular, might have felt that their interests were not central to those of the LA. Emphasizing subject knowledge, particularly of a scientific or technical nature,

Table 1.1 Former presidents of the Library Association by sectoral affiliation

	1877–1976	1977–1998
Public libraries	28%	50%
National libraries	20%	9%
Academic libraries	14%	14%
Non-professional worthies	16%	5%
Aristocrats	13%	–
Private libraries	4%	–
Cross-sectoral background	3%	4%
Library Schools	1%	18%

and the theoretical side of sophisticated information retrieval emerging from the infant information science, they tended understandably to gravitate to Aslib or the IIS. Arguably this situation was only satisfactorily addressed in 1994 with the establishment of the Special Libraries Committee.

On the academic side, in 1950 there was friction between LA Council and its University and Research Section Committee over negotiations with the Association of University Teachers that did not insist on LA qualifications in addition to academic ones for certain posts. The Council passed a resolution declaring LA qualifications 'desirable', the Section committee resigned, but then resumed office after a contested election (Munford, 1976: 268). This disagreement was resolved in time with a broadening of the LA's own interests and examinations and then with the spread of postgraduate diplomas in Library Schools. However, this took place only after a period of some 20 years when higher degrees were considered to be an alternative (and sometimes a superior one) to professional qualification, leaving a persistent influence on the culture and organization of academic libraries.

The most recent factor to impact on this complex professional culture is information technology which has had a primarily unifying effect that the old professional structures are still struggling to catch up with. For example, no longer is online information retrieval the particular concern of the special or even academic sector, but the common currency of all information professionals. IT has also augmented the professional body of knowledge and contributed to professionalization. Graduates with a first degree in Information and Library Studies have always made successful careers in the special sector but used to find it difficult to gain entry to university career grades: 'The common preference for a good honours graduate from a conventional "scholarly" discipline has been justified by many' (Smethurst in Thompson, 1980: 69). There are signs that this is changing, particularly in posts with high IT skills requirements, such as systems librarians and webmasters. The impact of networked information in particular was reflected in answers given by subject librarians to TAPin (see Chapter 12) on whether academic staff perceptions of their role had changed:

'Our information retrieval skills are being acknowledged.'

'They view me now as a real contributor to the teaching and learning process.'

CULTURAL DIVERSITY AND ITS ROOTS

Currently UK universities are deemed to be equal but, for the purposes of comparison, the cultural substrate on which networked libraries are building must be divided into five categories: ancient foundations; civic; 'new' or plate glass; ex-colleges of advanced technology and ex-polytechnics. It is not always easy to remember that most of these groups were called 'new' at some time. For Herklots in *The New Universities* (1928), there were but two types – the old and the new – and, for the moment at least, quite enough of the latter:

> The ancient is collegiate: in the modern the unit is generally the university itself. The ancient is largely masculine. The modern is almost unrestrainedly co-educational. The ancient is withdrawn from the busiest commercial life. Most modern universities are lost in great centres of population. ... In view of the fact that universities are under-staffed and that few of them possess the funds greatly to improve their position, one cannot but deprecate the attempts that are being made to found new universities up and down the country. Local patriotism is largely responsible for this. ... It is a little anomalous that at the time when the University of Leeds is launching an appeal for £500,000 to erect new buildings, in the next Riding men should set to work to establish a wholly new University College at Hull. ... (Herklots, 1928: 4, 87–88)

The ancient foundations of Oxford and Cambridge (thirteenth century), St Andrews (1411), Glasgow (1451), Aberdeen (1495) and Edinburgh (1583) share characteristics inherited from their medieval foundation. Their basis is collegiate and consequently their control, wealth, staff, possessions, and physical fabric is decentralized in a way which makes visitors to Oxford, for example, ask 'Where is the University?'. Their conception as centres of excellence engendered by the medieval idea of *studium generale* has resulted in the accumulation of large, rich, old and often unique collections for which responsibility is often fragmented. These conditions are not necessarily propitious to the promotion of networked information, although they are sometimes the ones that stand to benefit most from the integrative possibilities of networked resources and computer-mediated communication (CMC). Oxford, for example, has almost 100 independently managed library units, and the Director of University Library Services has no managerial control over the college libraries because they are legally and administratively independent institutions. Since a committee of inquiry into library services in 1987, however, libraries at research, faculty, departmental, and college levels have participated through committees in advising on key policy areas. A director of University Library Services is now preparing proposals for an integrated library system for the University for the new millennium and, meanwhile, an associate director for staff development, user education, and liaison has been appointed. For this group of libraries a thoroughly holdings-oriented ethos is often combined with quite widely dispersed staff and collections.

The background against which the civic universities emerged is well delineated in a recent history of the University of Leicester:

> The second half of the nineteenth century in England and Wales saw a huge expansion in education at all levels. New universities appeared throughout the century, starting with 'London University' now University College London in 1827. In 1836 the University of London (by then consisting of University College and King's College) was granted the power to confer its own degrees, and in 1858 ... London degrees were opened to any candidate, anywhere in the world, who could fulfil the academic requirements laid down by the University. (Burch, 1996: 1)

The civic universities were all first established as university colleges, granting external degrees of the University of London for a period before gaining independence, and were founded in two waves: the first over the second half of the nineteenth century comprised Manchester (1851), Newcastle (1871), Leeds (1874), Bristol (1876), Birmingham (1880), Liverpool and Nottingham (1881), Sheffield (1887) and Wales (1893); the second, in the early decades of the twentieth century comprised Southampton and Reading (1902), Leicester (1918), Exeter (1922) and Hull (1927). One important outcome of this common origin was that, despite their roots in local civic initiative, a certain homogeneity emerged from this shared constraint. They taught a quite similar range of subjects (arts and the three medieval professions supplemented by science, engineering, economics, business and, where appropriate, agriculture); embraced the residential model, but in the main without the collegial structure; adopted similar modes of governance comprising a council, senate, and vice-chancellor; and guaranteed one another's standards through a system of external examiners. This group's number and relative longevity have led its being regarded to some extent as the norm against which higher education innovations have been measured. Much of their political power has resided at the level of the individual department often wielded by the head or, in earlier times, the so-called god-professor and, for the vice-chancellor, managing them has often been a matter of skilfully obtaining consensus. In many institutions it has been felt necessary to create a non-professorial staff association. Achieving an overall information and library strategy in such institutions has often been hampered by the existence of large pockets of decentralized power.

The first university to be set up with the power to grant its own degrees from the outset was Keele in 1949. This marked the beginning of a national realization that a number of factors were working together to make growth in educational provision necessary: an increase in the birth rate after the Second World War, a backlog of those who had missed out on higher education because of the war, an increasing desire among young people to take up higher education, and the need for a more highly educated and trained population to help the UK maintain its position in the world. To coincide with the expected 'bulge' in demand in addition to increasing the capacity of existing universities, the government approved the establishment of seven genuinely new 'plate-glass' universities opening in the mid-1960s, as follows: Sussex (1961), East Anglia and York (1963), Essex, Lancaster and Warwick (1964), and Kent at Canterbury (1965). The Robbins Report (University Grants Committee, 1963) confirmed the need for these new foundations, but revised upwards the pre-existing student target numbers, at the same time recommending the upgrading to universities of colleges of advanced technology (CATs) and Scottish central institutions (discussed below) and one further new foundation of Stirling (1964).

The 'plate-glass' universities began with all the advantages that a fresh start can give and, by their nature, attracted many innovative and adventurous staff. They were able to move more quickly in some areas than the older universities simply because it is easier to create new structures and methods than it is to change old ones. New thinking in educational philosophy and methods brought change to the curriculum, teaching and academic organization. There was a renaissance in seminar and tutorial use, a broadening of the undergraduate curriculum, and a new emphasis on interdisciplinary studies resulting in units called schools of studies which were more broadly based than traditional departments. Sussex was a good example of this:

> Suffice it to say here that much of our thinking was characterised by the conviction that our undergraduate courses and academic organisation should provide for the full exploitation of interdisciplinary studies. Hence the formation of Schools of Studies rather than Departments, and the commitment to 'Contextual' studies on the Arts and Social Studies side of the University and to the 'Major/Minor' degree structure on the Science side. (Blin-Stoyle, 1986: xiv)

The methods of governance of 'plate-glass universities' also tended to have more democratic structures than their predecessors, and Sussex went so far as to commission a report from McKinsey and Company into its government, organization and administrative methods which was the first of its kind in a British university and, in 1967, resulted in substantial constitutional changes

9

(ibid.: 15). This group of universities also immediately entered into the public domain in a way not common in the past, and tended to arouse wide interest and a sense of ownership in the communities in which they were established. They further benefited from being sited on adequate land space secured for their planned future growth, although the networked future makes it likely that they were the last generation that need concern itself unduly about this. York, Kent and Lancaster chose to follow the earlier collegial model. On the library and information front most university librarians seem to have been given considerable freedom to experiment with new staffing structures, new techniques, and building up new collections, which was probably an advantage, since they needed to create research collections from scratch and at considerable speed with inadequate start-up finance from the University Grants Committee (UGC). Fortunately, in the early years these institutions gave their libraries an above average share of their recurrent grant and, with few exceptions, did not indulge in the expensive luxury of departmental or college libraries. With hindsight it may appear that the plate-glass universities were established slightly too early to benefit from the culture change from holdings to access, which would have made the transition to networks easier. As it was, although great emphasis was put on a service orientation rather than a custodial one, collection-building was given a very high priority, and the growth in collections was remarkable in the context of the short timescale and limited finance. The use of a subject-specialized staff structure in every library at the outset and the considerable importance accorded to classification to the extent of using mixed and in-house schemes in three of them (Reid, 1973) are further indicators of a subject expert culture in these libraries as a group.

The ex-CATs identified for university status by Robbins had had their beginnings in a variety of institutions such as polytechnics, polytechnic institutes, technical schools and technical colleges and had progressed towards providing advanced-level technical education. Aston, Bath, Bradford, Brunel, Chelsea, City, Loughborough, Salford, Surrey and the University of Wales Institute of Science and Technology received their charters in 1966–67, after Strathclyde, two years earlier, in 1964. Unlike the plate-glass universities, the ex-CATs were not given grants earmarked for collection development, presumably because they had existing collections. However, these were technical college libraries and the efforts of their librarians to enhance them into research collections commensurate with university status were not always helped by long-serving staff who continued to regard them as adequate. A further provision problem arose from the fact that competition for students in the 1970s led most ex-CATs to diversify their subject range from the original science, technology, social science and management into such areas as law, literature, modern languages, European studies and so on. Against this background, the percentage of total university expenditure devoted to the library between 1965 and 1974 was 3–4 per cent for ex-CATs against 5–7 per cent for plate-glass universities (Statistics of Education, 1965–1974). Furthermore, cancellations from already slim periodicals subscription lists in ex-CAT libraries continued to be reported throughout the 1970s and later. One result of this was a heavier than usual reliance by these libraries on what is now the British Library Document Supply Centre in Boston Spa, and they became amongst the heaviest users of that service in the country. The long-term result was that this group of libraries developed what was in fact an access culture long before it became fashionable to talk about it and certainly before computer networks were widely available to support it. At that time it manifested itself primarily in a heavy emphasis on access tools such as abstracting and indexing services (which were often given purchase priority over primary materials) and online information retrieval services and other information services, including current awareness and selective dissemination of information (Vincent and Seals, 1975), all of which were backed up with quick and effective document delivery.

The polytechnics (31 in England, six equivalents in Scotland and one in Wales) were established mainly between 1969 and 1971. The policy intention was to provide degree-level courses which would not only meet the shortfall in university places for sixth-form applicants, but also provide mainly vocationally-oriented practical education to full-time, part-time and sandwich students focusing on the local community and industry. Typically they were based on amalgamations, sometimes over considerable periods of time, of a number of tertiary colleges in a particular geographical area. For example Birmingham Polytechnic (now the University of Central England in Birmingham) was formed in 1971 out of five colleges: Birmingham College of Art, Birmingham School of Music, Birmingham College of Commerce, South Birmingham Technical College, and North Birmingham Technical College. In 1975, as part of national reorganization of teacher education, the City Council added to the Polytechnic three further colleges: Anstey College of Physical Education, Bordesley College of Education and the City of Birmingham College of Education. In 1988 Bournville College of Art merged with the Polytechnic's Faculty of Art and Design and in 1989, along with all other Polytechnics, Birmingham Polytechnic became a corporation with charitable status, independent of the local education authority. It achieved university status in 1992 when all polytechnics were empowered to adopt the title of university and has expanded once more in 1995 with the absorption of the Birmingham and Solihull College of Nursing and Midwifery and the West Midlands School of Radiography.

The role of the polytechnics – now 'new' universities – has been the subject of lively discussion ever since their creation by Tony Crosland in the mid-1960s. Donaldson argued that the polytechnics' practice had drifted considerably away from the original policy objectives for their establishment specifically that their local engagement was 'limited and declining'; that there was increasing emphasis on 'intellectual and conceptual rather than practical course contents'; that economic forces were working against part-time and sandwich courses; and that 'the student body of at least some of the polytechnics [was] as high in social class composition as [was] that of the universities'. (Donaldson, 1975: 15). He further quotes Burgess and Pratt (1970: 176) with approval:

> In the absence of specific efforts to prevent it we should expect the polytechnics to begin shedding their part-time and thus working-class students, to turn their backs on their technical college traditions and to become mere copies of the universities. (Ibid.: 176)

In view of the fact that it has taken barely 20 years for them to *become* universities, it is difficult not to concede that there has been at least some movement in the direction of 'embourgeoisement' predicted here.

Recent history ensures that polytechnics are generally large, multi-sited and with vestiges of local authority bureacracy and ethos, all of which leaves them in search of a clear corporate identity and unified culture. However the multi-sited nature of polytechnics and their small, modern book stock encouraged polytechnic libraries to develop fully integrated library management systems with online catalogue access before most of the traditional universities. In addition, this sector has no shortage of vigour, and often entrepreneurial flair, although there is little of the collegial in management styles. Writing particularly about the 'new' universities, Warren (1994: 48) regrets 'the loss of collegiate authority over educational policy and resourcing issues, the increasing alienation of lecturers from their own knowledge and personal standards of quality, and the replacement of peer-group control and autonomy by top-down managerial control'. He argues, using Durkheim's distinctions between mechanical solidarity (community) and organic solidarity (contractual association), that the medieval university is collegiate, the modern university a professional bureaucracy, and the ex-polytechnics hybrid professional/machine bureaucracies. He further concludes that new managers, often from non-academic backgrounds and anxious to respond to external pressure for cooperation with industry and the state, are exercising a degree of social control formerly wielded by the LEAs which is driving ex-polytechnics towards the machine bureaucracy with its 'typical dysfunctional effects'. Whatever view one takes of this as a general theory for the ex-polytechnic sector, it is difficult not to agree that some of the most deleterious effects of the stresses and strains put on UK higher education in recent years have appeared in this sector. Despite this, however, ex-polytechnics have led the way in delivering a wide range of courses to an increasing number of students, especially mature students and part-timers. Furthermore, they are also now undertaking, albeit through necessity, more research, much of which is highly relevant to the professions.

Applied to the TAPin institutions, the categories described in this section would identify one civic university (the University of Birmingham), one plate-glass (the University of Warwick), one ex-CAT (Aston University) and three ex-polytechnics (Coventry, Central England, and Wolverhampton). It should be noted here, however, that such detail was inappropriate for the micro-analysis involved in that project which categorized the ex-polys as 'new' and the remainder as 'old'.

THE SPECIAL LIBRARY SECTOR

As noted at the beginning of this chapter, special LIS are more varied, fragmented and subject to radical change in response to market conditions, particularly in the industrial and commercial sector. In the 1960s English Electric had, arguably, the finest technical LIS in the country. Now it would be towards the pharmaceutical industry that one would look for some of the best examples (Sherwell, 1997). Professionally this sector may look to the Institute of Information Scientists, Aslib, or the Library Association Industrial and Commercial Libraries Group, but it will very frequently use a peer group network either informally as in the case of insurance company LIS or formally as is the case with the Association of Information Officers in the Pharmaceutical Industry (AIOPI).

Research associations have had to meet external change in the form of radically altered customer requirements – RAPRA with their globally marketed databases and TWI in offering their image database via the World Wide Web. Government department libraries are vying to establish quality websites spurred on by the government's avowed commitment to open government and freedom of information. Desktop access to information both from intranets and external networks has become so widely anticipated that it has transformed special LIS, setting up new internal tensions, but also creating new opportunities and (some may argue) a new discipline of 'knowledge management'. These dynamic issues are explored with other elements of the special LIS environment in Chapter 10.

REFERENCES

Blin-Stoyle, R. (ed.) (1986), *The Sussex Opportunity: A New university and the Future*, Brighton: Harvester Press.
Brichford, M. (1991), 'The context for a history of the American Library Association', *Libraries and Culture*, **26**(2), 348–56.

Bryan, H. (1998), 'Dietrich Borchardt, scholar-librarian', *Australian Library Journal*, **47**(1), 6–8.

Burch, B. (1996), *The University of Leicester*, Leicester: University of Leicester.

Burgess, T. and Pratt, J. (1970), *Policy and practice: The Colleges of Advanced Technology*, Harmondsworth: Penguin.

Clapp, B.W. (1982), *The University of Exeter: A History*, Exeter: University of Exeter.

Donaldson, L. (1975), *Policy and the Polytechnics: Pluralistic Drift in Higher Education*, Farnborough: Saxon House.

Goode, W.J. (1961), 'The librarian: from occupation to profession?', *Library Quarterly*, **31**(4), 306–20.

Goode, W.J. (1969), 'The theoretical limits of professionalization' in A. Etzioni, (ed.), *The Semi-professions and their Organization*, New York: Free Press.

Herklots, H.G.G. (1928), *The New Universities: An External Examination*, London: E.Benn.

Leeper, A. (1900), *A Scholar-Librarian*, Adelaide: Government Printer.

Library Association of Australia (1961), Board of Examiners Minutes of meeting, Resolution 14/1961, unpublished.

Munford, W.A. (1976), *A History of the Library Association 1877–1977*, London: Library Association.

Rayward, W.B. (1989), 'Metcalfe, John Wallace' in H. Bryan (ed.), *Australia's Library, Information and Archives Services: an Encyclopedia of Practice and Practitioners*, Volume 2, Sydney: ALIA, 126.

Reid, B.J. (1973), Trends in recataloguing and reclassification in British university libraries, *Research in Librarianship*, **4**(24), September, 183–93.

Sherwell, J. (1997), 'Special sector: reaching for the virtual library', *Library Association Record*, **99**(7), July, 376–77.

Statistics of Education (1965–1974), *Universities*, London: HMSO.

Thomison, D. (1978), *A History of the American Library Association*, Chicago: American Library Association.

Thompson, J. (1977), *A History of the Principles of Librarianship*, London: Bingley.

Thompson, J. (1980), *University Library History: An International Review*, London: Bingley.

UNESCO (1971), 'Recommendation concerning the International Standardization of Library Statistics', in *Records of the General Conference*, 16th Session, Paris 12 October–14 November 1970, VI Resolutions (Record no. 114046), 143–48.

University Grants Committee (1963), *Committee on Higher Education. Higher Education: Report* (Robbins Report), London: HMSO.

Vincent, I. and Seals, J. (1975), 'A manual current awareness service at the University of Aston', *Aslib Proceedings*, **27**(6), June, 247–61.

Warren, R.C. (1994), 'The Collegiate Ideal and the Organisation of the New Universities', *Reflections*, 6 August, 39–55.

2 Organizational models for managing academic information

Bruce Reid

INTRODUCTION

The organizational model chosen by an LIS for managing academic information is informed by cultural assumptions about the nature of information, of information staff, of infomation users, and about the relationships between them. The chosen model, in turn, creates, strengthens or perpetuates the cultural assumptions it embodies. This chapter explores the principal models used (defined primarily by the subject versus function expertise polarity) and their cultural consequences in interaction with professionalism.

THE ROLE OF THE INFORMATION PROFESSIONAL

In higher education institutions (HEIs) the role of the information professional has attracted a great deal of attention since the impact of IT has apparently transformed it, but the organizational model within which that role is played has been the subject of serious discussion and experiment for most of the twentieth century. The core tasks and obligations may, nevertheless, still be matched for the mid-century and end-of-century environments, even if the language to describe them is different because of changes in modes of information resource storage, detection, retrieval and delivery. The recent neologism RADAR (resource access detection acquisition and retrieval) provides as good a framework as any for comparative analysis (see Table 2.1). To these should be added the core responsibility of advice and teaching, properly appearing in both columns, but probably assuming an increased importance in a time of rapid change. It is also important to acknowledge that, in today's information environment, the acquisition responsibility takes on a new complexity and demands a group of related research, financial and managerial skills further discussed by Reid and Rafferty (1996) and well summarized by Corrall:

Purchase decisions may involve cost/benefit analysis of the relative cost-effectiveness

15

Table 2.1   Comparative scope of the information profession in *c.*1950 and *c.*2000

	c.1950	*c.2000*
Access	Ensuring and using bibliographic control	Ensuring and using bibliographic control, connectivity, appropriate hypertext links, and bookmarking of appropriate uniform resource locaters (URLs)
Detection	Finding, identifying and assessing relevant resources for routine use enquiries or current awareness	Finding, identifying and assessing relevant resources for routine use enquiries or current awareness
Acquisition	Purchase and transport	Purchase and transport or downloading or password provision
Retrieval	Internal classification, subject indexing and physical arrangement	Internal classification, subject indexing and physical arrangement. Integration of chosen networked resources into internal retrieval tools, e.g. OPAC, intranet.

of print versus electronic resources, standalone versus networked, locally mounted versus nationally or regionally networked. The information professional will need to use techniques of investment appraisal and life cycle costing, as well as negotiating and influencing skills for striking the best deal with suppliers. (Corrall, 1994: 25)

Finally, it is interesting to note that one increasingly significant effect of the pervasiveness of networked information is that distinctions between assuring access and fabricating internal re-retrieval mechanisms for local objects are beginning to break down.

TYPES OF ORGANIZATIONAL MODEL

The essential question on which all construction of, and discussion about, organizational models for delivering the above services turns is how to apply the principle described in economic theory as the division of labour. In economic terms this principle allows the greatest advantage to be taken of the individual's natural abilities and training and the maximum benefit to be made of systematic, mechanized or automated work practices, but it is limited by three factors: the suitability of the work to subdivision, the extent of the market and the risk of counterproductive effects because of boredom. In academic LIS the following traditional work has been done across a range (often a very wide range) of subject areas: stock selection; liaison with academic departments; acquisitions;

cataloguing and classification; shelf arranging; borrowing services; document delivery; enquiry and advisory work; literature searching and current awareness services; and user education. The question to be settled for the organizational structure in any large academic library is the degree to which staff are assigned to working in these important functional areas of professional work, as against working in a range of these activities within a particular subject or subjects with which they may be familiar, or indeed in which they may themselves be expert.

In management terms this is an important question. There is a substantial and thoughtful professional literature on the subject and two major surveys of the situation with regard to UK universities (excluding ex-polytechnics) have been drawn on for this chapter (Woodhead and Martin, 1982; Martin, 1996). However, in the context of this book, the way in which the organizational question is resolved is important as a cultural indicator rather than as measure of operational efficiency or effectiveness. That it is a culture-sensitive issue is suggested by the fact that other Anglo-Saxon countries (notably Australia and the United States) have shown a published interest in what Scrivener (1974), with a slight implication of kinkiness, calls 'British practices', but no inclination to adopt them (for a primarily negative US stance, see Johnson, 1977; Wilkinson, 1983; Hay, 1990), whereas there has been interest and practice in some African countries (see Bandara, 1986; Avafia, 1983). The close analogy between the British subject organizational approach and German *Fachreferenten* (see, for example, Ostrem, 1966) is no accident (see below) and furnishes further evidence for cultural significance. Moreover, if any factors are likely to provide a touchstone of organizational culture, then attitudes to professionalism and the nature of knowledge and expertise are likely to be among them. This may become true *a fortiori* if some post-modernist analyses of knowledge in education find long-term acceptance. The 'blurb' of a recent book entitled *The End of Knowledge in Higher Education* succinctly formulates the current dilemma:

> There is no longer an easily identifiable foundation for our knowledge of the world and ourselves. The pre-eminence of science in providing objective knowledge is increasingly questionable. Post-modernism has attacked the idea of social improvement brought about by rational thought. The utilitarian ethos of competency, with its emphasis on skills, performance criteria and measurable outcomes, has begun to take hold in universities. The concept of higher education, based upon the acquisition of knowledge and understanding, is a precarious one in the light of these shifts of thought and belief. (Barnett and Griffin, 1997)

The information professional, as knowledge engineer, might be thought to face a daunting task in this situation of epistemological confusion. However, the role might well prove to be one of vital ally to the academic, if the conclusions of the book about a knowledge strategy for universities are to be pursued:

> Academics rest their legitimacy on their knowing capacities. But now, these capacities

17

have to be continually reasserted, secured and legitimated in and by the wider world. Academics are epistemologists; but the modern world requires that they be practical epistemologists. (Ibid.: 179)

To return to organizational models, the emphasis on a subject- rather than function-oriented approach to organization in British university libraries 'owes a great deal historically to R.W. Chambers, who introduced at University College, London something of the German Seminar Library approach' (Reid, 1968: 24) and to Richard Offor at the University of Leeds, whence it spread to a number of other university libraries in a somewhat dynastic-like fashion well described by Smethurst (1980: 65–66) and Naylor (1980: 236–37). However, the way in which the concept was implemented in different institutions was very varied and can be best understood by reference to the five-category classification used by Martin and Woodhead, based on that proposed by Scrivener (1974), but with refinements.

1. Functional

All functions of the library are performed on a centralized (i.e. non-subject) basis rather than some of them being subdivided among several senior members of staff (that is assistant librarians and above) by subject.

2. Dual

Some members of the senior staff perform certain functions of the library which have been subdivided among them by subject. Other members of the senior staff perform the remaining functions (i.e. those which are run on a centralized basis).

3. Hybrid

Some or all members of the senior staff perform certain functions of the library which have been subdivided among them by subject. Each member of staff who has such 'subject' duties is also responsible for one or more of the remaining functions (that is, those which are run on a centralized basis).

4. Three-tier

All or most of the senior members of staff perform functions which have been assigned to them on a subject basis. The remaining functions (that is, those performed on a centralized basis) are the responsibility of a middle grade of staff, commonly senior library assistants, supported by junior assistants and clerical staff.

5. Subject divisional

There are subject teams consisting of both senior and supporting staff, each team being located in, and responsible for, a physically separate portion of the central library collection. Underlying this arrangement there will normally be a supporting structure performing those functions which are centralized. (Woodhead and Martin, 1982: 98; Martin, 1996: 160–61)

A number of interesting changes emerge from Martin's comparison of numbers of libraries following each model in 1982 and in 1996: those libraries that feel able to escape a purely functional arrangement seem to be doing so; there is considerable movement away from both hybrid and three-tier models; and there is a strong movement towards the dual model which now accommodates some 63 per cent of respondents.

These quantitative results are certainly significant in themselves, but it is the qualitative data reported from these surveys and elsewhere and articulating attitudes to policy, practices and reasons for change that convey a sense of cultural context. In 1982 a certain degree of unease was expressed by respondents with the term 'subject specialist' and a variety of alternative terms were reported to be in use, including the widely used 'subject librarian'. By 1996 about 50 per cent of respondents used the term 'subject librarian', but a number of new terms had appeared.

1982 alternatives	*1996 (new terms only)*
subject librarians	faculty librarians
subject responsibility	subject support officers
School librarians	academic librarians
liaison officers	link librarians
subject assistants	information librarians
subject consultants	information specialists
reference librarians	
liaison librarians	
readers' advisers	

These listed terms certainly display a proper caution about pretending to specialist subject knowledge that their bearer may not have, and the new terms with their emphasis on 'information' and 'support' may well be attempts to describe the new role of the information professional described by Fielden (John Fielden Consultancy, 1993: 26) and elsewhere.

ACADEMIC AND UNIVERSITY LIBRARIES

The main differences in the models used for the survey lie in the *degree* to which functional operations are separately performed on a subject basis and the debate has centred on where on the continuum is the best place to be. It is also this debate that is most interesting culturally. We have seen in Chapter 1 that, for a significant period from the 1950s to the 1970s senior appointments were made to many British university libraries without a requirement for professional qualifications. However, it would be misleading to suggest that they were completely discounted; they were merely regarded as one among several useful qualifications and not necessarily the most important.

I was given career advice by a university librarian in 1967 to the effect that a first degree was not enough and that you needed a higher degree, professional qualifications or to be a poet or something! This period coincided with the development and/or introduction of subject specialist structures into some civic and most of the 'plate-glass' universities which placed a premium on the depth of subject knowledge denoted by the doctorate. At its best, subject specialization provided a university department with a scholar in the library who could select materials, classify them, build up their collection and offer bibliographic help and advice as well as, if not better than, they themselves and might, in addition, contribute to their research programme. Understandably, the collection-building aspect was especially attractive to the 'plate-glass' universities and to those 'civics' that were establishing entirely new subject departments from scratch. One of the most vigorous proponents of subject specialization was the late W.L. Guttsman who used it very successfully at the University of East Anglia to build up entirely new collections.

Thompson (1975) claims to have built up, as English Literature specialist at East Anglia, 'one of the best and least accidental collections in that field'. This thoroughgoing subject specialist structure corresponds to Martin's three-tier category and is concisely described by Taylor:

> To 'learned librarians', enjoying parity of esteem and rewards with their teaching colleagues, would be delegated the principal part in selecting library material. They would have a consultative role in administration, but non-graduate staff would run the functional departments on a day-to-day basis and act as cataloguers. (Taylor, 1998: 267)

It should be added that, in many cases, the non-graduate staff in this model would be professionally qualified so, viewed from one perspective, this could be seen as the return of the scholar-librarian after professionalization had taken place.

Even during a period when the subject specialist structure was most widely in favour there were sceptical voices such as those of Evans (1979) and Lester (1979) at a SCONUL Information Services Group Conference on Subject Specialisation into the 1980s. Presaging a term that would be widely used as a job title in the 1980s and adopted for 'subject librarian' at Aston University Library in 1986, Lester held:

> ... our libraries increasingly need '*information* specialists' and not '*subject* specialists'. An academic must find in his or her subject specialist librarian, first and foremost someone with a wide and competent knowledge of librarianship; who knows, or at least knows where to find out, about all those specialised areas of librarianship that the academic is ignorant of. (Quoted in Woodhead and Martin, 1982: 102)

It is clear from the Martin surveys cited above that a kind of *de facto* consensus has settled in academic libraries on the desirable degree of subject specialization (in the absence of other overriding factors such as size or physical separation) and that this is represented by the dual model. My observation also suggests that some degree of accord has been achieved in practice on the functional areas to which division by subject should best be applied or – more easily enumerated – best *not* applied. From the list of functions given in Table 2.1 those that generally remain firmly centralized are acquisition (of non-networked materials), cataloguing and classification, and loan and document delivery services. However, the cultural legacy of attitudes to knowledge formed by these historical variations in structure should not be underestimated, and they are certainly among the factors slowing down the adoption of newer models.

Martin identifies a number of key factors for the move away from his three-tier organizational model: increasing size and scale of operations; increasing professionalization; decreasing importance of book selection; and, significantly, 'the growth in information technology [which] had brought in a different style of librarianship' (Martin, 1996: 162). These are also the principal shapers of new organizational models. From the literature, and from observation, it is possible to discern some salient trends in these new models which also apply in the ex-poytechnics excluded from the Martin survey, but it would be overstating the case to suggest that there is a consensus on how to respond to what is a turbulent, if not chaotic, environment. There is a move towards flatter, less hierarchical structures and to teamworking in which front-line staff are in more direct communication with the decision-making process. This often takes the form of school or faculty teams comprising a range of staff levels and, in merged institutions, a range of professional expertise and background. There is sometimes an element of 'matrix management' in which formal and informal structures and links cut across one another and the individual wears a variety of different hats depending on the service need being addressed. An important factor is the proliferation of new tasks associated with mediating electronic resources: identification, choice of delivery mode, mounting, licensing, interface selection or creation, platform advice, promotion and training to name but a few. They seem to have determined that, in many LIS, subject knowledge as such has become secondary and subject responsibility has become what it always has been in many environments – a convenient means of assigning limited areas within which knowledge of resource need and availability can be developed to a high degree of compass and depth. This is certainly the direction in which Fielden thought that the subject librarian role would develop further, embracing:

- course planning and design
- tuition on subject resources and how to access them
- academic audit and quality assurance in the LIS dimension

- support of academic staff in awareness and best use of electronic and hard-copy resources
- tailored navigational support in accessing relevant electronic text and databases worldwide
- production of resource guides in a variety of formats (John Fielden Consultancy, 1993: 26).

THE SPECIAL LIS

In Chapter 1 of the first edition of the *Handbook of Special Librarianship and Information Work* (1955) Wright says of special libraries 'They supply information rather than material, draw attention to its existence and so evoke the demand for it. This calls for special techniques connected with the filing and dissemination of information' and of the Information Officer that when he is also a technical specialist '[he] may go so far as to interpret for the technical staff of his parent organization the information contained in the literature'. This information emphasis is usually achieved through a specialist collection of materials fully catalogued, classified and subject-indexed often with the use of an in-house thesaurus and sometimes involving analytical indexing of content, even of journals. This will often provide the basis for current awareness and selective dissemination of information services for users, and sometimes even an abstracting service. The latter is more likely if the LIS is a centre of excellence in its field and is thus able to defray the expense by selling it externally. The Rubber and Plastics Research Association and its *RAPRA Abstracts* is a good example of this.

Special LIS were also amongst the earliest and most creative users of online information retrieval systems. BP for example had the Chemical Abstracts Service mounted on its in-house mainframe computer long before distributed searching became available by packet switching. It is therefore not surprising that it was to special libraries that academic libraries looked for example and inspiration at the end of the 1960s when there was a general feeling that the latter needed to improve their information services and become more proactive (MacKenna, 1980: 96–97). In the context described above, it is understandable that many information officers in the past have had subject knowledge of direct relevance to the organizations in which they worked and also skills in abstracting that were not required in many other areas of the information profession. Furthermore, users of most special library services in the past were accustomed to a culture in which the information they required was provided for them on request, rather than their having to find it for themselves. In his introduction to *The End-user Revolution*, Biddiscombe (1996) explains that in the book's chapters '[libraries] from the academic sector are in the majority ... because it is in this sector that the empowerment of the end-user is most evident, so far'. However, the nature of this impact of networked information in special libraries has also been far-reaching, though perhaps less homogeneous and evenly spread, because of the absence of a common catalyst such as the universities' Joint Academic Network (JANET).

Some indicators of the changing nature of special library work can be found by looking at the contents pages of the seven successive editions of *The Handbook of Special Librarianship and Information Work*. In 1955 the topics were: the special library and information service; administration; acquisitions; cataloguing and indexing; classification; filing and storing material; binding; library planning; service routine; reference and information work; and abstracting. By the third edition in 1967, three additional topics were thought to be of sufficient importance to warrant chapters of their own: literature searching, information retrieval and technical report literature. The effects of government policy to close the science and technology achievement gap supposedly indicated by Sputnik may be seen at work here. The new topics certainly reflected the contemporary concerns of the National Lending Library for Science and Technology (NLL), Boston Spa and the content of its highly influential courses on the structure and use of literature.

Management, foreign languages, and document delivery are given their own chapters for the first time in the fourth edition, 1975, although library planning had figured in earlier editions. The first edition not now to seem primarily of historical interest is the fifth, which was published in 1982. For the first time there is a chapter devoted to networks and it is accompanied by *debut* chapters on computerized information retrieval, dissemination, computer-based housekeeping systems and information management.

The sixth (1992) and seventh (1997) editions both provide more chapters on more specific topics than their predecessors. For example, the sixth edition has no chapter entitled 'Management', but three which cover this area under the headings: 'Analysing and understanding an organisation's information needs'; 'Achieving beneficial outcomes'; and 'Managing human resources'. It also has no fewer than four chapters on specifically technological topics, namely: 'Automation options'; 'Technology overview'; 'Optical information systems'; and 'IT interfaces'. Other chapter topics appearing for the first time are: 'Business and commercial information'; 'Records management'; and, most significantly, 'End-user searching'. The most recent seventh edition (1997) has been completely revised yet again and, this time, the theme of networks is all-pervasive – for example, the end-user searching chapter has become 'Understanding end-users'. There are also chapters on 'The role of the special librarian in the electronic era'; 'Knowledge management'; 'The Internet'; and 'Towards the Electronic Library'.

Finally, there are six case studies which convey well by their coverage the five major impact areas of networked information: intranets; electronic publishing; computer-assisted learning (CAL); external database searching; and integrated housekeeping automation systems. The current special LIS environment is fully delineated in Chapter 10 of this book.

PERSISTENCE OF THE CULTURAL SUBSTRATE

Some writers refer to the study of the way in which users interact with networked information and one another in the CMC context as 'social informatics' in order to call attention to the complex and unprecedented nature of this new cultural phenomenon (Bishop and Star, 1996). It is because of this complexity and genuine novelty that the pre-existing culture can have great influence on institutional responses to quite suddenly available networked digital resources. The foregoing brief sketches of cultural context for different categories of university and for special libraries could not, of course, hope to capture the multitude of differences between individual institutions, but they do perhaps go some way to explaining some of the differences in response to networks perceptible not only in the attributed and anonymized case studies drawn on in this book, but in the wider literature.

REFERENCES

Avafia, K.E. (1983), 'Subject specialization in African university libraries', *Journal of Librarianship*, **15**(3), 183–205.

Bandara, S.B. (1986), 'Subject specialists in university libraries in developing countries: the need', *Libri*, **36**(3), 202–10.

Barnett, R. and Griffin, A. (eds) (1997), *The End of Knowledge in Higher Education*, London: Cassell.

Biddiscombe, R. (1996), *The End-user Revolution: CD-ROM, Internet and the Changing Role of the Information Professional*, London: LAPL.

Bishop, A.P. and Star, S.L. (1996), 'Social informatics of digital library use and infrastructure', *Annual Review of Information Science and Technology*, **31**, 301–401.

Corrall, S. (1994), 'Middle managers – a defunct species?', *Library Manager*, (1), November, 25.

Evans, A.J. (1979), 'The case against subject specialisation: what is the alternative?' unpublished paper given at the SCONUL ISG conference on subject specialization into the 1980s, 9–11 March 1979. Quoted in Woodhead and Martin (1982: 102).

Fletcher, J. (ed.) (1985), *Reader Services in Polytechnic Libraries*, Aldershot: Gower for COPOL.

Handbook of Special Librarianship and Information Work (1955), Wilfred Ashworth (ed.), London: Aslib.

Handbook of Special Librarianship and Information Work (1962), Wilfred Ashworth (ed.), (2nd edn), London: Aslib.

Handbook of Special Librarianship and Information Work (1967), Wilfred Ashworth (ed.), (3rd edn), London: Aslib.

Handbook of Special Librarianship and Information Work (1975), W.E. Batten (ed), (4th edn), London: Aslib.

Handbook of Special Librarianship and Information Work (1982), L.J. Anthony (ed.), (5th edn), London: Aslib.

Handbook of Special Librarianship and Information Work (1992), Patti Dossett (ed.), (6th edn), London: Aslib.

Handbook of Special Librarianship and Information Work (1997), Alison Scammell (ed.), (7th edn), London: Aslib.

Hay, F.J. (1990), 'The subject specialist in the academic library: a review article', *Journal of Academic Librarianship*, **16**(1), 11–17.

John Fielden Consultancy (1993), *Supporting Expansion: A Report on Human Resource Management in Academic Libraries* for the Joint Funding Councils' Libraries Review Group, Bristol, HEFCE, July (revised September 1993).

Johnson, E.R. (1977), 'Subject-divisional organization in American university libraries, 1939–1974', *Library Quarterly*, **47**(1), 23–42.

Lester, R.G. (1979), 'Career prospects for subject specialists', unpublished paper given at the SCONUL ISG conference on subject specialization into the 1980s, 9–11 March 1979. Quoted in Woodhead and Martin (1982: 102).

MacKenna, R.O. (1980), 'University library organization', in J. Thompson (ed.), *University Library History: An International Review*, London: Bingley, 96–97.

Martin, J.V. (1996), 'Subject specialization in British university libraries: a second survey', *Journal of Librarianship and Information Science*, **28**(3), September, 159–69.

Naylor, B. (1980), 'The libraries of London University: a historical sketch', in J. Thompson (ed.), *University Library History: An International Review*, London: Bingley, 236–37.

Ostrem, W.M. (1966), 'The Ruhr University Bochum Library', *Wilson Library Bulletin*, **41**, 418–20.

Reid, B.J. (1968), 'An outline of staff subject specialization at Leicester University Library', *News Sheet*, **9**(1), Library Association of Australia, University and College Libraries Section, 18–24.

Reid, B.J. (1973), 'Trends in recataloguing and re-classification in British university libraries', *Research in Librarianship*, 4(24), September, 183–93.

Reid, B.J. and Rafferty, P. (1996), 'The changing role of professional education for information professionals' in R. Biddiscombe (ed.), *The End-user Revolution*, London: LAPL, 173–86.

Scrivener, J.E. (1974), 'Subject specialization in academic libraries: some British practices', *Australian Academic and Research Libraries*, **5**(3), 113–22.

Smethurst, J.M. (1980), 'University library staffing in the United Kingdom' in J. Thompson (ed.), *University Library History: An International Review*, London: Bingley, 65–66.

Taylor, B. (1998), 'Obituary: Willi Guttsman', *Library Association Record*, **100**(5), May, 267.

Thompson, J. (1975), 'The argument against subject specialisation, or, Even a good idea can fail', *ARLIS Newsletter*, **22**, 3–6.

Wilkinson, J.P. (1983), 'Subject divisionalism: a diagnostic analysis', *Advances in Library Administration and Organization*, **2**, 21–38.

Woodhead, P.A. and Martin, J.V. (1982), 'Subject specialization in British university libraries: a survey', *Journal of Librarianship*, **14**(2), April, 93–108.

Developments in technical services: cultural change and organizational management

3

William Foster

INTRODUCTION

It is generally recognized that:

> ... there is scope for information systems (ISs) to play an increasingly important role in the development of higher education. The sector will continue to be at the forefront in the innovative use of information systems both by building on current facilities, to ensure they are properly exploited, and by continuing to take part in farsighted and imaginative research and development. (Joint Information Systems Committee, 1995: 5)

The electronic library presently being implemented in many higher education (HE) institutions will form a central role in supporting the new teaching and learning strategies currently being developed to deliver courses of study across global networks. The importance of the library's role in the rapidly changing HE environment demands that its services and operations be managed effectively. The heart of the library's operational management has traditionally been referred to as technical services. Technical services departments have always been concerned with the processes of library housekeeping, such as the acquisition and cataloguing of stock, and were in existence long before the use of computers. However, the use of computers for bibliographic control, enabling libraries to share and exchange catalogue records, was of considerable benefit to overstretched cataloguing departments in the 1970s. Cooperative cataloguing agencies, such as OCLC in the USA and BLCMP in the UK, played a significant role in shaping the early development of library automation in their respective countries, and they continue to do so. The widespread implementation of automated library systems in academic libraries during the early 1980s provided libraries with more streamlined housekeeping operations and significantly improved the management of library stock. The systems of the mid- to late 1980s began to incorporate industry standard, rather than proprietary, networking technology, with the ability to distribute both housekeeping functions and library services to any connected site, thus allowing technical services to be decentralized and, more significantly, library services to be delivered across an organization.

From the 1980s onwards a number of key issues and developments have taken place, which have substantially altered the role of the technical services department and the way in which it supports the services that libraries provide to their customers. During this period academic libraries in particular have gradually moved, as Dempsey has suggested, from an era of bibliographic control (BC) to an era of access and delivery (AD) (Dempsey, 1992). This chapter discusses some of these developments in the context of cultural change and organizational management. Ironically, with the recent explosion of the Internet and, in particular, the World Wide Web (Web), a principal focus of attention within technical services is once again bibliographic control, as libraries come to terms with cataloguing and utilizing a very wide range of electronic resources, many of them located outside their own institution and therefore beyond their direct control.

Library systems are increasingly performing a central role within developing HE campus networks as electronic access to teaching and learning materials becomes commonplace. Consequently, many institutions have perceived the need to merge their separate library and computer services, to provide both economies of scale and a broader spread of expertise to support the delivery of an increasing volume of information and associated services. The topic of convergence is discussed in detail in Chapters 5 and 6.

THE LIBRARY MANAGEMENT SYSTEM (LMS) MARKETPLACE

The first fully integrated library management systems (LMSs) appeared in the UK in the early 1980s, and the history of these early systems has been well documented by Tedd (1987) and Leeves (1995), among others. Despite the small size of the UK library sector there was comparatively little change within the systems market during the 1970s and 1980s, although some companies disappeared and others remarketed themselves under different names in line with changes to their systems. Surprisingly, many suppliers have managed to survive with very few customers, although a number have attempted to expand their customer base by moving into different sectors, particularly the secondary and primary school market, or by 'diversifying into other value-added services such as facilities management, consultancy services and training' (Muirhead, 1997b: 22). In a market where the customers do not have sufficient money to pay for customized computer systems, the development of LMSs is largely in the hands of the systems suppliers' strategic policies, although many do support user groups in which customers have some say in development priorities. The complexity of current systems, and the increasing need for library systems and services to fit in with overall organizational information strategies, has meant that, in the 1990s, some suppliers and their respective systems have struggled to meet the demands of the modern library and have found their customers drifting away. Consequently, a number of American and European companies have seized the opportunity to take over ailing British companies and provide themselves with a sizeable British customer base.

OPEN SYSTEMS

The first LMSs, like most commercial software in the 1960s and 1970s, were developed for particular manufacturers' hardware platforms, which severely limited libraries' ability to develop the system in customized ways, exchange data with other campus computers or link the library system to their institution's network to provide a campus-wide public access catalogue. As librarians realized that their present systems would not last forever, they began to consider replacing them with systems that could run on any hardware platform. Many library suppliers suddenly found their existing customers looking elsewhere and hastily began to convert or rewrite their systems to be more hardware-independent. These so-called third-generation systems are based on the adoption of industry-wide, open systems utilizing standards such as Unix, Microsoft Windows NT or the ISO OSI model (Broome, 1994). This may prove to be particularly important, because, over the years, LMSs, partly because of the small market size, have generally failed to keep pace with industry-standard developments in either software or hardware, often providing disappointing performance and sometimes reflecting badly on the library service. Muirhead (1997b) suggests that the potential benefits of third-generation systems include: shorter development cycles, faster processing, network interoperability, portability, improved front-ends and better management information. All of these will be essential in the development of the electronic library. A number of EU-funded projects have resulted in a range of software tools that can help implement and maintain an LMS (European Union, DG-XIII-E4). As network interoperability is so important today, future LMS developments may depend on the willingness of library suppliers to forsake a little competitive edge and work together to develop high-quality products to benefit the profession as a whole. Three of Europe's major suppliers, ALS International (UK), Sisis Gmbh (Germany) and Pica (Netherlands), forged a technical alliance in 1998 called EuroLIB to coordinate system development and produce exchangeable system components which will fit seamlessly together (Anonymous, 1998b).

MIGRATION AND EVOLUTION

Perhaps the most significant market for LMSs has been the HE sector where the size of system required is often as large as those found in the public library sector and the demands of the users can be as significant as those in the special library sector. Many HE libraries are now using their second or even third computerized system – a reflection of the fact that many systems have been unable to offer an adequate upgrade path. The migration process involved has given many systems librarians a difficult time as they wrestle with the choice between staying with their existing supplier or moving to a new one. Muirhead emphasizes that the IT revolution in libraries – as far as library management systems is concerned – has not exactly been bloodless:

> There are many published accounts of 'forced' migrations in which 'push' factors have been the main reason for the acquisition of a replacement system. These push factors include: unacceptable response times, costly maintenance on obsolescent hardware, dissatisfaction with software support, lack of vendor support for old products and vendor take-overs/insolvency'. (Muirhead, 1997b: 14)

A potential problem for libraries, when migrating, is the conversion of their database from one system to another, especially where the records come from a variety of different sources.

As academic libraries increasingly choose new systems to support their involvement in the electronic library, it has become important that the LMS is compatible with the very wide range of other systems within the organization, can interoperate with the systems of bibliographic utilities and book suppliers (for exchanging bibliographic and acquisitions data), and deliver information directly to the desktop of the rapidly increasing number of users. This can only be achieved through the development of a coherent, long-term strategy (Gallimore, 1997b). Gallimore (1997a) emphasizes that

> … in the global networking culture which is now evolving, all organizations will be interlinked and their strategies will need to be coherently linked together. It is essential that every library service develops a clear IT strategy, concentrating on the strategic use of IT systems as part of the overall management strategy of the library service.

CD-ROMS: THE DRIVING FORCE OF NETWORKED INFORMATION

When CD-ROM – a format designed specifically for storing large amounts of electronic information – was developed in the mid-1980s, libraries saw the possibility of using the new format for providing improved access to commercial databases (Tedd, 1995). Where a particular database was heavily used it often made sense to subscribe to it in a format that could be run on a locally networked system, thus removing the need for an expensive telecommunications connection to the USA or Europe, and generally improving response time. A significant benefit of using a locally mounted CD-ROM product, paid for by subscription rather than on a pay-as-you-go basis, is that it becomes free at the point of use. This means that users can undertake searches for themselves without the fear of incurring heavy charges; indeed many libraries actively encouraged their users to do so. However, this places a burden on the library to provide appropriate training, documentation and support, either in person or electronically, to the inexperienced users who would previously have expected the library staff to undertake searches on their behalf.

As CD-ROM use by libraries began to increase, a small number of publishers began to develop full-text electronic journals collections on CD-ROM, although many were clearly worried about whether such provision would reduce their revenue from printed subscriptions. Libraries, too, were wary of moving away from print to electronic sources for a number of reasons: use of electronic resources places an increased dependence on networking technology; and electronic subscriptions need to be continued in order to maintain a particular resource – if the subscription is stopped the library stock disappears because there is no print version remaining. Nevertheless, in 1992 Aston University decided to subscribe to the ADONIS document delivery service, providing access to 500 electronic journals but at the loss of 75 printed journals. At the time their ADONIS supplier did not envisage the system being used as a replacement for printed subscriptions. The royalty payment system imposed for printing from ADONIS made financial planning difficult, especially as many of the extra journals were only peripheral to Aston's teaching and expected use could not easily be calculated (Cameron, 1996).

For many libraries the installation of an independent, locally maintained CD-ROM network was their first taste of using industry-wide networking standards such as Novell's Netware. Because of the large storage capacity of the CD-ROM it was necessary to use additional software that could support CD-ROMs across a network. Technical services librarians began to acquire expertise in the installation and maintenance of networking software and also in the delivery of electronic information. Some libraries were offering 50 or more CD-ROMs in this fashion, although they were generally text-based and running under DOS rather than the Windows-based multimedia CD-ROMs that were just beginning to appear (Akeroyd, 1989; Black, 1992; Lambert, 1994). As more flexible campus networks began to be developed in the 1990s, the possibility of linking the library CD-ROM network to the campus network became a reality and enabled users to access some of these resources directly from their offices and, in some cases, from student halls of residence. Unfortunately, some libraries were unable to make all their CD-ROMs available in this way as certain titles, perhaps based on superseded standards, stubbornly refused to be networked beyond the library. Many libraries discovered that some CD-ROM producers were charging a prohibitively expensive licence fee for networked CD-ROMs because of the potentially large number of simultaneous users. Consequently, some libraries were forced to set a system limit on the number of simultaneous users in order to keep the producer's licence fee to an acceptable level, but this often led to frustration on the part of users if they had to wait for another user to log-off before they could gain access.

The average number of CD-ROM titles per university in the UK rose from three in 1988 to 43 in 1996 (East and Leach, 1998) but its use as a vehicle for information provision may have peaked. An alternative approach taken by some libraries has been to abandon the CD-ROM where the database is available across the Web, but access can be very slow (Haydock and Craft, 1997). Many database suppliers have enhanced the functionality of their Web service and offer a range of features such as: Web administration tools, integrated full-text content, tailored current awareness services, document delivery and links to a wide range of other electronic library collections. More recently, the falling price of hard disks has encouraged a number of institutions to cache CD-ROMs on to a local hard disk which can improve access to the information, although negotiating licences with CD-ROM suppliers to do this can be problematic. Nevertheless, as caching becomes more widespread across the Internet, it is likely to become a central part of the electronic library, particularly as a means of accessing regional and national digitized resource collections. Caching allows the library:

> ... to create a copy of a resource that is in some way ... more local to the end user than the original, canonical copy of the resource. ... the hope is to improve the retrieval performance for the end user, and it also has the advantage of reducing demands on congested links in the network and on the resource's server. (Kirriemuir and Knight, 1997).

CAMPUS-WIDE INFORMATION SYSTEM (CWIS): THE PROTOTYPE INTRANET

With the introduction of campus-wide networks many HE libraries saw the opportunity to network their catalogue across the campus, and some library suppliers began to offer a community information (CI) module within their library management system. Some of these early versions operated like broadcast videotext or teletext systems, offering a limited number of pages with access by page number. Although they were primarily used to provide basic information about the library and its services, libraries quickly realized that they were in a good position to act as coordinators of the increasing range of general information needed within an educational institution.

Universities saw the potential for delivering a wide range of information, both academic and administrative, within a campus-wide information system (CWIS) (Rothnie, 1993) designed as 'an interactive networked information retrieval system, providing access to items of information pertaining primarily to a particular academic institution and its members' (Work, 1993: 41). However, such were the limitations of the early CWISs that priorities on what to include needed to be established. In 1990 the UK's Inter-University Information Committee (IUIC) and SCONUL produced a report on computer-based information services in universities. Subsequently the IUIC set up a subgroup, the Information Services Working Group (INFSWG), to look specifically at the content of a CWIS. Topics generally agreed for inclusion in a CWIS included: diary of university events, library service information, computer service information, e-mail/ telephone directory. Other generally desirable, but perhaps less critical, topics included: university calendar, student union activities, diary of cultural events, diary of sporting events, newsletter, institutional rules and regulations, course information, community information, travel information, networked information services, research interests, useful contacts (Work, 1993: 50). The fact that not all the above information was included as standard – all of which today would be considered an essential part of any CWIS – illustrates how far information networks have developed in the last ten years.

After the University of Minnesota developed its gopher software in 1991 many HE libraries rapidly installed the software to provide their users with gopher-based menu systems offering seamless links to other gopher-based campus systems and OPACs across the Internet. The use of gopher was short-lived and soon overtaken by the widespread use of the World Wide Web software developed by Tim Berners Lee at CERN in Switzerland. This huge worldwide take-up of the Web galvanized many institutions into reassessing information provision on their campus network. It soon became clear that some information – for example, on local transportation and cultural events – was now available on the Web directly from its source. It also became evident that some general information about the institution needed to be made available to external Web users, and that an institution's Web presence was becoming essential as a marketing tool in the scramble to attract more students. Many HE institutions are also developing intranets – in-house or internal networks – based on standard Internet technologies (Bevan and Evans, 1996; Blackmore, 1997). A 1998 report from Ovum indicates there are 1.06 million intranet servers currently in operation worldwide (Anonymous, 1998c).

Whereas early CWISs and gopher-based systems were mainly instigated by libraries, other departments within the institution have become much more

33

involved in the design of information pages as a consequence of intranet development. A major focus of the intranet is its use as a vehicle for teaching and learning where it can be used for the dissemination of institutional information, as a discussion forum, for the provision of course materials, and as a gateway to external information sources. However, the potential difficulties associated with the establishment of intranets include: deciding who has overall responsibility; curbing vested interests or local enthusiasms; overcoming apathy of users and potential content providers; maintaining the site; and the provision of adequate navigation. White says:

> Without a good content strategy that reflects the information needs and uses of the different business functions in the organization, potential users quickly become frustrated and disillusioned. ... For users particular issues of concern include: relevance of the information, potential information overload, the information's currency and authority, ease of connectivity, scope of the intranet – the balance between external and internal information. (White, 1998: 3)

The importance of providing informed access to external websites has become critical as academic staff and students increasingly use the Web as their initial source in their quest to find information relevant to their researches. The library pages often provide the most useful starting-point for users seeking information beyond their own institution, and most academic libraries have taken the opportunity to reformat and restructure their original CWIS information pages for the Web. A number of libraries have been involved in the provision of subject-specific gateways, and some of the important eLib projects in this area are explored in detail in Chapter 4. A 1998 analysis of 86 university and college library websites showed that the average size of an academic library website was 4.6 MB, with one particular site achieving 133 MB. Academic library sites are generally larger than public library sites, making greater use of dynamic Web technologies – a potential problem for users with older versions of Web browsers (Anonymous, 1998f).

An important spin-off from the Web technology is the development of a Web interface to the library catalogue. Most LMSs now offer a WebCat module which allows the library to provide a catalogue compliant with their users' standard browser. The Royal Postgraduate Medical School is a typical example of a small library utilizing standard Web technology to ease the burden of providing networked access to a graphical OPAC:

> The difficulty of distributing, maintaining and supporting potentially hundreds of copies of the GUI client ... meant that this was only available on computers in the library. Remote users had to be content with the character-based, terminal-type interface provided by telnet access. (Davis and Stone, 1997: 77)

The majority of UK HE library catalogues are now available across the Internet and the NISS (National Information Service and Systems) maintains a list of these. The means of access to them is divided almost equally into those catalogues providing a Web interface and those providing a traditional telnet interface.

Libraries still need to provide terminals and/or computers within the library building, despite the increasing number of users accessing the OPAC from their desktop. Making the choice can be difficult when budgets available for hardware purchases are small. The University of North London has decided to install network computers (NCs) rather than full-scale personal computers in order to:

> ... minimize the administration and support overheads by eliminating the need to individually configure and update each workstation. Other important factors include the requirement for a Java Virtual Machine and a good graphical interface running on a web browser. (Anonymous, 1998e: 157)

TOWARDS THE ELECTRONIC LIBRARY

The widespread use of IT by academics, researchers and students has forced libraries to adopt a more proactive approach with regard to IT provision in the library. The HEFC's Joint Information Systems Committee (JISC) has encouraged the library community to embrace and exploit IT more fully, both for administration and the delivery of resources (Joint Funding Councils, 1993; Joint Information Systems Committee, 1995). Recognizing that, in many institutions, the library is the department that is open for the most hours during the week, many libraries have established open access computer laboratories for students to use – in some cases with 24-hour access. This has placed an enormous burden on the LIS staff in terms of technical support. Nevertheless with students increasingly required to access electronic teaching and learning materials, this is clearly the way forward and some institutions have invested substantial sums in developing new learning resources centres (Godwin, 1998), utilizing Web technology to provide some form of 24-hour enquiry service (Gleadhill, 1997) and providing improved short-loan management (Dugdale and Howat, 1997). Some smaller and subdegree course institutions have already developed intranets which provide extensive course material, resulting in the replacement of most of the shelves of books in the library with banks of personal computers. Where textbooks are still the normal means of information dissemination, a number of libraries have moved to self-service issue to improve efficiency (McDonald and Stafford, 1996). The franchising of HE courses and the need to support lifelong learners with a range of intellectual and physical abilities are of increasing concern to HE institutions and their libraries (Brophy and Goodall, 1997). There are a number of projects such as REVIEL (Resources for Visually Impaired Users of the Electronic Library) which are trying to ensure that electronic library services will be accessible to all potential users, including those with disabilities.

In the long term, the individual IT initiatives that HE libraries currently provide will form part of a much broader electronic library which might be described as the utilization of one or more networks to deliver a broad range of electronic information to the user's desktop. Its success will depend on the digital content provided, and upon organizational, cultural, technical and financial factors. The first project to build a working electronic library for use by students in a UK university was the ELINOR project which ran from 1992 to 1996 at De Montfort University (Ramsden, 1998). The main impetus behind it was the likelihood that, in the future, not all their campus sites would be able to afford to keep sufficient copies of all books for all courses.

> Elinor was a two phase pilot project with three overall goals: first to create a pilot system and, in so doing address some of the issues involved (technical, copyright, selection [and] acquisition of materials), and the user aspects; second, to investigate the expansion of a small-scale electronic library to a larger distributed library; and third, as of necessity, to develop a more efficient and effective means of accessing and sharing resources within a networked multi-campus institution. (Ramsden, 1998: 1)

Many UK university libraries now provide access to a wide range of electronic resources and document delivery services (Fecko, 1997). Library catalogues are being made available to different groups of users through subject or regional collections of catalogues or clumps. 'The term "clumps" refers to groups of distributed catalogues, or "metadata resources" which can be searched together as though they were a union catalogue' (Nicholson et al., 1998: 75). A number of clumps projects were funded under Phase 3 of eLib, including: Cairns, Music Online and Riding (Pinfield, 1998a). A wide range of electronic journals is available across the Web and is beginning to be used by academic staff (Tomney and Burton, 1998).

A significant problem facing libraries is the need to integrate conventional bibliographic records and electronic resource identifiers such as URLs (uniform resource locators) into a single online catalogue. URLs present particular difficulties because, although they uniquely identify an individual resource, they represent items not formally published and which could disappear from the Internet entirely or be moved to another Internet location at any time. The potential use of metadata for describing electronic resources is currently being investigated by OCLC, the World Wide Web Consortium (W3C) and the UK Office for Library Networking (UKOLN), among others. OCLC and other bibliographic agencies have investigated the use of the USMARC 856 field, *electronic location and access*, for including URLs, but the facility within the metadata structure to additionally include resource format, ownership and platform details may prove to be more beneficial in the long term. At the time of writing, however, there are various competing metadata standards and it remains to be seen which will emerge as the ideal version for the majority of electronic libraries.

A range of electronic national data service providers (DSPs) and their collections, such as BIDS, MIDAS, EDINA are available to the UK academic community across the universities' own network, JANET. These form part of the Distributed National Electronic Resource, supported by the JISC, which 'acts as a facilitator and enabler – it creates the conditions in which UK HE teaching and research can take a maximum advantage of developments in information technology and information services' (JISC, nd). One particular JISC initiative is CHEST (the Combined Higher Education Software Team) which is able to negotiate advantageous licence agreements on behalf of the whole university sector. Thus most of the JISC resources are free at the point of use to the end-user, having been paid for, through a CHEST agreement, at the institution or library level (East *et al.*, 1998). Usage of these resources has grown considerably as academic staff and researchers become more aware of their availability and gain confidence in their use (Pinfield, 1998b). Indeed, because of the huge growth in the use of worldwide electronic resources, volume charging was introduced for the first time for the institutional use of JANET transatlantic links in August 1998 (Anonymous, 1998a), encouraging libraries to make more use of the UK national cache provided by JISC for heavily used US sites (Hadland, 1998).

JISC-funded licence agreements are available to relatively few libraries, and subscription charges continue to be a major problem for most libraries in the UK and elsewhere. The International Coalition of Library Consortia (ICOLC), representing a combined membership of over 5000 libraries worldwide, have published a Statement of current perspective and preferred practices for the selection and purchase of electronic information (ICOLC, 1998). This urges publishers to develop sensible, multiple-pricing models and asserts that 'publishers cannot expect libraries to bear all development costs today for incomplete product features and unstable systems' (Anonymous, 1998d).

Most of the electronic resources currently available to library users, whether via the Web or other systems, are text-based and, even here, a considerable portion of material that will provide useful content in the electronic library remains to be digitized. Long-established universities with rare collections are beginning to exploit the latest technology to improve access to older material (Simpson, 1997), although many are still at the stage of creating detailed descriptive cataloguing records of their holdings (McDonald, 1998). In fact, a 1997 survey showed that at least 28 million catalogue records representing 6 million items in UK HE libraries still await retrospective conversion (BLRIC, 1997). Multimedia resources will become more common as digital content is created, particularly in the arts; the eLib Project Patron has explored a wide range of issues in the delivery of multimedia performing arts material (Lyon, 1996).

How the hardware and software platform of future LMSs will develop to support the electronic library is not yet clear. In the UK a number of HE institutions and eLib projects have adopted the MODELS information architecture (MIA) developed by UKOLN and others. In this environment the user is presented with:

> ... a 'landscape' which hides some of the underlying differences between resources, collates returned results and supports a higher quality of service than unmediated access to end-resources themselves would. Resources accessed may be 'metadata' (library catalogues, subject services, and so on) which point to a mixture of print and electronic resources, or, in due course, a range of resources themselves. Such intermediate systems will be provided by libraries, 'aggregators', publishers, data centres, and others. Some will be quite simple (a parallel searching facility); some will add value in other ways (incorporating user profiles, service descriptions, and so on). (Russell and Dempsey, 1998: 231)

MANAGEMENT INFORMATION

Increasingly, the main issues surrounding electronic resource provision concern not the nature of the content itself, but problems of design and format, intellectual property, management and control, all of which will be of concern within the electronic library and which may need to be tackled within the management information part of the LMS (Kidd, 1997; Lyon, 1996). Controlling the remote use of institutional resources has become a major issue as staff and students increasingly use the Internet to access the campus network. There is a growing need to provide reliable authentication procedures to prevent unregistered or unauthorized users gaining access to CD-ROMs and other electronic resources and consequently infringing the institution's licensing agreement. In 1997 the NISS developed ATHENS which is now widely used by JISC data service providers and HE institutions. 'ATHENS combines a user authentication service with a resource authorization management facility. Its key features are a "single sign-on" to multiple resources, together with a distributed management of user accounts' (ATHENS, 1998).

Monitoring the use of expensive electronic resources, whether held internally or accessed externally, will be essential for long-term financial planning. Rights management systems will have to be installed if libraries are to avoid being sued for failure to pay intellectual property rights (IPR) holders their dues. A number of European research projects such as CITED, TOLIMAC, IMPRIMATUR (sometimes IMPRIMATEUR), have been exploring issues of what has come to be called ECMS (electronic copyright management systems). The results from these may help to deal with one of the principal weaknesses of most LMSs – their inability to deliver adequate management information. Even in the 1980s, writers such as Lancaster (1983) and Hawks (1988) outlined the potential benefits of a good management information module which include 'the enhanced ability to monitor processes, to collect, structure, analyze, and report critical or useful data previously unavailable or extremely difficult or costly to obtain' (Hawks, 1986: 246). More recently Lancaster and Sandore have stated that: 'Regrettably, most libraries do not consider better management/decision making as a major reason for automation, and the system vendors certainly fail to emphasize their capabilities in this area' (Lancaster and Sandore, 1997: 3). Where this is the case some libraries have exported their housekeeping data into industry-standard products such as Microsoft Access or Microsoft Excel to provide better analysis of the information. The EU-funded project Minstrel developed system-independent software which enables 'library staff at all levels of management to obtain relevant and reliable management information from automated and non-automated data sources' (Adams, 1997: 394). With the move towards the electronic library the ability to generate and act upon management information will become much more critical, and some systems suppliers have developed executive information systems (EIS) to present management information in a more visually appealing way.

In the long term some measurement of the performance of the electronic library will be crucial to determine its effectiveness, but what should be measured and how will it be achieved? Brophy and Wynne (1997) have drawn together the principal, recent contributions to the development of library performance indicators, but have focused on the library manager's requirements which include not only information on evaluation and review, but also operational management and forward planning. However, it may be too early yet to develop an appropriate evaluation model, as user groups, information-seeking behaviour, the role of the library and available datasets will all change as the electronic library develops.

THE SYSTEMS LIBRARIAN – TECHNICIAN OR MANAGER?

The huge changes that have taken place in the technical services of academic institutions in the last ten years have placed a considerable burden on the systems librarian who has traditionally been responsible for maintaining the LMS. The technology has developed exceptionally fast, and the systems librarian has been forced to take on board a range of new and complex technologies demanded by library users. Fortunately there are a number of Mailbase electronic discussion lists where systems librarians can discuss with each other the problems of implementing the latest technologies such as client/server networking, Z39.50 protocols, the World Wide Web, intranets and Java™. However, systems librarians are increasingly also having to take on more of a management role in what is rapidly becoming an electronic library incorporating a wide range of services (Dempsey, 1996). The question is whether the systems librarian is now more of a manager than a technician.

We can identify a number of factors that suggest this may be the case including: the increased number of staff working in technical services (in some cases working within converged services); the need to negotiate licensing agreements with publishers and suppliers to allow information to be networked around the organization; the need to make policy decisions about what should be accessed and what should be held (some of this to be negotiated with other libraries); possible involvement with a regional network or metropolitan area network (MAN), such as CALIM (Mendelsohn, 1995), MidMAN or the London MAN, or national digitized collections or datasets.

In the 1980s many systems librarians, particularly in academic libraries, were promoted from within, either from positions of subject librarian or more frequently from cataloguer. As many universities made their first foray into automation by converting the catalogue to machine-readable form perhaps this is not surprising. Warlow (1994) has discussed how the role of systems librarian has evolved at Manchester Metropolitan University. During the 1990s that role has changed significantly as it has in most HE institutions. As Dunsire says:

> A typical mission statement or job function of the systems librarian might indicate a role in leading and developing automated information services for the library and its clients. If the accent is on coordination and consolidation, passive rather than active, and there is no compensation elsewhere in the staff structure, then the mission will fail and the job malfunction. Coordination cannot be achieved without development, nor consolidation without leadership. (Dunsire, 1994: 74)

Dunsire goes on to ask whether the opposite of what has been suggested may be true – namely, '… is the library manager evolving into a systems manager by acquiring technical expertise and familiarity with system concepts?' This echoes Dearing's view that HE managers should combine a deep understanding of communications and information technology (C & IT), with senior management experience (National Committee of Inquiry, 1997). In the short term some institutions will have managers turned systems librarians; others will have systems librarians turned managers. In the long term a new kind of information professional will probably emerge, combining the high-quality skills, both technical and managerial, that are required in a distinctly culturally changed organization and information environment.

REFERENCES

Adams, R. (1997), 'The Minstrel management information transformer' in A. McDonald and J. Stafford (eds), *Self-service in Academic Libraries: Future or Fallacy? Proceedings of a Conference Organized by Information Services, University of Sunderland, in Conjunction with SCONUL in June 1996*, Sunderland: University of Sunderland Press, 393–99.

Akeroyd, J. (1989), 'CD-ROM usage and prospects: an overview', *Program*, **23**(4), 367–76.

Anonymous (1998a), 'Academic libraries and Janet bandwidth charging', *Library Technology*, **3**(5), November, 67.

Anonymous (1998b), 'European suppliers form technical alliance', *Library Technology*, **3**(2), April, 23.

Anonymous (1998c), 'Market research update: intranets – facts and figures, *Dialect*, **1**, 10 (quoted from an unreferenced Ovum report).

Anonymous (1998d), 'Preferred practice statement released', *Library Technology*, **3**(3), June, 42.

Anonymous (1998e), 'University of North London uses network computers for TalisWeb', *Program*, **32**(2), April, 157.

Anonymous (1998f), 'Webwatching academic library sites', *Library Technology*, **3**(3), June, 43.

ATHENS (1998), *Glossary*, http://www.athens.ac.uk/info/glossary.html

Bevan, S. and Evans, J. (1996), 'Managing the library intranet at Cranfield University', *Managing Information*, **3**(9), September, 38–40.

Black, K. (1992), 'CD-ROM networking: the Leicester Polytechnic experience', *Aslib Information*, **20**(7–8), 288–90.

Blackmore, P. (1997), 'The development of an intranet within a college of further and higher education', *Aslib Proceedings*, **49**(3), March, 67–72.

BLRIC (British Library Research and Innovation Centre) (1997), *Making the Most of our Libraries: The Report of Two Studies on Retrospective Conversion of Library Catalogues in the United Kingdom, with Recommendations for a National Strategy*, British Library Research and Innovation Report, 53, London: BLRIC (also available at: http://www.ukoln.ac.uk/blri053).

Broome, J. (1994), 'Market influences and the role of the systems librarian', in G. Muirhead (ed.), *The Systems Librarian: The Role of the Library Systems Manager*, London: Library Association, 78–93.

Brophy, P. and Goodall, D. (1997), 'The role of the library in franchised higher education courses', *Library & Information Briefings*, (72), July.

Brophy, P. and Wynne, P. (1997), *Management Information Systems and Performance Measurement for the Electronic Library*, Electronic Libraries Programme Studies MIEL 2, London: Library Information Technology Centre.

Cameron, A. (1996), 'CD-ROM and document delivery', in R. Biddiscombe (ed.), *The End-user Revolution: CD-ROM, Internet and the Changing Role of the Information Professional*, London: Library Association, 119–34.

Davis, E. and Stone, E. (1997), 'A painless route on to the web', *Library Technology* **2**(4), August, 77–78.

Dempsey, L. (1992) 'The future of library systems: integrated or insulated', paper given at the 1992 Library Networking Conference, University of Bath

Dempsey, L. (1996) 'Towards distributed library systems: Z39.50 in a European context', *Program*, **30**(1), January, 1–22.

Dugdale, C. and Howat, A. (1997), 'Speedy answer to high demand', *Library Technology*, **2**(5), November, 98. See also the Reside site at: http://www.uwe.ac.uk/library/itdev/reside/

Dunsire, G. (1994), 'A life in the week ...' in G. Muirhead (ed), *The Systems Librarian: The Role of the Library Systems Manager*, London: Library Association, 62–77.

East, H. *et al.* (1998), 'Charging for access to university-wide networked database services in British academic libraries', *Aslib Proceedings*, **50**(10), November–December, 299–307.

East, H. and Leach, K. (1998), 'The continuing prominence of CD-ROMs in academic libraries: the findings and evaluation of a survey', *Aslib Proceedings*, **50**(8), September, 208–14.

European Union, DG-XIII-E4, Telematics for Libraries, http://www2.echo.lu/en/software.htm

Fecko, M.B. (1997), *Electronic Resources: Access and Issues*, London: Bowker Saur.

Gallimore, A. (1997a), *Developing an IT Strategy for your Library*, London: Library Association.

Gallimore, A. (1997b), 'Get IT sorted', *Library Technology*, **2**(3), June, 63–64.

Gleadhill, D. (1997), 'Does the Nerd have the answer?', *Library Technology*, **2**(2), April, 35–36. See also the Nerd site at: http://www.ncl.ac.uk/library/

Godwin, P. (1998), 'IT flagship or word-processing shed? The LRC at South Bank University', *Multimedia Information & Technology*, **24**(3), August, 182–88.

Hadland, S. (1998), Transatlantic bandwidth: how to save money on your costs', *Ariadne*, (18), December, http://www.ariadne.ac.uk/issue18/bandwidth/

Hawks, C.P. (1986), 'The Geac acquisitions systems as a source of management information', *Library Acquisitions: Practice & Theory*, **10**(4), 245–53 (quoted in Lancaster and Sandore, 1997: 47).

Hawks, C.P. (1988), 'Management information gleaned from automated library systems', *Information Technology and Libraries*, **7**(2), June, 131–38.

Haydock, I. and Craft, E. (1997), 'Whither the CD-ROM network?', *Managing Information*, **4**(10), December, 35–36.

ICOLC (International Coalition of Library Consortia) (1998), *Statement of Current Perspective and Preferred Practices for the Selection and Purchase of Electronic Information*, http://www.library.yale.edu/consortia/statement.html

JISC (Joint Information Systems Committee of the Higher Education Funding Councils for England, Scotland and Wales and the Department of Education for Northern Ireland), http://www.jisc.ac.uk/

Joint Funding Councils' Libraries Review Group (1993), *Report*, Chairman: Professor Sir Brian Follett, Bristol: HEFCE, http://www.ukoln.ac.uk/services/papers/follett/report/, (Follet Report).

Joint Information Systems Committee (1995), *Exploiting Information Systems in Higher Education: An issues paper*, Bristol: JISC.

Kidd, T. (1997), 'Electronic journals management: some problems and solutions', *Managing Information*, **4**(10), December, 25–26, 31.

Kirriemuir, J. and Knight, J. (1997), 'Mirroring and caching network-based resources', in C. Davies and A. Ramsden (eds), *Electronic Library and Visual Information Research: ELVIRA4*, London: Aslib, http://hill.lut.ac.uk/People/jonpubs/Elvira97.html

Lambert, J. (1994), 'Managing CD-ROM services in academic libraries', *Journal of Librarianship and Information Science*, **26**(1), March, 23–28.

Lancaster, F.W. (ed.) (1983), *Library Automation as a Source of Management Information*, Urbana-Champaign: University of Illinois, Graduate School of Information Science.

Lancaster, F.W. and Sandore, B. (1997), *Technology and Management in Library and Information Services*, London: Library Association.

Leeves, J. (1995), 'Library systems then and now', *Vine*, (100), September, 19–23.

Lloyd, L. (ed.) (1992), *Campus Wide Information Systems and Networks: Case Studies in Design and Implementation*, Westport: Meckler.

Lyon, E. (1996), 'A moving performance', *Library Technology*, **1**(5), August, 97. See also the Patron web site at http://www.surrey.ac.uk/library/research/patron.html

McDonald, A. and Stafford, J. (eds) (1997), *Self-service in Academic Libraries: Future or Fallacy? Proceedings of a Conference Organized by Information Services, University of Sunderland, in Conjunction with SCONUL in June 1996*, Sunderland: University of Sunderland Press.

McDonald, B. (1998), 'The Stella project: a retrospective conversion at Trinity College Dublin', *Catalogue & Index*, (127), Spring, 1–5.

Mendelsohn, S. (1995), 'Sharing the load', *Library Manager*, (5), March, 18–19.

Muirhead, G. (1994), *The Systems Librarian: The role of the Library Systems Manager*, London: Library Association.

Muirhead, G. (1997a), 'If it ain't broke, fix it anyway', *Library Technology*, **2**(4), August, 81–82.

Muirhead, G. (ed.) (1997b), *Planning and Implementing Successful Systems Migration*, London: Library Association.

National Committee Of Inquiry Into Higher Education (1997), *Report* (Dearing Report), Chairman: Sir Ron Dearing, London: HMSO.

Nicholson, D. *et. al.* (1998), 'Cairns that go clump in the night', *Library Technology*, **3**(5), November 75–76.

Pinfield, S. (1998a), 'Hybrids and clumps', *Ariadne*, (18), December, http://www.ariadne.ac.uk/issue18/main/

Pinfield, S. (1998b), 'The use of BIDS ISI in a research university: a case study of the University of Birmingham', *Program*, **32**(3), July, 225–40.

Ramsden, A., (ed.) (1998), *ELINOR: Electronic library project*, London: Bowker Saur.

Rothnie, L. (1993), 'Campus wide information system development at three university libraries', *Vine*, (93), December, 18–30.

Russell, R. and Dempsey, L. (1998), 'A distributed national electronic resource? MODELS workshop 6 report, 5–6 February 1998, Bath', *The Electronic Library*, **16**(4), August, 231–37.

Simpson, J. (1997), 'Rare books on the web', *Library Technology*, **2**(3), June, 61–62.

Tedd, L.A. (1987), 'Computer-based library systems: a review of the last twenty-one years', *Journal of Documentation*, **43**(2), June, 145–65.

Tedd, L.A. (1995), 'The changing face of CD-ROM', *Journal of Documentation*, **51**(2), June, 85–98.

Tomney, H. and Burton, P.F. (1998), 'Electronic journals: a study of usage and attitude among academics', *Journal of Information Science*, **24**(6), 419–29.

Warlow, A. (1994), 'More by accident than design, or, The rise and rise of a chief cataloguer?', in G. Muirhead (ed.), *The Systems Librarian: The Role of the Library Systems Manager*, London: Library Association, 129–45.

White, M. (1998), 'Information gurus: intranets and the role of the information manager', *Dialect*, **1**, 3–4.

Work, C.K. (1993), 'The future developments of campus-wide information systems: towards the virtual campus', *Journal of Information Networking*, **1**(1), 41–52.

The Electronic Libraries Programme: a vehicle for academic cultural change

4

William Foster

INTRODUCTION

The Electronic Libraries Programme (eLib) was a direct response to the 1993 Libraries Review commissioned by the UK Higher Education Funding Councils (HEFC). The review was critical of UK higher educational libraries' failure to embrace technology for the development of networked electronic information services, in order to alleviate some of the problems brought about by declining book funds. The review made clear that 'there needs to be a sea-change in the way institutions plan and provide for the information needs of those working within them. The traditional view of the library as the single repository of information needed for teaching, learning and research is no longer adequate' (Joint Funding Councils, 1993: 5). The review also suggested that university libraries should be more involved in helping shape university information policy for, as Watson says, 'information services contribute to the institutional development through the activities of information management, information technology and learning support' (Watson, 1998: 6). Consequently, the primary aim of the eLib Programme was 'to engage the Higher Education community in developing and shaping the implementation of the electronic library' (Joint Information Systems Committee, 1997: 2). Since the eLib Programme began, a number of UK government-initiated reports have highlighted the need for academic institutions at all levels to utilize technology more fully, and to integrate it into their programmes of study to improve teaching and learning for an ever growing student body of lifelong learners (Department for Education and Employment, 1997; Fryer, 1997; Further Education Funding Council, 1997; National Committee of Inquiry, 1997). Together with the development of a more competitive, client-focused ethos, a greater emphasis on research and publication by academic staff and a focus on teaching quality assessment, the UK HE sector is undergoing a radical culture change.

THE ELECTRONIC LIBRARY

The move away from providing and maintaining a physical, print-based collection to the provision of a networked library of digital resources will clearly bring with it a culture shift for both librarians and their users. A short supporting eLib study in 1997 addressed the issue of whether eLib had 'created appropriate preconditions for longer-term cultural change, since little explicit cultural change could be discerned from the available material' (Davies *et al.*, 1997: iii). The report concluded that eLib is only one contributor to the general cultural change which is taking place in HE and that training and awareness activities, although impressive, needed better targeting with more involvement from library schools.

One of the central tenets of the electronic library is the delivery of information, whenever required, to the user's desktop, wherever that may be. Librarians, therefore, will increasingly need to provide their services in some electronic form rather than expect face-to-face contact with their customers. As academics become more willing and more accustomed to using electronic information on a regular basis, they will become increasingly dependent on technology for information access. An additional factor is that, in networked environments, information providers can supply their information directly to the end-user and so bypass the library entirely. Thus the move to an electronic information environment will radically alter the way in which a library operates and interacts with its customers, and librarians will need to consider their own future role as intermediaries (Brodie and McLean, 1995).

The electronic library will form a crucial part of an institution's information service provision and is likely to have a much wider remit than that of the traditional library. Electronic libraries will need to provide a range of new value-added services for internally generated and externally acquired academic and scholarly information, and may be involved in the delivery of administrative information as well. However, the primary aim of the electronic library will be to support the institution's teaching and learning which might change significantly with an increasing number of part-time students entering HE and the gradual progression to more student-centred learning.

The quality of the information content of the electronic library will be crucial to its success, as will its promotion to, and support of, different client groups (Steele, 1997). Electronic resource delivery can only be guaranteed when a sufficiently robust, transparent, high-bandwidth network is in place. Unfortunately, individual campus networks in many institutions still remain a hotchpotch of interconnected local area networks. One of the early pioneers of the electronic library, Tilburg University in the Netherlands, suggested that the central elements of a successful electronic library are 'an infrastructure based on a campus-wide accepted computer architecture, integration of services and personally controlled information management' (Geleijnse, 1994: 10). In summary, the success of the electronic library will depend on reliable access to user-required resources, combined with an intuitive and customizable front-end – referred to by some commentators as *connectivity, content and competencies* (MacDougall, 1998).

THE ELECTRONIC LIBRARIES PROGRAMME (eLIB)

The Electronic Libraries Programme (eLib) was funded by the Joint Information Systems Committee (JISC), the body funded by the HEFC 'to stimulate and enable the cost effective exploitation of information systems and to provide a high quality national network infrastructure for the UK higher education and research councils communities' (Joint Information Systems Committee, 1998).

The JISC was responsible for creating the Joint Academic Network (JANET) which links the UK's universities and major research establishments. Many universities are now connected to its latest incarnation SuperJANET, and it might be argued that the electronic library will only be successful when network speeds similar to those available through SuperJANET can be delivered to the desktop itself. The current Internet has shown itself to be inadequate to meet the demands placed on it and is clearly not capable of delivering large digital files which will be the cornerstone of the electronic library. Nevertheless the World Wide Web (Web), a key development of the Internet in the second half of the 1980s, has been essential for the delivery of many eLib project outcomes, as a means of providing users with a simple browser interface to a rapidly growing worldwide collection of electronic resources. However, the technical infra-structure supporting the electronic library will clearly improve over time.

The eLib Programme, with an initial budget of over £15 million, funded over 60 projects in phases 1 and 2, exploring different models of information delivery within the electronic library (Electronic Libraries Programme). Phase 3 was initiated in 1997 to explore issues directly relevant to the implementation of the electronic library, including the interim potential of hybrid libraries (Electronic Libraries Programme, Phase 3, nd). The eLib Programme was divided into a number of programme areas, each of which was intended to explore issues surrounding the development of the electronic library. These included the following, some of which will be considered in detail:

● access to network resources (ANR)
● digitization
● electronic journals
● electronic short loan

- on demand publishing (ODP)
- electronic document delivery
- pre-prints
- quality assurance
- training and awareness.

ACCESS TO NETWORK RESOURCES

What is of most concern to the electronic library user, whether academic staff or student, is the range of resources and services provided within it. We have seen that 'in a relatively short period of time, electronic resources have expanded from a few dozen computerized bibliographic databases to include the overwhelming information available on the Internet' (Fecko, 1997: ix). This last point is important. In March 1998 the Internet was estimated as providing access to 275 million Web pages (Bharat and Broder, 1998). However, only a small proportion of these have any real scholarly value to the academic community. Simple searches undertaken using one of the many search engines available will retrieve references to thousands of items, many of which will provide inadequate bibliographic information, some of which will be unavailable, and most of which will be irrelevant to answering scholarly enquiries. For traditional library users, used to well organized, carefully selected, high-quality printed resources, this is clearly unsatisfactory.

Anticipating the difficulties that many users would have in using electronic and unfamiliar resources for the first time, a number of the access to network resources (ANR) projects were concerned with the creation of subject-based information gateways (SBIGs) designed for particular disciplines. One factor in promoting their use was ensuring the quality of the selected resource links, to demonstrate that they were a substantial improvement on what was generally on offer via the Internet. Macleod *et al.* (1998) point out that:

> ... the subject based information gateways ... are hand crafted. The resources in their searchable databases have been examined by teams of experts who identify, describe and classify each item. Resources are only included in the SBIG databases if they fulfil the criteria according to usefulness, relevance, and subject content. (Macleod *et al.*, 1998: 206)

A number of the academic disciplines chosen for SBIGs were those in which computers have not traditionally been used by academics or students, such as Art and Architecture, Music, Urban Design and Social Sciences. Some of these subjects make extensive use of non-text resources, but there is a rapidly growing digital resource base of non-text material available to the academic communities in these subject areas. The starting-point for these projects was the provision of an introductory set of Web pages offering guidance and support, and links to preselected websites for users within those subject areas. It was hoped that the availability of a ready-made starting-point would encourage use of the gateway in particular and the Internet in general. ADAM, the art SBIG, recognized that many organizations and individuals were already making art and design information available over the Internet, but the quality of these varied and there was also considerable duplication. The emphasis therefore needed to be on selection. ADAM also recognized that attempting to catalogue these resources to any degree was going to be uneconomic in the long term and expected that:

> ... the emphasis of projects such as ADAM will begin to shift away from resource discovery and descriptions as these are increasingly dealt with by information producers and technological solutions, and will move increasingly towards the quality control, classification and peer review functions that users seem to value so highly. (Tavistock Institute, 1997: 30)

Any user reluctance to make use even of these dedicated subject resources might be overcome by providing access to resources familiar in hard-copy format, subject-specific websites, and prepackaged collections of materials either in html format or some other widely used format such as Word or PDF (portable document format). EEVL, the engineering SBIG, developed a number of additional services for its gateway including the Engineering Newsgroup archive – a searchable 40-day archive of news articles from 100 engineering newsgroups – and the Offshore Engineering Service which provides details of publications and meetings (Macleod, 1998). EEVL has subsequently been evaluated to examine the ways in which its service meets its users' needs (Kemp and Davenport, 1998).

An important advantage of electronic resources over printed materials is that they can be updated easily. However, the benefit may be lost if the user is unaware that a change to the resource has been made. The use of electronic mail as an alerting service for changed URLs or resources is possible, and the long-term use of electronic resources may require a combination of different electronic methodologies to provide a comprehensive service to the user. While intelligent software agents working on an individual's behalf might be the long-term solution to this, in the meantime some sort of tailored alerting service would provide a possible solution. The aim of the Newsagent project was to create a user-configurable electronic news and current awareness service for the LIS field, together with a selection of refereed articles, reviews and editorial matter.

ELECTRONIC JOURNALS

One way to convince academics and researchers that a move to the electronic library is worthwhile is to provide desktop access to the scholarly journals already available within the library. A number of electronic journal services have appeared in the last few years including: JournalsOnline (BIDS), Electronic Journal Navigator (Blackwells), SwetsNet/SwetScan (SWETS), Information Quest (IQ), FirstSearch Electronic Collections Online (OCLC) (Fecko, 1997; Thompson and Henley, 1997). Some services are based upon whether or not a library or regional cooperative subscribes to the printed version. There are clearly substantial funding issues here regarding central subscriptions versus departmental or individual pay-per-view charges and also of an appropriate access versus holdings policy. However, once such services become established, users may become dependent on them and may be reluctant to forgo them even if budgets become tight. Ideally, electronic journals should be delivered to the desktop via a single user interface or access point, but this may be difficult if journals are being supplied by different publishers. Any electronic journal service should be a well organized and indexed service, offering free access to tables of contents, with either free or pay-per-view access to the journals themselves depending on subscription arrangements.

It is perhaps no surprise that the largest number of eLib projects were concerned with aspects of the electronic journal, still the cornerstone of most academic activity. One of the eLib supporting studies has explored some of the economic implications of the scholarly electronic journal concluding that:

> The advent of electronic full-text journals affords the opportunity to take a fresh approach, recognizing that any risk to publishers in the new electronic age is likely to fall on the small players in the sector, particularly learned societies which are operating on restricted budgets. (Fishwick *et al.*, 1998: iii).

However they recognize that 'offering individual as well as bundles of articles to a world-wide academic community linked to the Internet may well increase demand' (ibid.: iii).

Alongside the establishment of electronic versions of existing print journals, the electronic library will see the development of multimedia-enhanced versions of print journals and also completely new hypermedia journals which can fully exploit the new dynamic Web technologies. The rapid growth of institutional intranets and the ease with which Web pages can be developed has encouraged a number of academics to create new web journals which would otherwise not have been published.

A good example of a multimedia-enhanced journal is the parallel electronic version of the Royal Society of Chemistry's journal *Chemical Communications*. The Internet Archaeology project has produced an entirely new journal, publishing the results of archaeological research, analyses of large datasets, visualization, geographic information systems, computer modelling and other computer software. The archaeologists recognized that, as with many other image- and data-rich disciplines, conventional publications cannot do justice to the rich diversity of archaeological information. On the other hand, *The Journal of Information, Law and Technology* was designed to promote a discursive electronic culture through the establishment and development of a brand new hypermedia and multimedia e-journal.

Nevertheless, academics may still only be willing to use electronic journals if they are published in parallel with printed versions, or the electronic journals are peer-reviewed. In the early development of the electronic library, peer review will be an important consideration for publishers and academics alike. The CATRIONA II project examined approaches to the creation and management of electronic research and teaching resources at Scottish universities. The survey results showed that a large number of academics (85 per cent) regarded desktop access to resources created at other institutions as either important, very important or essential (Nicholson and Smith, 1998).

A potential difficulty with regard to electronic journals is the choice of format for storage and delivery. Until academics and students become accustomed to using e-journals, the integrity of the printed journal look and layout may need to be retained. There are a number of different formats that might be used to retain the layout of a printed journal, none of which is yet a universal standard, although Adobe's PDF (portable document format) is now widely used (Brailsford, 1998). Additional software may be required to allow a particular format to be handled, which may prevent its use or hinder its acceptance by a desktop user. In the long term, Web developments such as Java should allow the electronic journal and the required viewing software to be delivered to the desktop simultaneously. In the meantime, though, this is a significant problem and a potential barrier to the use of e-journals among academics. Russell agrees that the take-up of electronic journals has been disappointing.

> The eLib Electronic journals projects have exploited important potential in new technologies but have also discovered significant constraints. Although many projects are creating new and innovative mechanisms for scholarly interaction – many of which could not be achieved in the print medium – most funded projects have not acted as catalysts for other electronic journal ventures in their disciplines. Instead those involved have found reluctance amongst academics to contribute articles to electronic journals. The majority of the academic community have preferred the safety of traditional journal titles and print culture. (Anonymous, 1997: iii)

In the long term academics will surely begin to accept the electronic journal as an adjunct to, or even a replacement for, existing print journals (Bell, 1997). Once they do, they will start demanding desktop access to all the journals and resources held by the library, as well as new services which were not previously available. These may centre not just around providing journals but also packages of information to meet the needs of staff and students in particular disciplines. The Biz/ed project has developed an extensive and searchable database of wide-ranging electronic resources in business and economics designed for academic staff and students up to first-year undergraduate level.

ON-DEMAND PUBLISHING AND ELECTRONIC RESERVE (ODP/ER)

In the long term many electronic resources may not be published in the traditional sense, but only on demand. These may be made available through some electronic reserve system (the traditional short-loan collection) or supplied in some tailored form for a particular individual. Users may be able to pick and mix information content to retrieve a self-selected and individually created journal issue. Instead of taking out an expensive subscription to journals of marginal interest, or paying for complete journal issues, only those articles deemed to be of relevance to the courses being studied need be selected and paid for.

On-demand publishing (ODP) is likely to be a significant component of the electronic library but it is heavily dependent on the stated needs of academics, researchers and students regarding required material, and the cooperation of publishers (Armstrong and Lonsdale, 1998). This will require both providers and users of information to rethink their approach to information handling. A number of just-in-time electronic article delivery services have been established, many of them in the United States, and are experimenting with desktop journal provision on an as needed basis (High Wire Press, 1998). However, as value-added services may possibly attract extra charges over and above any basic services, the need to control individual departmental library budgets and careful avoidance of unnecessary ODP duplication may therefore be important to their success.

Most of the eLib projects in the ODP programme area were concerned with ODP for students, where the potential for making high-usage material, such as standard textbooks and mainstream journal articles, more easily available can be seen. Project Phoenix (South Bank University) highlighted the current problems.

> Keeping pace with the volume demands of student needs, as expressed by the contents of the module reading lists, is a constant battle; a problem compounded by increasing numbers of students, reduced budgets, and an increase in the speed at which paper based books and journals are produced and updated. (Lloyd-Owen, 1997: 2)

The use of the Web as an alternative publishing medium may be significant here. The ERIMS project explored 'the longer term delivery of marked-up texts by working with selected academics authoring new texts' (Joint Information Systems Committee, 1997: ERIMS project flyer). Eurotext coordinated the development of a national electronic resource bank, relating to the European Union, which allows lecturers to combine documents from Eurotext with locally produced Web or printed materials.

Not only will the content of the electronic library be held electronically, but the management of the individual resources will also need to be handled electronically. Electronic administration systems must be developed which can handle, among other things, copyright clearance and royalty payments. Project eOn focused on the establishment of a suitable model for ODP which incorporated cataloguing, copyright and charging mechanisms and which could be integrated into current educational provision. ODPH (On-Demand Publishing for the Humanities) developed a model for networking copyright texts, and SCOPE (Scottish Collaborative On-demand Publishing Enterprise) developed a model for negotiating and clearing copyright. The five electronic reserve (short-loan) projects – ERCOMS, Project Acorn, Project PATRON, QUIPS and ResIDE – explored a number of practical and procedural issues relevant to the needs of part-time students and distance-learners who are presently disadvantaged by the restricted loan periods of current short-loan collections (SLCs).

A supporting eLib study examining the impact of ODP/ER on students, teaching and libraries and exploring the technical issues involved in all the eLib ODP/ER projects was carried out in 1997. This produced a number of important recommendations which will be necessary to the long term success of ODP/ER, many of them to do with operational standards and agreements (Halliday, 1997). Subsequent to this study, the JISC funded a further eLib project 'to develop a national database and resource bank of electronic texts which will widen access to course materials and improve the quality of learning throughout HE' (ibid.: v).

ELECTRONIC DOCUMENT DELIVERY

We have seen that one of the principal benefits of the electronic library will be the ability to deliver information services to the user's desktop to save them from visiting the library at all. If material is only available electronically then users might just as well access the resources from their own desks. How important this culture change is perceived to be by the individual will depend on the social aspects of the visit to the library, but undoubtedly the transition to an electronic information environment will radically alter the way in which a library operates and interacts with its traditional customers. Electronic document delivery is a relatively new idea for most libraries, although some regional and national document supply services have developed delivery mechanisms incorporating some electronic elements, particularly for document request. However the eLib Document Delivery Programme area has been rather low-key compared to many of the others.

In order to meet the growing demand from academics for access to a wider range of electronic materials we are likely to see more cooperative library ventures with shared or *quid pro quo* services. The LAMDA project is one example of a cooperative structure designed to provide document delivery services to academic libraries in London and Manchester. Journal articles not available in the 'home' library are routed firstly to other libraries in the city, then to libraries in the second city and finally to the British Library Document Supply Centre (Blunden-Ellis, 1996). The existing service is only designed for requests for printed journal articles but clearly can be adapted to accommodate electronic journal delivery. LAMDA has now developed from a closed research project into a fully-fledged service available to all UK HE institutions.

For the increasing number of part-time students, electronic delivery to the home will be of major significance. One of the eLib document delivery projects, EDDIS, has produced an integrated document discovery, location, request and supply service for non-returnable items as well as for the more traditional returnable items, such as books (Larbey, 1997).

TRAINING AND AWARENESS

The reliability of the physical network and the provision of adequate scholarly resource content are critical to the success of the electronic library, but no electronic library in the world will be of any consequence if users are neither aware of its existence nor have sufficient training to use it. If users are unable to gain access to the resources to meet their need or, once connected, are unable to use the electronic resources, then the electronic library will be considered a failure. In the long term both librarians and library users will have to be trained to use the electronic library efficiently and effectively, and be kept up-to-date with important changes to both content and interface. Good initial training may also help users compensate for possible weaknesses that will inevitably be present during the development phases of the electronic library.

Collectively, the eLib training and awareness projects explored a range of issues. These included: Internet current awareness (Ariadne); skills required by LIS workers (SKIP) (Garrod and Sidgreaves, 1997); skills required by LIS trainers (Edulib, Netlinks); skills required by academic users (TAPin); networking training programmes (Netskills); professional development programmes (Netlinks); networking training packages (CINE, Netskills); establishment of a body of network skills accredited trainers (Edulib 1998); and identification of good practice (Netlinks). A further complementary study, IMPEL2, a successor to the non-eLib-funded IMPEL1 project, has looked at the impact of the electronic library on both libraries and academic institutions as a whole. Assessing the culture change brought about by the increased use of networked information has been particularly important to this programme. The IMPEL2 and TAPin case studies reflected a range of HE institutions and, even during the short lifespan of the projects, a number of institutions and individual departments showed a significant change in their awareness and use of networked information. The IMPEL1 and IMPEL2 project findings have been widely published and disseminated, with a number of well attended regional workshops held throughout the UK (Edwards *et al.*, 1993; Edwards *et al.*, 1998; Walton and Edwards, 1997). A number of short IMPEL guides have been produced to 'provide direction and key points on relevant issues facing Higher Education electronic library service providers' (Day *et al.*, 1998). The TAPin project, discussed in detail in this book, looked specifically at the needs of academics regarding access to, and use of, networked information and their interaction with the subject librarians who support them. This brought about a significant culture change not only for the academics and librarians who participated directly in the project, but, in some cases, also for the students of the academics, the rest of the library staff and the institution as a whole.

One of the spin-offs of the training and awareness programme is that the fruits of some of its projects have fed into others. *Ariadne* was a monthly Internet magazine produced in both print and electronic form to reach the widest possible audience. As an added attraction to encourage users to access the Internet, each issue of the Web version included additional articles not available in the print version. By August 1997 the number of monthly hits of the Web version was almost 250 000 (UKOLN, 1997: 17).

The Netskills project was intended to provide a comprehensive national network skills training programme aimed at shifting the culture within HE institutions towards awareness and widespread use of networked information resources. It has produced a number of information and training packages, such as TONIC, which have been used by the other training projects and have been made available through gateway services provided with the ANR programme. By September 1998 over 25 000 individuals had registered to use the original version of TONIC. As an alternative to the more traditional training materials the CINE project explored the potential of brief animated sequences as a medium for training. Topics ranged from the widely applicable, such as search technique improvement, to the more specific – understanding how the Z39.50 protocol works.

HYBRID LIBRARIES

Much of the current research is exploring the long-term implications of a fully functioning electronic library, but in the short term most educational libraries will probably be maintaining a mixture of both traditional printed resources and electronic resources. Indeed Follett Funding has paid for a number of new physical libraries in the second half of the 1990s. Rusbridge (1998) has written in detail about the contribution of the early eLib projects to the hybrid library, but the later projects should provide a better view on how best to manage them and organize the resource collections for the benefit of end-users. HYLIFe is exploring the practicalities of delivering the mixture of print and electronic services required in future educational libraries with economical maintenance. The focus here is not technological, but on the needs of specific non-standard customers and the required institutional, social and educational support. These customers include part-time students, remote users, practitioners/students and franchised colleges. Malibu is developing appropriate management models for the hybrid library including the migration from current library structures to the new ones. BUILDER is developing a model of the hybrid library within both a teaching and a research context at Birmingham University. The project is investigating the use of metadata indexing for all resources including CAL packages. It is also exploring a number of teaching and learning issues such as integration of materials, support for teaching staff in the creation of intranet packages and the involvement of the University Press in the publication and digitization of materials.

CONCLUSION

The electronic libraries programme has involved most of the university libraries of the UK and consequently has had a significant impact on the library workforce. Thus the cultural impact on the libraries of the UK's higher education service has been high. Not all the projects have had a direct impact on the users of those libraries and some projects have clearly been more successful than others. Collectively, though, the programme has shown that the electronic library is feasible and that, with sufficient training and awareness, people will use it. That training will need to continue as the technology of the electronic library changes. The momentum generated by the various projects will need to be maintained, training and awareness materials updated and networked information users more heavily involved than they have hitherto been. The skill level among librarians is high but, in many institutions, is likely to diminish once the effects of the programme wear off, unless a mechanism for periodically updating those skills is put in place. If librarians are to play a greater role in learner support then this becomes imperative. The SKIP project identified a common theme running throughout the literature – namely that:

> ... libraries need to acquire new skills and knowledge as a matter of urgency. Failure to do so, through apathy or procrastination, could amount to professional suicide ... the digital era requires staff who thrive on change and who are proactive in terms of both their approach to work and their own professional development. Equally, organizations need flexible structures if they are to be effective; structures which are

based on a matrix to facilitate cross-functional teamwork, and which are responsive to rapid change. (Garrod, 1998: 244–45)

REFERENCES

Anonymous (1997), *Impact of Electronic and Multi-media Journals on Scholarly Communications: Two eLib Study Reports*, Electronic Libraries Programme Studies E4, London: Library Information Technology Centre. This comprises two separate reports: Alsop, G. *et al.* (1997), *A Study of Human Communication Issues in Interactive Scholarly Electronic Journals*; Esson, K. *et al.* (1997), *A Comparative Analysis of the Role of Multi-media Electronic Journals in Scholarly Disciplines.*

Armstrong, C. and Lonsdale, R. (1998), *The Publishing of Electronic Scholarly Monographs and Textbooks*, Electronic Libraries Programme Studies G5, London: Library Information Technology Centre.

Bell, A. (1997), 'The impact of electronic information on the academic research community', *The New Review of Academic Librarianship*, **3**, 1–24.

Bharat, K. and Broder, A. (1998), 'Measuring the web', http://www.research. digital.com/SRC/whatsnew/sem.html

Blunden-Ellis, J. (1996), 'LAMDA: a project investigating new opportunities in document delivery', *Program*, **30**(4), September, 385–90.

Brailsford, H. (1998), 'Parallel publishing and the scholarly journal', *Library and Information Briefings*, (82), May.

Brodie, M. and McLean, N. (1995), 'Process reengineering in academic libraries: shifting to client-centered resource provision', *CAUSE/EFFECT Magazine*, **18**(2), Summer, 40–46. Also available in different formats from: http:// www.educause.edu/pub/ce/cem95/cem952.html

Davies, C. *et al.* (1997), *Early Impact of eLib Activities on Cultural Change in Higher Education*, Electronic Libraries Programme Studies E1, London: Library Information Technology Centre, July.

Day, J.M. *et al.* (1998), *IMPEL Guides*, Newcastle: University of Northumbria at Newcastle.

Department for Education and Employment (1997), *Connecting the Learning Society: National Grid for Learning: The Government's Consultation Paper*, London: DfEE.

Edwards, C. *et al.* (1993), 'Key areas in the management of change in higher education libraries in the 1990's: relevance of the IMPEL project', *British Journal of Academic Librarianship*, **8**(3), 139–77.

Edwards, C. *et al.* (eds) (1998), *Monitoring Organisational and Cultural Change: The Impact on People of Electronic Libraries*, Electronic Libraries Programme Studies G4, London: Library Information Technology Centre.

Electronic Libraries Programme, (eLib) Phase 3, (nd) The eLlib Phase 3 Programme: hybrid libraries and large scale resource discovery ... and digital preservation. http://www.ukoln.ac.uk/services/elib/background/pressreleases/summary2.html

Fecko, M. B. (1997), *Electronic Resources: Access and Issues,* London: Bowker Saur.

Fishwick, F. *et al.* (1998), *Scholarly Electronic Journals: Economic Implications,* Electronic Libraries Programme Studies E2, London: Library Information Technology Centre.

Further Education Funding Council (1997), *Learning Works: Widening Participation in Further Education,* (Kennedy Report), Chair: H. Kennedy, Coventry: Further Education Funding Council.

Fryer, R.H. (1997), *Learning for the Twenty-first Century: First Report of the National Advisory Group for Continuing Education and Life-long Learning,* no publisher.

Garrod, P. (1998), 'Skills for new information professionals (SKIP): an evaluation of the key findings', *Program,* **32**(3), July, 241–63.

Garrod, P. and Sidgreaves, I. (1997), *Skills for New Information Professionals: The SKIP Project,* Electronic Libraries Programme Studies G3, London: Library Information Technology Centre.

Geleijnse, H. (1994), 'A library of the future', *Library Association Record,* **96**(2), February, 10–11.

Halliday, L. (ed.) (1997), *The Impact of On-demand Publishing and Electronic Reserve on Student, Teaching and Libraries in Higher Education in the UK,* Electronic Libraries Programme Studies E3, London: Library Information Technology Centre.

High Wire Press (1998), 'Just-in-time(sm): electronic article delivery services', http://www.public.iastate.edu/~CYBERSTACKS/Just.htm

Joint Funding Councils' Libraries Review Group (1993), *Report,* (Follet Report), http://www.ukoln.ac.uk/services/papers/follett/report/

Joint Information Systems Committee (1997), *Electronic Libraries Programme,* edition 3.

Joint Information Systems Committee (JISC), (1998), http://www.jisc.ac.uk/

Kemp, B. and Davenport, E. (1998), 'Executive Summary', in R. McLeod and L. Kerr *A User-centred Qualitative Evaluation of the EEVL Service: A Summary,* http://www.eevl.ac.uk/evalsumm.html

Larbey, D. (1997), 'Project EDDIS: an approach to integrating document discovery, location, request and supply', *Interlending and Document Supply,* **25**(3), 96–102.

Lloyd-Owen, R. (1997), 'On-demand publishing – researching its application to some library problems: Project Phoenix', *Library and Information Briefings,* (74), August, 1–21.

MacLeod, R. *et al.* (1998), 'The EEVL approach to providing a subject based information gateway for engineers', *Program*, **32**(3), July, 205–23.

MacDougall, A. (1998), 'Supporting learners at a distance', *Ariadne*, (16), July, 6–7, http://www.ariadne.ac.uk/issue16/

National Committee of Inquiry into Higher Education (1997), *Report*, (Dearing Report), Chair: Sir Ron Dearing, London: HMSO.

Nicholson, D. and Smith, M. (1998), 'Electronic resource creation and management at Scottish universities: survey results and demonstrator service progress', *Ariadne*, (14), March, 9–10, http://www.ariadne.ac.uk/issue14/ (See also the CATRIONA website.)

Rusbridge, C. (1998), 'Towards the hybrid library', *D-Lib Magazine*, July–August, Also available as http://mirrored.ukoln.ac.uk/lis-journals/dlib/dlib/dlib/july98/rusbridge/07rusbridge.html

Steele, C. (1997), 'Managing change in digital structures', in D. Raitt (ed.), *Libraries for the New Millennium*, London: Library Association, 148–68.

Tavistock Institute (1997), *Evaluation of the Electronic Libraries Programme: Synthesis of the Annual Reports*, London: Tavistock Institute, Evaluation Development and Review Unit.

Thompson, S. and Henley, J. (1997), 'JournalsOnline: the online journal solution', *Ariadne*, (12), November, 1. Also at: http://www.ariadne.ac.uk/issue12/

UKOLN (1997), *Annual report 1996/97*, Bath: University of Bath.

Walton, G. and Edwards, C. (1997), 'Strategic management of the electronic library in the UK higher education sector: implications of eLib's IMPEL2 project at the University of Northumbria at Newcastle' in D. Raitt (ed.), *Libraries for the New Millennium: Implications for Managers*, London: Library Association.

Watson, L. (1998), 'Information services: a mission and a vision', *Ariadne*, (14), March, 6–7, http://www.ariadne.ac.uk/issue14/

eLib PROJECT SITES

The following is a list of eLib project sites discussed in this chapter. The entries include project acronym, full project name, lead institution, URL (last checked on 1 February 1999).

ADAM (Art, Design, Architecture and Media), The Surrey Institute of Art and Design, http://www.adam.ac.uk/

Biz/ed: Business Education on the Internet, University of Bristol, http://www.bized.ac.uk/

BUILDER (Birmingham University Integrated Library Development and Electronic Resource), Birmingham University, http://builder.bham.ac.uk/

CATRIONA II, Strathclyde University, http://catriona2.lib.strath.ac.uk/catriona/

CINE (Cartoon Images for Network Education), King's College, London, http://www.kcl.ac.uk/projects/cine/

The CLIC Consortium Electronic Journal Project, Imperial College, http://www.ch.ic.ac.uk/clic/

EDDIS (Electronic Document Delivery – the Integrated Solution), University of East Anglia (no website identified via UKOLN)

EduLib (Educational Development for Higher Education Library Staff), http://www.hull.ac.uk/edulib/

EEVL (Edinburgh Engineering Virtual Library), Heriot Watt University, http://www.eevl.ac.uk/

eOn: Inter-institutional networking of learning materials, University of East London, http://www.eon.uel.ac.uk/

ERCOMS (Electronic Reserve Copyright Management Systems), De Montfort University, http://www.iielr.dmu.ac.uk/Projects/ERCOMS/

ERIMS (Electronic Readings in Management Studies), Templeton College, Oxford, http://www.templeton.ox.ac.uk/www/college/library/erims/intro.htm

Eurotext, Hull University, http://eurotext.ulst.ac.uk/

HyLife (HYbrid LIbraries of the FuturE), University of Northumbria at Newcastle, http://www.unn.ac.uk/~xcu2/hylife/

IMPEL2 (IMpact on People of Electronic Libraries), University of Northumbria at Newcastle, http://ilm.unn.ac.uk/impel/

Internet Archaeology, Council for British Archaeology (with the University of York), http://intarch.ac.uk/

JILT: The Journal of Information, Law and Technology, Warwick University, http://elj.warwick.ac.uk/

LAMDA (London/Manchester Document Delivery), University College, London, http://www.ucl.ac.uk/Library/lamda.htm

Malibu (MAnaging the hybrid LIbrary for the Benefit of Users), King's College, London, http://www.kcl.ac.uk/humanities/cch/malibu/

Netskills, Newcastle University, http://www.netskills.ac.uk/

Newsagent, South Bank University, http://www.sbu.ac.uk/~litc/newsagent/

ODPH (On-Demand Publishing in the Humanities), Liverpool John Moores University, http://www.livjm.ac.uk/on_demand/

Project ACORN (Access to Course Readings via Networks), Loughborough University of Technology, http://acorn.lboro.ac.uk/

Project PATRON (Performing Arts Teaching Resources ONline), University of Surrey, http://www.lib.surrey.ac.uk/Patron/Patron.htm

QUIPS (Quick Information for Part-time Students), Liverpool John Moores University (no web site identified via UKOLN).

ResIDE (RESearch Information DElivery), University of the West of England, http://www.uwe.ac.uk/library/itdev/reside/

SCOPE (Scottish Collaborative On-demand Publishing Enterprise), Stirling University, http://www.stir.ac.uk/infoserv/scope/

TAPin, University of Central England, http://www.uce.ac.uk/tapin/tapin.htm

5 Convergence: a review of the literature

Alison Sutton

INTRODUCTION

Technical convergence describes the ongoing evolutionary process, brought about by advances in the electronic storage and networking of academic information, in which there is a coming together and overlapping of the roles of libraries, computer centres and academic departments. The effect of this with regard to the two principal information services is twofold: first, the library has changed its function from the holding of information to one of providing access to it; and, second, the computer centre, no longer required to service large centralized computers, has a newer role in providing networking expertise to enable the flow of that information through the university. This is matched with a convergence of user need as academics and students exploit electronic information.

It should be noted that, in addition to the library and computer centre, converged services sometimes include a variety of other departments, such as audiovisual or media services, educational development, print services, teaching and learning initiatives, and even student counselling. However, it is the relationship of the library with the computing service which is the focus of this chapter. The make-up of the computer centre varies between institutions but usually comprises some or all of academic support, systems support, MIS (management information systems) and sometimes the telephone system.

IMPLICATIONS OF CONVERGENCE

In 1989 the significance of convergence for universities was stated strongly in *The Electronic Campus: An Information Strategy* – the proceedings of a major UK conference attended by senior librarians and academics (Brindley, 1989). It put the convergence debate firmly on the map stating that 'We are moving into an era ... when it will no longer be possible to consider these services in isolation from each other, or from the institution at large' (Sidgreaves, 1989: 71) and 'The concept of an electronic or wired campus will cause us to re-examine both the function and structure of these services ...' (ibid.: 72).

Convergence is continually evolving and 'The issue is what institutions decide to do about that fact [of convergence] in terms of their organisation and operations' (Williams, 1994: 69). Thus merging, or integrating, aspects of the library and computer centre, and sometimes other services, is a chosen response to the converging environment, bringing the convergent paths closer. Whilst *merging* should not be used interchangeably with *converging* it is sometimes necessary to use the varied terminology of the authors, when discussing their works, in order to quote accurately and to avoid redefinition.

Many institutions have responded by merging or integrating, in a variety of ways, some of their library and computer centre services, functions, staff or senior management. There are no current figures for the number of combined services in UK universities, possibly due to differing interpretations of what constitutes such a service. However, Foster (1995: 12) suggested '40 of around 100 mainstream universities', a year later Collier (1996: 72) estimated 'well over 30' and Pugh (1998: 3) more recently stated that a 'little over half of the university sector has undertaken some form of integration of provision' – an indication that there is widespread significant change in the management of information resources on campus.

THE CONCEPT OF INTEGRATED SERVICES

The merging of various services with the library is not a new idea. An intermingling of services in further education can be traced back to the 1950s (Armsby, 1994: 81). Learning resource centres were developed in some secondary schools in the 1960s (Sidgreaves *et al.*, 1987: 7) and in some further and higher education institutions from the mid-1970s – Brighton and Plymouth Polytechnics being early examples (Lovecy, 1994: 2). Initially, the learning resource centres did not include computing but usually combined media/audiovisual resources, library, educational development and educational technology. In these cases, integration may have been driven by the philosophy of resource-based learning.

Convergence is clearly occurring in sectors of information provision other than universities, and it is also not unique to the UK – similar movements are taking place in Ireland and Australia (Collier, 1996: 72). A literature search of *Library and Information Science Abstracts* also finds references to Europe and the Far East. However, the situation in other countries is not discussed below, with the exception of the USA where ground-breaking ideas had a great impact on the early UK convergence debate.

THE LITERATURE

The theory of converging libraries and computer centres originated in the USA, during the early 1980s, where it 'was founded in a faith in the evolving technology' (Sutherland, 1992: 13). The American literature, often referred to by UK authors, precedes the British interest which began in the mid-1980s because the application of information technology in libraries had an earlier impact in the USA.

The literature is not easily identifiable by searching only under the term *convergence*. It is a concept which permeates many aspects of academic library literature, such as computer services, learning resources, and staffing issues, and thus there is a vast amount of literature which is relevant. The following is a review of the key works only, which are discussed in chronological order, illustrating the history and development of the convergence debate. Most of the literature in both the USA and UK reiterates ideas put forward in previous publications and so it is sometimes difficult to assign ideas to one individual. Also, the authors of these works are senior librarians, rather than computing people, so the literature takes the library, rather than the computing, perspective.

THE US LITERATURE

The US debate in the 1980s and 1990s

Battin was one of the earliest proponents of combining the computer centre and library. She believed that a combination of the skills and facilities of both the library and computing service would allow the electronic library to be developed for the benefit of the student:

> The obvious answer to the Electronics Scholar's plight is the formation of a Scholarly Information Center by merging the Libraries and the Computer Center. ... The integration of Libraries and the Computer Center, each with its specific strengths and expertise, will provide one-stop shopping for the University community as well as a stabilizing planning mechanism for effective and flexible response to rapidly changing technologies. (Battin, 1984: 16–17)

In this way Battin introduced the fundamental concepts which were to dominate the convergence issue on both sides of the Atlantic during the 1980s: the electronic imperative and the perceived scholarly need for merging; and the institutional significance in terms of planning a combined information service. She acknowledged that there were problems with integration, one of the chief barriers against moving closer together being the two professions' respective images of each other (ibid.: 12) as well as the problems of funding such change, and inappropriate staff skills (ibid.: 17).

A year later, Moholt (1985: 286) explored these perceived differences between librarians and computing professionals and stated that libraries and computer centres already had many of the essential ingredients – that is, the overlapping and complementary areas of expertise and operations – to enable integration of the library and computing service. Similarly, Neff identified eight similar trends, based on overlapping electronic applications in libraries and computer centres, which he summarized as follows:

> ... the library is a repository of packaged information and the computer center stores and retrieves information: the library lends information and the center displays it; the library acquires and borrows information and the center inputs information. In one form of service or another, storage, retrieval, input and output of information are common to both. (Neff, 1985: 8)

Battin (1984) had suggested that organizational change might be necessary to bring about this close relationship between the library and computer centre, and Cimbala (1987) and Dougherty (1987) went on to propose contrasting theoretical models. Cimbala's was an *organizational model*, based on the concept of the overlapping functions of computer centres and libraries, already mentioned above. It basically consisted of an administrative merger based on carving up the old services and arranging their functions into a service branch – public or user services – and a technical branch for processes such as inputting catalogue records (Cimbala, 1987: 395). She also suggested that the development of a new kind of staff, 'a hybrid librarian–computer scientist may be the solution to the personnel dilemmas created by such an organization' (ibid.: 396).

Dougherty's solution was not an organizational model but a suggestion for cooperation. He proposed that:

> ... the two organizations will continue to have distinct, though closely related, identities for many years. In this context they can best serve their users by carefully constructed programmes of collaboration that recognize both their common links in information science and their historically different missions. (Dougherty, 1987: 289)

In 1987 Cargill suggested that experiences at Texas Tech University had revealed an alternative to merging – coexistence, within shared buildings, of the library and computing centre:

> If those responsible for the library and computer center will focus on the results – that is, providing effective access to information in different forms ... and not concentrate so much on the procedures and the mechanics, there will be a virtually seamless integration of both facilities. We – and our clientele – can embrace the new while still valuing the old. (Cargill, 1987: 347–48)

The concept of cooperation was further developed in the 1990s. In 1993 Creth suggested that administrative mergers of libraries and computer centres were no longer of primary concern, and called for the development of a '... truly collaborative culture in which librarians and computer professionals work together to develop mutually beneficial projects and a support structure to achieve a flexible and innovative response to the integration of information technology into all aspects of university life' (Creth, 1993: 15). She further proposed a model for pooling expertise: 'a collaborative, virtual organization – not administrative merger' (ibid.: 116). Creth saw these staff as partners, rather than as separate groups pursuing parallel paths (ibid.: 118).

The US literature since the mid-1990s

Although convergence continues to feature in the literature there have been few full-scale mergers in the USA, despite the intense interest of the previous decade. Young wrote that: 'Only a few large universities and perhaps a couple of dozen or more smaller institutions have placed the computer centre and the library under single management' (Young, 1994: 5). This largely confirmed what Brindley had earlier concluded, following a study tour to the USA in 1988:

> The issue of convergence, a hot topic two years ago, ... no longer seems to be centre stage. ... Cooperation across the two services [library and computer centre], rather than merger has become the focus, with the LIS still keeping a centre stage position in electronic information service provision. (Brindley, 1988: 2)

Eight years later Collier suggested that the reasons for this might be that:

> ... the reduction in unit of resource has not yet reached a stage in the United States where it has provoked a radical response, and also that faculty and professional structures are so strong relative to the executive that institutional change is not easily effected by strategic measures. (Collier, 1996: 72)

Thus, despite its early impact on the UK debate, convergence in the USA takes place in a very different cultural context in which alternative relationships to the administrative merger of libraries and computer centres predominate.

THE UK LITERATURE

The UK literature falls into the following broad categories: journal articles (theoretical and anecdotal); surveys and studies which are essentially primary evidence; and major reports which have influenced the debate.

The early UK debate: the late 1980s and early 1990s

After the 1988 conference reported in *The Electronic Campus: An Information Strategy* (Brindley, 1989), the first major work to deal specifically with convergence was a 1988 issue of the *British Journal of Academic Librarianship* devoted to the subject. This is an important publication because most of the important concepts which feature in later literature were introduced here. Of particular interest in this issue is an overview of convergence issues provided by Naylor (1988). Polytechnic South West and the University of Salford, together with Carnegie Mellon University, USA, and the National Institute for Higher Education, Limerick, are included as case studies.

One of the most obviously significant implications of the case studies is that the university libraries and computer centres featured all moved towards different merger models. In the first of the two UK examples the University of Salford computing services merged with the library (which already had responsibility for audiovisual media services) to form the academic information services. This was the first UK university 'to merge the major academic services at the operational level' (Harris, 1988: 147). The catalyst for the merger at Salford was the departure of the Director of Computer Services, and a further opportunity was created by the development of a new building intended to house both services. However, the justification for the process was the increasing technological overlap between the two services (ibid.: 148). The new service was headed by the librarian – Harris – who became dually titled as Director of Academic Information Services and Librarian, and was possibly the first case in the UK of a merged service with a single executive head (Lovecy, 1994: 1).

Harris's discussion of the regime at Salford is significant in that it explains the benefits of merging from an institutional perspective. He believed that the newly merged service must be 'more than simply the sum of the [constituent] parts' (Harris, 1988: 150). First, he saw that the reduction in competition between the two services, and increased consultation between the two, would result in a single view, so that planning would be easier and expenditure would not be duplicated. Second, the single information service at Salford would not only be able to respond to academic developments across the campus, but it could also take the lead (ibid.: 151). In other words, its profile and impact as a single entity became greater than that of the library and computer centre as separate bodies.

At Polytechnic South West, learning resources, computing services and student services were integrated into learning resources services. This was intended to provide a coordinated delivery of services to students under the assistant director (academic services) – Sidgreaves, previously the librarian. Despite their close association each element continued to be controlled by its own manager – for example, a librarian remained in charge of the library. This reorganization was seen as a response to the pressures of the higher education environment, in terms of demands posed by increased student numbers, the greater emphasis on student-centred learning and the pervasive use of IT in teaching (Sidgreaves, 1988: 136–37). The Polytechnic South West case is important in that it demonstrates the variety of services that can be brought together in a merger. As an example of a merging service it demonstrates that reorganization can begin with integration at the level of service delivery.

Naylor's paper in the *British Journal of Academic Librarianship*, is crucial to the early literature about convergence because it analyses, in a UK context, the theories and arguments which underpin the debate. Like much of the US literature it is preoccupied with the technological overlap of functions between the two services, but also draws attention to some of the human resources problems associated with a merged service. Staff would require new skills, and a 'different kind of person' may be needed from the traditional library and computing staff (Naylor, 1988: 183). Naylor also proposes that the uniqueness of the library be questioned and that it detach itself from its special custodial role and become a conduit for information provision (ibid.: 184–85).

Bebbington and Cronin (1989: 7–16) suggested that the library and computing centre had remained separate because of differences in professional cultures. They observed that it could be difficult for the computer centre to identify its purpose with that of the library because the library deals with *intangibles* – service being unmeasurable and difficult to quantify – whereas the computer centre deals with *tangibles*, such as computers and software. Furthermore, libraries are centrally funded whereas computer centres operate charge-back policies, which makes coordination of the two difficult, and a further barrier to cooperation is constituted by the professional hierarchy within libraries which is uncongenial to the computer centre staff. Bebbington and Cronin suggested that the cultural barriers to merger are reinforced by *organizational inhibitors*: the division of the institutional culture of universities into 'autonomous units has resulted in a failure to perceive the essential relationship between libraries and the appliance of information technology to the needs of the university as a whole' (ibid.: 8). However, despite their emphasis on the difficulties of cooperation, they suggested that: 'The foundation elements needed to create a powerful and appropriate information utility already exist' (ibid.: 10, as defined by Moholt (1985)). Libraries provide: user-friendly orientation, highly structured files and collections, uniformity of access and a high degree of subject expertise; and computer centres offer: 24-hour access, unlimited, cost-effective storage, easily manipulable files, and a high degree of technical expertise (ibid.: 11). In addition to looking at the functions of the library and computer centre, Bebbington and Cronin commented on the difficulty of staffing the new service – a point already raised by Naylor (1988). They concluded that 'Social engineering will be as important as either structural or electrical engineering in laying the foundations of the campus information utility' (ibid.: 13).

Breaks (1991) examined the development of library and computer cooperation in the UK, providing a summary of the organizational forces and university organizational structures which had kept them apart. Cultural differences and institutional barriers became more entrenched, he argued, as IT developments – uncoordinated in terms of standards and funding – took place within universities (Breaks, 1991: 142). Breaks also mentioned the forces drawing them together, such as interest shown by the University Funding Council for the submission of institutional plans which included a requirement for a university-wide information and computer strategy – an indication in itself of strategic thinking (ibid.: 144). Additionally, SCONUL (The Standing Committee of National and University Libraries) and IUCC (Inter-University Committee on Computing) set up a Joint Information Service Working Party to look at 'computer-based information services in universities, and how libraries and computer centres might co-operate over the installation, operation and use of these information services'(IUCC and SCONUL, 1990 cited in Breaks, 1991: 144).

Sutherland's (1992) survey, *The Management of Integrated Learning Resources*, examined learning resources in the literature and through case studies and is a valuable consolidation of both the US and UK literature described above. She summarized the factors influencing the restructuring of resources in learning services into four categories: changes in student profile; changes to learning and teaching; managerial; and technically converging activities (ibid.: 4–12). In her summary and conclusions she wrote that: 'If there is no established pattern and no single solution, there are nevertheless common problems and approaches that have been recognised and implemented by institutions' (ibid.: 51).

The UK literature: the mid 1990s

The Follett Report (Joint Funding Councils, 1993) gave new impetus to the convergence debate in the 1990s. It looked at the present and future role of libraries in UK universities in the light of changes in higher education and stressed the need for an institution-wide information strategy featuring the concept of the information service. It further suggested that the advantage of organizational convergence was that it enabled 'an integrated information strategy to develop' (ibid.: 29), but argued nevertheless that: 'Regardless of its management structure, each institution should seek to promote the coordinated planning of all its teaching and learning resources, bringing those responsible for library and information services into this work' (ibid.: 29). The Report also recommended that the senior person responsible for information services should take 'a leading role in the senior management of the institution' (ibid.). This prescriptive attitude from the Joint Funding Councils towards the organization of information services led some writers to conclude that 'Convergence of services is now actively being encouraged in the UK' (Edwards *et al.*, 1993: 158).

Following the Follett Report, the Fielden Report (John Fielden Consultancy, 1993) was commissioned by the HEFCE (Higher Education Funding Council for

England) Libraries Review to look at human resources in libraries. It examined various information services structures and identified two types of model: 'organisational or formal convergence' and 'operational or informal convergence' (ibid.: 15).

Also in 1993 a controversial correspondence in *The Times Higher Education Supplement* added spark to the convergence issue. Ratcliffe and Hartley of the University of Cambridge (3 March 1993) suggested that, apart from small institutions which needed to merge for financial reasons, 'At the very least the priorities and management needs in two such diverse bodies [as the library and computer centre] are incompatible'. They accepted that these two services could expand their remits into each other's territory but maintained that this hardly meant amalgamation was justified. They saw the library only as a department, like any other in the university, which was a user of the computer centre's technology. In a similar vein, Crocker (12 March 1993), whose letter was published a week later, feared that if the computer centre was merged with the library its independence in terms of providing the hardware and software infrastructure necessary for electronic development across all departments would be reduced. Such a move could mean that the computer centre would be 'inhibited by some expedient but ill-conceived management structure'. By contrast, and in the same issue, Lovecy (12 March 1993) suggested that the management needs of the two services were not incompatible but identical in some respects because their competition for resources caused a competitive overlap of interests. He believed that some form of coordination was justified in order to present a single, rather than a competitive, application for funding.

Williams (1994) after surveying the US and UK literature in detail, then went on to consider whether merger was inevitable by looking at the reasons for merging or not doing so, and the factors affecting the process and resulting models. He suggested that, for some universities, merger would be necessary and, for others, there would be a different model of service integration or an information service similar to that proposed by Cimbala (1987) (Williams, 1994: 69–70).

The same year witnessed the publication of Lovecy's (1994) overview of the state of convergence in the UK. Using the analysis in Bruce Royan's (1994) then recent survey of mergers in UK universities he observed that models at one end of the spectrum included 'the meeting between the heads of the services' in which they cooperate to 'agree priorities' and at the other 'the single service administered by one officer in which many staff cannot claim to be either Library or Computing Staff' (Lovecy, 1994: 2). Despite this diversity, Lovecy pointed out that the emphasis on information strategies by the funding bodies means that library and computing must work together regardless of how separate their structures remain (ibid.: 4). He also suggested that 'The degree to which convergence moves towards merger depends not on some ideological belief in the rightness of merger, but on the extent to which the needs of the University can be satisfied without it' (ibid.: 8).

A year later, Sidgreaves wrote the lead article in an issue of *Relay*, basing his ideas on the belief that convergence must display *service convergence* – that is, convergence in the operation and delivery of services at the user end (Sidgreaves, 1995: 3–6). This is consistent with his view in 1988, when he described the early stages of integration at Polytechnic South West (Sidgreaves, 1988). The justification for joining them together is indicated by 'the perceptions of students themselves as learners' (Sidgreaves, 1995: 4). From this perspective the library should be at the hub of a converged service, because from the students' viewpoint, the library has a history of service and is a 'crucial element in their study' (ibid.). However, he stressed that the success of convergence depends on mutual respect and that it shouldn't be regarded as a takeover.

Paterson (1996) added a refreshing angle to convergence in the UK by showing how cooperation can be a respectable response to convergence. He perceived information services as being divided into those which are converged according to various definitions, and those which simply co-exist, among some of which there is 'encouraging and developing cooperation' (ibid.: 196). He suggested that, at the University of Exeter, convergent destinies could be brought closer together through teambuilding and the careful pacing of change in the process of projects, such as the development of an information strategy for the university and the construction of web pages. In non-merged services he emphasized the importance of a 'structure which makes willingness to cooperate and the continued sharing of perceptions and plans an institutional expectation and a directorial imperative' (ibid.: 204).

The UK literature: the late 1990s

After the mid-1990s there were few publications that added a new dimension to the convergence debate, although a great deal of useful comment emanated from the literature of the eLib projects and from that inspired by the Dearing Report (National Committee of Inquiry, 1997). Articles by Brewer (1998), Garrod (1998), Clegg (1998), and Pugh (1998) are such examples. The only major contribution to the research in the late 1990s is Pugh's (1997) report, *Convergence in Academic Support Services*. He considered convergence, in the context of change management, by examining, through case studies, institutions where there had been real change to the status quo rather than collaboration or simply combined reporting lines of service managers to vice-chancellors. He found the following to be of great importance in achieving fully converged services: 'consultative processes, leadership, boundary spanning structures, teams, devolved management and decision making and a sharp focus on the learning process and customer services' (Abstract page). However, he did acknowledge that many of the universities which fell outside this definition did display many of the benefits of converged services.

This later period of the debate has been enlarged by electronic publications. This medium has become a vehicle for much of the eLib and post-Dearing comment and is a distinct body of literature because of its currency and because it so often discusses real-world situations. For example, there have been interviews with senior members of information services in the electronic journal *deLiberations* and short case studies in a regular discussion column, 'Down your way', in the dually published journal, *Ariadne*. Some of these articles discuss the provision of information services in new learning centres, thus illuminating the impact of new buildings on mergers – an aspect not featured in much of the literature discussed above.

CONCLUSION

One of the most useful overviews of UK convergence is Collier's (1996) chapter, 'The context of convergence', the conclusion of which serves well for the findings of this chapter – that the debate is still not stabilizing. He called for 'a coherent theory to be developed to provide a framework for management and development of such [merged information] services' (ibid.: 79).

REFERENCES

Ariadne, http://www.ariadne.ac.uk/
Armsby, A. (1994), 'Convergence of learning resource services in further education', *Coombe Lodge Reports*, **24**(2), 81–98.
Battin, P. (1984), 'The electronic library: a vision for the future', *EDUCOM Bulletin*, Summer, 12–17, 34.
Bebbington, L. and Cronin, B. (1989), 'Courtship and competition on campus: the convergence of university libraries and computing centres', *Library Review*, **38**(2), 7–16.
Breaks, M. (1991), 'Problems in managing the campus information utility', *IATUL Quarterly*, **5**(2), 142–49.
Brewer, G. (1998), 'Minotaur', *Ariadne*, (15), May, http://www.ariadne.ac.uk/
Brindley, L.J. (1988), *Libraries and the Wired-up Campus: The Future Role of the Library in Academic Information Handling: Report of a Study Visit to the United*

States 14–24th August 1988, British Library R & D Report 5980, London: British Library.

Brindley, L.J. (ed.) (1989), *The Electronic Campus: An Information Strategy*, British Library LIR Report 73, London: British Library.

British Journal of Academic Librarianship (1988), **3**(3). The entire issue is devoted to the topic of convergence.

Cargill, J. (1987), 'Cooperative cohabitation: libraries and computer learning centers', *Library Software Review*, **6**(6), 344–48.

Cimbala, D.J. (1987), 'The scholarly information center: an organizational model', *College and Research Libraries*, **45**(5), 393–98.

Clegg, S.M. (1998), 'Converged enquiry/help desks: rhetoric or reality?', *Relay*, **45**, 7–10.

Collier, M. (1996), 'The context of convergence' in M. Oldroyd (ed.), *Staff Development in Academic Libraries: Present Practice and Future Challenges*, London: Library Association Publishing, 68–80.

Creth, S.D. (1993), 'Creating a virtual information organization: collaborative relationships between libraries and computing centres', *Journal of Library Administration*, **19**(3–4), 111–32.

Crocker, P. (1993), Letter, *The Times Higher Education Supplement*, 12 March.

deLiberations, http://www.lgu.ac.uk/deliberations/

Dougherty, R.M. (1987), 'Libraries and computing centers: a blueprint for collaboration', *College and Research Libraries*, **48**(4), 289–96.

Edwards, C. *et al.* (1993), 'Key areas in the management of change in higher education libraries in the 1990s: relevance of the IMPEL project', *British Journal of Academic Librarianship*, **8**(3), 139–77.

Foster, A. (1995), 'The emergence of convergence', *Library Manager*, **11**, October, 12–13.

Garrod, P. (1998), 'SKIP: skills for new information professionals', *Ariadne*, (11), September, http://www.ariadne.ac.uk/

Harris, C. (1988), 'Academic information services at the University of Salford', *British Journal of Academic Librarianship*, **3**(3), 147–52.

IUCC & SCONUL (1990), 'A report by Inter-University Committee on Computing & Standing Conference of National and University Libraries Joint Information Services Working Party. Information technology penetration and co-ordination on university campuses', *British Journal of Academic Librarianship*, **5**(1), 1–30.

John Fielden Consultancy (1993), *Supporting Expansion: A Report on Human Resource Management in Academic Libraries for the Joint Funding Councils' Libraries Review Group*, Bristol: HEFCE, July 1993 (revised September 1993).

Joint Funding Councils' Libraries Review Group (1993), *Report*, (Follet Report), Chair: Professor Sir Brian Follett, Bristol: HEFCE.

Lovecy, I. (1993), 'Libraries IT role overdue?', Letter, *The Times Higher Education Supplement*, 12 March.

Lovecy, I. (1994), 'Convergence of libraries and computing services', *Library and Information Briefings*, **54**, 1–11.

Moholt, P. (1985), 'On converging paths: the computing center and the library,' *The Journal of Academic Librarianship*, **11**(5), 284–88.

National Committee of Inquiry into Higher Education (1997), *Report*, (Dearing Report), Chair: Sir Ron Dearing, London: HMSO.

Naylor, B. (1988), 'The convergence of the library and the computing service: the central issues', *British Journal of Academic Librarianship*, **3**(3), 172–86.

Neff, R.K. (1985), 'Merging libraries and computer centers: manifest destiny or manifestly deranged?', *EDUCOM Bulletin*, Winter, 8–12, 16.

Paterson, A. (1996), 'Surf and turf: issues in the development of academic services', *IATUL Proceedings (New series)*, **5**, 194–204.

Pugh, L. (1997), *Convergence in Academic Support Services*, British Library RIC Report 54, London: British Library Research and Innovation Centre.

Pugh, L. (1998), 'Dearing, IT and information services: two cheers (or one and a half?)', *Ariadne*, (13), January, http://www.ariadne.ac.uk/

Ratcliffe, F. and Hartley, D. (1993), 'Library services', Letter, *The Times Higher Education Supplement*, 5 March.

Royan, B. (1994), 'Are you being merged? a survey of convergence in information service provision', *SCONUL Newsletter*, **1**, Spring, 17–20.

Sidgreaves, I. (1988), 'The development of "academic services" at Polytechnic South West', *British Journal of Academic Librarianship*, **3**(3), 136–46.

Sidgreaves, I. (1989), 'The electronic campus – an information strategy: organisation issues' in L. J. Brindley (ed.), *The Electronic Campus: An Information Strategy*, British Library LIR Report 73, London: British Library.

Sidgreaves, I. (1995), 'Convergence: an update', *Relay*, **42**, 3-6.

Sidgreaves, I. *et al.* (1987), 'Supporting changing patterns of teaching and learning: Plymouth Polytechnic Learning Resources Centre', *Programmed Learning and Educational Technology*, **24**(1), 7–16.

Sutherland, P. (1992), *The Management of Integrated Learning Resources*, Brighton: Council of Polytechnic Librarians.

Williams, A.G. (1994), 'Where are we going? The development of convergence between university libraries and computing services', in C. Harris (ed.), *The New University Library: Issues for the 90s and Beyond: Essays in Honour of Ian Rogerson*. London: Taylor Graham, 55–72.

Young, A.P. (1994), 'Information technology and libraries: a virtual convergence', *CAUSE/EFFECT*, **17**(3), 5–6, 12.

6 Technical convergence and the response of the academic institution

Alison Sutton

INTRODUCTION

Despite the fact that there 'appear to be almost as many variations [of structures] as there are converged services' (Sidgreaves, 1995: 3) and that 'no one model has appeared as an indicator of successful joint working practices' (Huntingford, 1998: 3), a number of attempts have been made in the literature to categorize merged information services and to prescribe the criteria necessary for a successful response to technical convergence. These provide a variety of examples against which institutions considering merger can assess their own requirements. In this chapter my own qualitative case study research both illustrates and extends the concepts raised in the literature. As in Chapter 5, the focus is on the merger of libraries with computing services, and other services incorporated within mergers are not discussed.

CASE STUDY RESEARCH

In 1997 I carried out six case studies in both old and new (ex-polytechnic) universities – three in the South-east of England and three in the Midlands – four of which had merged their library and computing services. These and the two non-merged services were examined by means of visits, interviews or e-mail discussion with the information services' directors or senior managers, and through internal documents. The interviewees were contacted again in 1998 to obtain a brief summary of developments in the interim. For all the case studies the interviewees were of library origin, except in Case Study 1 and Case Study 5, in which managers of a computer centre background were also interviewed.

To preserve the universities' anonymity the case studies are referred to by number, as explained in Table 6.1. All the services are described as *information services* rather than giving them their true titles and, wherever possible, their constituent parts are known as *library* and *computer centre*. The case studies and

Table 6.1   Coding and profiles of the convergence case studies

Code for university	Type of institution	Convergence history
Case Study 1	• old university • large multi-site • old library/computing buildings • emphasis on research	• merged • merger was a senior university initiative
Case Study 2	• old university • medium multi-site • old library buildings • emphasis on research	• not merged • strong cooperation between library and computer centre
Case Study 3	• old university • medium multi-site • old library buildings • emphasis on research	• not merged • strong cooperation between the library and computer centre
Case Study 4	• old university • medium single site • old library/computing buildings • emphasis on research	• merged • senior university initiative
Case Study 5	• new university • large multi-site • new learning centre and old buildings • HE and FE environment	• merged • 1998 some disaggregation • university librarian's initiative • some Follett funding
Case Study 6	• new university • medium multi-site • includes learning centre and old buildings • HE environment	• merged • librarian and computing manager initiative

the literature are discussed side-by-side and, where examples are named, this information originates from the published literature. Information referenced to the literature is assumed correct at the time it was published although these institutions will since have changed.

MERGER MODELS

The models and descriptions identified below illustrate the many types and interpretations of merger, varying from operational cooperation and partial convergence, through to full merger. The following are not mutually exclusive and, indeed, some aspects of convergence may be exhibited by non-merged services.

ORGANIZATIONAL AND OPERATIONAL MERGER

The Fielden Report (John Fielden Consultancy, 1993) was one of the first attempts to categorize merged information services. Two broad types were identified: ' "organisational" or "formal convergence" in which the two services ... are brought together for management purposes. In its most limited form this may mean that one person is put in overall control of the two services with no other organisational change to the status quo' (ibid.: 15) and ' "operational or informal convergence" in which the detailed functions or operations of the two services change or are brought together ...' (ibid.).

Thus some institutions were considered to have merged managerially and sometimes organizationally. Other services were thought to provide coordinated delivery of services without change to the management structures of the services. Collier (1996) believed that simply bringing services together in one reporting line did not constitute a converged service and also disputed that it was possible for the two types of convergence to exist independently of each other: 'This is a fudge to allow for those situations where for political or other reasons real convergence has not happened' (ibid.: 76).

Collier's opinion reflects a belief that, for operational convergence to work, it must be underpinned by a change in managerial structure and by backing from the senior officers of the university. The interviewees at Case Study 1 considered this essential to the success of the tightly planned and large-scale merger at that university. Indeed, there would appear to be some interdependence of the two Fielden models in other universities' information services. For example, originally at Case Study 6 the success of operational convergence was very dependent on the cooperative relationship between the directors of the information service. Here, the merger was managerial only in the sense that the two managers of the original constituent services voluntarily merged their library and computer centre services. To a large extent, however, the previous demarcations of the original services remained and, although one was nominally more senior, if either of the directors had left the director interviewed felt that the university would have needed to create an extra management tier by appointing an overall director to secure the merger. In effect this has since happened. Internal management restructuring brought about the vacancy of one director's post, following which the other has become overall director.

MANAGERIAL AND ORGANIZATIONAL MERGER

Royan's (1994) electronically conducted survey identified a more detailed set of models than Fielden's. He found 'five broad patterns of convergent service management':

- the service heads cooperating through goodwill
- the taking of turns between the heads of the original services
- consultative committees for each service, sharing the same chairperson
- appointment of a pro-vice-chancellor to whom the heads of both services report
- one service head in overall charge – an information supremo (ibid.: 18).

Although this set of models deals with a very specific interpretation of convergence, it does describe the patterns of senior management found in the institutions of the four merged case studies. All are closest to the last category, although the merger at Case Study 6 originated with the first. However, there is a danger of overestimating the impact of these arrangements as, in some cases, convergence does not extend beyond these labels. There are examples of universities where a single director of the two services has been appointed but, apart from the merged line management, there is no convergence in terms of planning, cooperation or functional merger and therefore no vision of such. In these cases, the appointment of an overall director can simply be a cost-cutting exercise achieved by combining the separate posts of university librarian and director of computing.

It is also difficult to interpret organizational structures. The limitations of these were highlighted by Priestley (1996) in his preface to *Working Papers on University Library Staffing Structures* – a collection of staff structure charts. He believed that they did not show the complexities and flexibilities of a service, the convergence at the Universities of Birmingham and De Montfort, for example, being difficult to interpret. Similarly, Brewer has written that: 'To categorise services as converged or not merely on the basis of their line management is almost meaningless without reference to the operational practicalities for staff and users' (Brewer, 1998: 1). This is illustrated by case study research: the reporting lines in the 1997 staff structure chart for Case Study 6 do not show that the library systems manager was reporting to one director despite being a member of the other director's team. Neither is the detail of operational convergence shown, such as the setting up of Web pages with input from both library and computing teams.

Lovecy, whose categories are similar to Royan's, described a further type of merger – that is, institutions in which a specific aspect of service is jointly administered but other functions remain separate (Lovecy, 1994: 2). This is similar to Fielden's operational convergence but differs from looking at merger across the whole of information services, by acknowledging that it may only affect parts of the library and computer centre functions. Examples were identified by Foster (1995).

OPERATIONAL MERGER

Foster (1995) described four areas in which operational convergence was possible:

- liaison with academic departments
- enquiry desk services, particularly suited to a shared building and providing potential for multi-skilling
- joint training of users in IT skills between the library and computing services
- collaboration between library and computing staff on development projects and information services (ibid.: 12–13).

These are present in the case studies which have managerially merged services but also feature in those which do not. For example, at Case Study 2 the library and computer centre provide joint induction sessions for freshers. There have also been joint training sessions at management level and some reciprocal job shadowing by library enquiry desk and computer help desk staff. Here the computer centre is also very supportive of a number of library initiatives – for example, in making complex data files available on the Web and in a project to incorporate personal portable computers in the library. The non-merged Case Study 3 also fits this category: despite the lack of vision and coordination at senior university management level, there is a high degree of cooperation between the library and computer centre at functional level, evidenced by the housing of personal computer clusters in the library and the sharing of scarce IT resources.

PHYSICAL MERGER

Another category of merged services is illustrated by the cohabitation of the computing and library service, possibly with the separate management of services. In effect it allows operational convergence of front-line services. For example, at the University of Bath, the library, its staff and the user services section of the computing services occupy the library and learning centre. The staff are not converged 'but work closely on shared interests, such as the operation of the complementary help desks' (Stark, 1997: 1). With the recent removal of academic computing from the merger at Case Study 5, a similar situation will occur here. The enquiry desk will be dually staffed by members of the now separate services of library and academic computing support, and the two teams will work alongside each other within the same building much as they had done before this deconvergence.

Another example, Thames Valley University, has a converged Centre for Complementary Learning (UCCL) within which there are, amongst other services, five learning resource centres (Irving, 1998: 11). In this particular model the constituent parts retain their individual identities but their operations are brought together when needed. For example, library services and computing and other services remain separately managed within the learning resource centres but are available under the same roof at the learning centres, thus providing an example of physical and operational convergence.

FULL MERGER

Fully merged models combine many of the above definitions but are also characterized by a cultural and educational commitment to teaching and learning – a vision shared by the senior managers of the services and the university at pro-vice-chancellor level. Collier proposed a list of criteria for a wide-ranging model for fully converged services, which would cut across traditional boundaries and whose structure would stem from the perceived needs of the user:

> The most convincing approaches to convergence appear to be those where services to users are looked at from the user point of view, deconstructed from their historic service structures and reassembled into more helpful constructs. (Collier, 1996: 75)

He specified a one-stop approach to customer services. In terms of administration an avoidance of overlap of resources or competition, and a flexibility of resource allocation across services according to customer needs was required. Management should be integrated and human resource management should be flexible across services. With regard to staff, there needed to be a breakdown of the barriers of professional demarcation, teams were to be multi-disciplinary and staff multi-talented (ibid.: 75).

Pugh (1997) looked at the key features of convergence situations in the context of a framework of organizational development. These are similar to Collier's and emphasize: a preference for delivery of core support services at one physical location; integrated or unified administration; structural change to break down demarcations; devolved decision-making to strengthen ownership; transformational leadership; and cultural change (ibid.: 23).

Case Study 1 is the only example studied here which fulfils these criteria, in that it has integrated management and finance structures, mixed teams of computing and library staff, a change of nomenclature and new job descriptions. Here there are five mixed-profession teams covering acquisitions, computer support, learning and research, administration and front-line services. The staff structure is fully merged and the former professional demarcations are no longer obvious in the staffing structure, with the teams being mixed, some headed by librarians and others headed by computing professionals. Staff development and recruitment is also merged. The new vertical structures are linked by cross-team working parties. The devolved budgetary model means that the allocation of funds is divided between the new teams showing an integrated approach to economic management rather than separate allocations to the different professional groupings of services. There is a one-stop approach to users, with dually staffed enquiry points in the main centre, and the library and computing services jointly liaise with the academic schools.

LONG-TERM MODELS

Corrall and Lester (1996) criticized the Fielden model as simplistic. They also raised the point that at some time in the future a physical information centre may no longer be of paramount importance. Their models are more futuristic than the models discussed above and concentrate on the whole converging environment. The authors focused on 'the blurring of boundaries and convergence of interests and activities between "professionals" [broadly speaking librarians and computing specialists] and "professors" [academic staff]' (ibid.: 85). They said that it was for each institution to decide the direction it will take and questioned whether there can be a future generic model. However, they believed that 'there are sound reasons for retaining the concept of the centrally managed library and information service, which includes commitment to a corporate approach to planning and developing the IT infrastructure' (ibid.: 99).

NON-MERGED MODELS

Another approach to convergence is characterized by the decision not to merge managerially or organizationally. However, some literature takes the contrasting view that some degree of merger is inevitable and that non-merged management structures will have to catch up with the operations of their information services:

> Despite the controversy surrounding convergence it is evident that it is now a dominant factor in the development of learning support services and will not be reversed. The trend will be towards more convergence in institutions and it will increasingly be underpinned by management restructuring. (Collier, 1996: 79)

With an acceptance of the inevitability of operational cooperation and collaboration between libraries and computer centres it may become increasingly artificial to describe information services as converged or non-converged models. Observations of the IMPEL2 research data suggest that 'within both converged and non-converged structures there were widely varying models and degrees of convergence' (Brewer, 1998: 1). Possibly, the labels of *converged* or *merged* information service are taken to indicate a successful response of an information service to the electronic environment, with the opposite judgement applied to non-merged services. However, it is interesting to note that the interviewees of the non-merged Case Studies 2 and 3 did not believe that their students were suffering as a result of the present arrangements, because they believed there was sufficient co-operation between the library and computer centre – that is, a degree of operational convergence.

The fact that a university has not merged its information services and is therefore not converged according to the above models does not necessarily mean that it has not acknowledged the issue of convergence by some other model. South Bank University is one such example. It has combined the computing support and electronic library in one building – the Learning Resources Centre – leaving the print-based library in another building. It was not physically possible to combine both in one location, and the new centre is an attempt to provide a seamless integrated electronic library service to customers in which library and computing staff are employed in mixed teams, using cross-professional skills (Clegg, 1998: 7).

REASONS FOR MERGER

The motives for merging are significant because they influence the type of merger model which develops and provide an indication of the expected benefits of merging. Bluck suggested that: 'Convergence should provide the organization with improved information management, a combined skills base to deliver services and managerial and operational economies' (Bluck, 1996: 98). Similar findings in the literature and case studies have determined the five principal reasons for merger as listed below:

- technical
- pedagogic
- economic
- strategic
- political.

However, to some extent, their classification is artificial, many of the imperatives being interlinked and all institutions having a combination of motives. For the purposes of this discussion, however, the five reasons for merger are discussed separately below.

TECHNICAL

Some see the technical overlap between the library and computer centre as an incentive for rationalizing their resources and skills base by merging, as summed up by Naylor:

> The crucial question that seems to arise ... is whether it is preferable to let the technological developments and their exploitation make the pace, or whether the organisation's structure should be changed so as to force the pace. (Naylor, 1988: 180)

This technical imperative was heavily opposed by Ratcliffe and Hartley (1993) who thought that the management needs of the library and computer centre were incompatible. Looking at user needs, Smith (1995), then Head of Computing Services and Learning Technology at the University of Central Lancashire, suggested that although users would need the new and different skills of the staff of the separate services, 'neither these new skills, nor their underpinning technologies, are any logical reason for merging Libraries and Computing Services' (ibid.: 8).

The findings in the case studies suggest a different picture. Library and computing managers at Case Study 1 and Case Study 5 both felt the converging technologies and the converging provision of information to be the prime reason for convergence, although not the sole reason. Generally, the librarians interviewed did not focus as much on the technical imperative as the computing interviewees did, possibly reflecting the librarians' traditionally greater interest in the staffing and managerial issues surrounding information provision.

Views in the literature since the mid-1990s have become more consistent in accepting the significance of the shared technological areas of library and computing services:

> ... the overlapping interests and the level of collaboration needed between library and computing services in the electronic information environment are now such that it is becoming hard to conceive an institution without some form of operational convergence. (Brewer, 1998: 1)

This interpretation is also consistent with all the pedagogic, economic, strategic and political reasons for convergence described below.

PEDAGOGIC

This originates in the support that learners are perceived to need in the electronic environment – support enabled by the collaboration of librarians and computing staff, whose combined skills and pooled resources can be used to develop user-centred services. The pedagogic imperative or convergence of customer needs is not just based on an ideal but is also a response to the pressures of the changed student profile – part-time, mature, increased numbers of students – which needs more support in a fast-changing electronic environment: 'Changes in teaching and learning methods demand new arrangements for the delivery of support services. Learners ... have no respect for the increasingly artificial barriers between these services' (Foster, 1995: 12). Here also is the justification for

85

Battin's one-stop-shop for learning support services – the *scholarly information centre* which, in a sense, marries the technical and pedagogic imperatives.

Whilst the importance of approaching convergence from the service perspective has been promoted since the mid-1990s by, for example, Sidgreaves, Collier, Bluck and Brewer, it has also been noted that 'pedagogic issues are no longer so much cited in the justification for convergence' (Brewer, 1998: 2). This has been well borne out by the case study research, with the exception of Case Study 6 at which the convergence of customer needs was given as a principal reason for merger, along with the convergence of skills and technology, and political expediency.

ECONOMIC

The expansion of higher education, not matched by an increase in resources, has also influenced economic and strategic thinking: 'In some instances restructuring may be motivated as much by cost savings as by a desire to create an improved service' (Huntingford, 1998: 1). In a similar vein, the director of the library service at Case Study 4 felt that, in most cases, merger would be inevitable due to financial necessity. Merger can reduce duplication of resources and allow a pooling of expertise between the library and computer centre, in effect realizing economies of scale, perhaps even achieving more than the sum of the separate services (Sutherland, 1992: 7–8; Harris, 1988: 150). However, it is doubtful whether it can actually save money except where the roles of computer centre director and librarian are combined, resulting in one less salary. In the short term, extra investment may be required to finance start-up activities, such as training and recruitment. Furthermore, where there has been insufficient investment in either of the separate services it is unlikely to provide a remedy, especially if the services have entirely different economic structures which would be difficult to combine. Lovecy believed that if libraries and computer centres had enough resources they would choose to remain separate:

> Convergence ... is in the first place a matter of economics and power ... not ... a power struggle between the Library and Computing Services, but the question of who is going to set priorities. If funds were unlimited the Computing Service and the Library could follow their own agendas, and each could offer all the support the other needed. (Lovecy, 1995: 7)

Economies of scale feature in most of the case studies. At Case Study 6 the merger resulted in the formation of a large department which no longer suffered from internal competition for resources as the constituent parts had previously done. At Case Study 4 the merger took place primarily as the result of a budget deficit within the university, which forced consideration of economies of scale on the information services. Nevertheless, this factor was considered to be a catalyst rather than the sole cause and it was thought that the merger would have taken place in the future anyway. However, the library and computer services were consequently confronted by merger earlier than they might otherwise have expected and are having to deal with the implications in retrospect.

STRATEGIC

There is pressure from the HEFCs for universities to rationalize information provision and to provide information strategies which encompass the whole range of printed and electronic information, its storage and retrieval. This can be seen, for example, in the Follet Report (Joint Funding Councils, 1993), and in the 1995 JISC guidelines (Joint Information Systems Committee 1995, revised 1998) for those designing information strategies. Thus the merger of library and computer centres is one possible strategy. More recently, the Dearing Report (National Committee of Inquiry, 1997) has emphasized the importance of efficiency and strategic planning of the whole university, the information service being a major department within this plan. Strategic coordination was among the reasons given for convergence at Case Study 1. At Case Study 2 the appointment of the new post of overall director of information services is part of the restructuring of senior management within the university, in line with the Dearing recommendations that senior managers should combine a deep understanding of communications and information technology with senior management experience. However, despite appearances of a merger this has not been the intention and it will not affect or combine the separate executive roles of the librarian and computer centre director.

POLITICAL

Political expediency has already been mentioned with reference to Case Study 6. Here there was an incentive for the library and computer centre to merge before merger was imposed from above. At Case Study 3 it was suggested that the fear of creating a powerful director of information services, as can be the case in a merged service, may be discouraging some senior officers within the university from merger. Indeed, merger seems unlikely here; the library and computer centre now has less overlap in strategic representation because the library and IT committees, which were once chaired by the same pro-vice-chancellor, now have separate chairs. However, despite appearances, this reorganization was not necessarily the result of a political or strategic decision: the second pro-vice-chancellor was appointed in an effort to share the heavy workload. Furthermore, the librarian and director of the computing services do actually report to the same senior university officer.

FURTHER INFLUENCES ON THE NATURE OF MERGERS

The following issues affect the likelihood or success of merger but they are not principal motives in themselves.

OPPORTUNISM: NEW BUILDINGS

The Follett funding for new learning centre buildings increased the potential for housing the library and computing services in one, purpose-designed centre and so encouraged physical merger. This opportunity was a strong incentive for merging services at the University of Hertfordshire. Here, the advantages of using one building were seen to be improved services and more efficient use of resources, such as: services being available over longer hours and delivered by a single team; being able to satisfy, in one building, the increasingly similar building requirements of libraries and computer centres; a single management team for easier liaison with faculties; and new services supported by the skills of both types of staff (Macartney, 1995: 3). These constitute the advantages of physical merger, although most of these aspects can be achieved without occupying new or shared buildings.

OPPORTUNISM: SENIOR STAFF VACANCIES

Opportunities for merging were originally created at Case Study 5, with the retirement of the computer centre manager, and at Case Study 1 with the departure of the university librarian. There are also numerous similar examples in the literature. However, vacancies seem to be catalysts when merger is already a favoured option, rather than a *prima facie* reason for merging.

ACADEMIC CULTURE

The academic culture of Case Study 3 was given as one of the official justifications for not merging the information services. One view was that the distinct roles of library and computing were still required because some of the academic departments were seen to make use of the separate services in their own right – the library for the large book-based research collections and the computer centre for the heavy specialized use of the IT infrastructure by, for example, the School of Computing. This is the same viewpoint as taken by Ratcliffe and Hartley (1993), and Smith (1995), mentioned above. However, these objections should not be seen as absolute obstacles since they could have applied equally to the academic culture of the now wholly converged information service at Case Study 1.

CUSTOMER FOCUS

It has been noted above that libraries and computer centres have distinct missions and that their customers have specific needs. However, this is further complicated by the fact that, at many institutions, the customer base of the computer centre is wider than that of the library. It is also unlikely that the two separate services can be neatly slotted together if their management and economic organizations differ. At Case Study 2 it was noted by the interviewee that the library's and computer centre's customer base did not coincide exactly and so their purposes differed – the library serving the academic community and the computer centre additionally supporting administrative departments. This situation varies between institutions and depends on which areas of administrative and academic support is provided by the computer centre. The recent disaggregation at Case Study 5, in which the management of academic computing support has been devolved to the campuses and managerially removed from the combined information service, suggests that some aspects of computer centre services may need to be more specifically focused than some merged structures allow. Here, the library remains merged with systems support for networking and MIS.

COOPERATIVE ENVIRONMENT

There is a belief that administrative or managerial merger will have little success in achieving a coherent operational merger in universities where there is no pre-existing cooperative relationship between the computer centre and the library:

> Convergence through common line management may be needed when people cannot or will not collaborate, but it is doubtful that this will necessarily and of itself bring about a well integrated, seamless service. (Brewer, 1998: 2)

PHYSICAL AND ADMINISTRATIVE STRUCTURE OF THE UNIVERSITY

The size and geographical dispersion of the university may affect the ease and rationale for a merged service. At Case Study 1 the size of the combined services of over 200 people across at least 15 buildings was a significant complicating factor, but not a deterrent.

UNIVERSITY SUPPORT AND LEADERSHIP

The support of the university's senior officers is essential for successful merger. The status of the librarian and computing director within the university management tiers also affects the support for, and their influence in, the proposal and process of merger. Sutherland recommended representation of the service on the institution's most senior decision-making body, and concluded that successful merger was dependent on the commitment of senior management and the institution (Sutherland, 1992: 53). The Follett (Joint Funding Councils, 1993) and Dearing (National Committee of Inquiry, 1997) Reports also suggested that the information service should have senior representation within the university's management and policy-making bodies. The findings of the IMPEL2 study showed that 'strong central initiative and support helps to facilitate the design and operation of a more coherent and effective service' (Huntingford, 1998: 3). The backing of senior officers at Case Study 1 was seen as a major contributor to success. The director of the service now sits on the vice-chancellor's executive committee and on other key bodies, reflecting this support and ensuring a common understanding of the future development of the service. The importance of leadership qualities of the director of the information service has been debated in the US and UK literature. Fleit concluded that a computer *czar* was not necessary. What was needed was an *enabler* – somebody with flexibility and vision about the potential for IT rather than detailed technical knowledge, and someone who could expand horizons and opportunities (Fleit, 1986: 30).

STAFFING PROBLEMS IN MERGED SERVICES

Staffing issues are the biggest obstacles to merging and, as the staff are both the main resource of the service and the executors of the merger, it is vital to overcome personality clashes and cultural divisions:

PERSONALITY CLASHES

Sidgreaves, whilst not subscribing to them, summarized the traditionally stated inherent differences as:

> Librarians are described typically as being comfortable with order and structure, willing to accept organisational hierarchies, and generally preferring a predictable pattern in their work. Computing staff ... are more creative, enjoy developing new ideas, will work in teams on clearly defined projects, though some are happier working with machines in isolation. (Sidgreaves, 1995: 5)

These stereotypes were studied in the US by Allen (1995: 653–54) who concluded from various research that there were no consistent personality types found in the large majority of librarians or computing personnel, and so consequently there could be no substance to the belief that these professional groups were personally incompatible.

CULTURAL DIVISIONS

Professional backgrounds

Some sources suggest that the cooperation or integration of library and computing staff is made difficult by their lack of understanding of each other's professional cultures and functions (Bebbington and Cronin, 1989). This is partly because staff at an operational level rarely get a chance to work with each other before merger, resulting in poor or non-existent communication within the new service (Huntingford, 1998: 3). There is also the fear that merger means takeover, that each will be made to do the other's jobs, that their roles will become diluted, and that status and grading may be affected. For example, at the Aldham Robarts Learning Centre at Liverpool John Moores University (Anonymous, 1996) computing staff feared loss of status by being associated with the library, even worrying that they may have to shelve books!

Such views are consistent with the apprehensions of some staff in the case studies. At Case Study 5 each professional grouping had fixed opinions about what the other did – for example, that librarians were not technically-oriented and that computer people were not user-oriented. In the event, the merger brought about a synergy, fostering an exchange of skills and breaking down prejudices, so that, despite disaggregation, it became difficult and unnecessary to unravel the close working arrangements already established.

Service environment

The case studies found that library staff in merged services benefited from having the technical expertise of the computer staff more readily available, but some of the computer staff expressed considerable unease. This seemed to relate to the fact that the newly merged service appeared to be taking on the cultural identity of the library in that it is a people-centred, service-oriented environment.

Two case studies illustrate computing staff dissatisfaction. In the initial stages at Case Study 1 the computing staff did not recognize the significance of the merger and felt that it was being imposed by the library. However, at this particular university there was already a significant degree of customer service orientation in the academic support section of the computer centre and, even before the merger, some staff disliked this type of environment. Thus the resentment was not strictly limited to the merger.

At Case Study 4 much work remains in getting the computing systems staff to recognize the impact of their actions on the service users and to adopt a more positive approach to customer care. Here, the main groups which were to be integrated were the systems team from the library and the systems support team from the computer centre. Thus the lack of understanding is not based on ignorance of each other's technical skills, it is purely a difference of approach. First, the library staff serve their customers' needs in a service designed around customer need, rather than the provider's convenience. Second, there is also a difference in the way individuals of different professional cultures operate within teams. The library staff here were used to the traditions of sharing information through meetings and of shared decision-making and planning, but the computer centre staff were accustomed to direction from above whilst they themselves concentrated on technical tasks and viewed other involvement in the organization as a distraction from these duties. This means that staff originating from the computer centre who have been moved to managerial positions within the new structure have little experience of such roles. However, the personalities and willingness of these staff to adapt to the role is seen as compensating for any deficiencies of experience.

Despite the above generalizations, computing staff come from a variety of backgrounds. Some will be used to technical, project-based tasks, and will still be needed in this role, whereas others may have been employed to provide computer support and run courses for students and staff, and so will fit more easily into the service culture.

Library takeover

The fact that convergence as a management issue features in the library literature, rather than that of computing, may give the impression that it is a library initiative. However, the interest of the library profession is an extension of the fact that librarians have traditionally written about management issues, whereas computing professionals have tended to write about technical aspects. One computing manager interviewed stressed that convergence was of interest to everyone involved in the strategic management of information – whether librarians or computer staff. Merged information services can be headed by managers with a library background, such as at Case Study 1 or by a computing director as at Case Study 5. Whilst these are strategic appointments, possibly with some control over resourcing bids, very often the executive decision-making and running of the library and of the computer centre will remain within the remit of the university librarian and computer centre manager respectively.

TYPE OF STAFF REQUIRED IN A MERGED SERVICE

The types of staff needed by information services, whether merged or not, have been the subject of several eLib projects, following the focus in the Follett (Joint Funding Councils, 1993) and Fielden (John Fielden Consultancy, 1993) Reports.

The Fielden Report looked at the kind of library staff needed for the future and stated that: 'When universities prepare strategic plans for their LIS, they should also consciously plan for the people who will put the plans into effect' (ibid.: 6). It was suggested in the report that they will need teaching skills, database navigation skills, customer care knowledge and a team working ability (ibid.). While the ability to work across professions can provide a flexible staff, able to provide a seamless service to users, it does raise the issue of which skills should be acquired and to what level.

MULTI-SKILLED STAFF

Collier (1996) and Pugh (1997) recommended multi-talented staff as a feature of their fully converged models. Specific areas of work, such as a dually staffed enquiry desk, provide an opportunity to exchange skills. Clearly, this is most likely in cases of physical merger. However, it is not generally accepted that a single person would be able to combine the skills of both a librarian and computing professional, beyond the very simplest level. In her research, Sutherland found that:

> A change in professional roles to the extent of creating hybrid posts on a wide scale is not advocated. On the whole institutions seem at present to favour a preservation of professional career structures and responsibilities, with additional training to enable an enhanced awareness of the skills of colleagues. (Sutherland, 1992: 54)

The interviewees in the case studies reflected this view, all agreeing that the specialist skills of the two services were necessary in their own right. The director of the information service at Case Study 4 felt that, for some time to come, there would be a spectrum of staff ranging from those focused on content and retrieval, through those comfortable with all areas, to those comfortable primarily with hardware and software. The interviewees believed that, although some hybrid staff will evolve through working in environments such as merged learning centres, there will also be a need for specialists and staff should continue to develop their own areas of expertise, rather than attempt to become complete all-rounders. At Case Study 1 it was suggested that senior staff should expand their cross-profession awareness and learn about each others' professions, not at an operational level, but enough to manage a mixed professions team.

One issue related not only to mergers but also to the development of the electronic library is the skills needed by library staff. The SKIP project examined this, and its interim findings suggested that the IT skills required differed between the remits of different jobs. In a few cases 'managers embraced the concept of the hybrid information professional, and stated that for some posts people with either IT or library backgrounds would be acceptable' (Garrod 1996: 99). Evidence from the final SKIP studies suggested that, for staff, flexibility, customer orientation and an appropriate personality were the most essential requirements. Staff should be able to think critically and solve problems but IT skills could be taught (Garrod, 1998: 2).

DESKILLING AND DILUTION

At Case Study 2 it was felt that the two groups of staff would work best together if they shared an understanding of the strategic importance of information, that the skills of the two professions were becoming more specialized and that multi-skilling would dilute them, although a multi-skilled individual at a basic level was possible. This fear of dilution and deskilling, shared by both library and computing staff, was also voiced by Clegg: 'I think learning resource managers need to ask what multi-skilling does for students and for the staff. ... Does multi-skilling enrich everyone, or does it reduce all to lowest common denominator and a resulting low grade service?' (Clegg, 1995: 4).

Clegg later referred to experience at South Bank University where people were rotated between work areas in order to gain maximum exposure to new skills but, as a result, began to feel either deskilled or unskilled. This consequently led to the question whether they could still identify with a particular part of the service and build up confidence and specific skills (Clegg, 1998: 8–9).

The dual staffing of enquiry desks, although providing an opportunity for multi-skilling, can give the staff a sense of deskilling. At Case Study 5 computing staff and librarians felt that the enquiries were of a low level with about 80 per cent being of a basic technical nature, and so their skills were underused. At this university the problem has been alleviated by using some student assistants at the enquiry point and by the academic computing support service employing a new member of staff, who is happy with this work, for the computing position.

Multi-disciplinary teams

Multi-disciplinary teams are also recommended in Collier's (1996) and in Pugh's (1997) models. At Case Study 1 there are teams, staffed by computing and library people, which are organized on a faculty basis to liaise with the academic schools; some are managed by former computing centre staff and others by librarians. Indeed mixed professions teams are a means by which barriers between staff of different backgrounds can be broken down. These may take the form of permanent teams or may be groups which come together for a specific task, such as user education or Web page projects. The University of Limerick illustrates the latter: the library and computing centre there have merged, and working relations between the two professional groups have benefited from pooling their skills and working together on an external project, EDUCATE (O'Riordan, 1997). It should be remembered that such cooperation may also be a feature of non-merged information services such as at Case Study 2 where joint freshers' induction lectures, Web projects and staff training sessions are commonly held.

Nomenclature

Related to the concept of multi-skilling and hybridity are changes in job title, in which words like *library* or *computing* often do not feature. However, although this strategy nominally removes traditional divides, it can be unhelpful to users. For example at Anglia Polytechnic University, 'staff still refer to themselves as "library" staff or "computing" staff. ... In the main our users have very different distinct needs and need to identify staff accordingly' (Dye, 1997: 1).

THE PROCESS OF MERGING STAFF

Most of the literature suggests that planning is important before a merger is embarked upon, but the extent of this varies. The summary of the 1996 BUFVC (British University Film and Video Council) Conference in the March 1996 issue of *Audio-visual Librarian* stated the most necessary element for an institution which was planning a merger was 'a vision of the right direction' which could be edged towards 'step by step as finance, personnel and expediency allowed'. However, there was also a recommendation for some detailed planning: 'There is a need to do a people audit before embarking on convergence, whatever structure is chosen, because only people can make it work' (Godwin, 1996: 125). Pugh looked at the theoretical aspects of change management and stated that:

> ... the general health of the resulting organizations, and the ease of acceptance of the change, depend solidly on the presence of certain crucial characteristics, such as leadership, motivation, communication and teams. (Pugh, 1997: 8–9)

The management of the staff before, during and after the process of merging the two information services seems to be the most challenging task in a merger. Pugh remarked that, within convergence, there were all the reasons for resisting change. He summarized these as follows:

> It changes the way jobs are done, it breaks up existing group structures, it can be seen as a takeover, it reduces the influence of some individuals, it changes the power structure and moves the centres of decision making. It is sometimes seen as a threat to continued employment. ... (ibid.: 10)

According to Pugh (1997: 9), merger is essentially a top-down process which must be accompanied by consultation, dissemination and communication. At the Aldham Roberts Learning Centre at Liverpool John Moores University

(Anonymous, 1996), the staff were talked to about the merger in small groups, and an effort was made to make them aware of their opposite numbers' jobs. All the library assistants became information assistants and were regraded to the level of their computing assistant colleagues (ibid.: 2). However, overpreparation and consultation may cause anxiety as at Case Study 5, where the staff became more apprehensive of the merger rather than reassured. At Case Study 6 there were meetings with all levels of staff and manager and, because the computing staff feared that the library was taking over, it was stressed that separate professional disciplines would be respected and that individuals were to keep their own professional identities. Clearly, in some merger models such assurances are not appropriate.

The recruitment and reallocation of staff is another way of easing the merger of staff structures. At the University of Hertfordshire the staffing issue was tackled by recruiting a new staff team with job descriptions which were associated with neither library nor computer centre (Macartney, 1995: 3). This was also one of the strategies used at Case Study 1 where some staff were moved to other sites and many had to re-apply for positions because jobs were changed and new posts created with new job and person specifications. Reallocation was made easier by the recruitment of extra staff. Obviously, this is not a method suited to those universities where the merger is a result of a cost-cutting exercise and where there is no funding for new posts. However, in these cases staff could be moved or replaced when vacancies occur.

THE SUCCESS OF MERGERS

An evaluation should start by considering whether the reasons for, and expected benefits of, merger have been achieved. Formative evaluation could take place at various key stages throughout the merger, following which changes could be made during the process, before the merger is completed. Alternatively, a summative evaluation could assess the outcomes at the end of the merger, albeit drawing conclusions from evidence collected on various aspects and at various stages throughout the process. However, there is no evidence in the literature or in my research of any monitoring assessment plans in operation which can measure the success of mergers. This may be because, in some cases, it would be difficult to formulate an evaluation plan for a number of varied, practical reasons.

First, some mergers are not planned on a massive scale but develop as need and opportunity arise over a long period, as is seen in the fluctuating merger at Case Study 6 where, over the years, a number of aspects have been added to, or removed from, the merged structure to accommodate change and development within the university. Deconvergence at Case Study 5 also shows that merged structures are not static. Thus a method of assessment could not use a fixed set of criteria.

Second, it is difficult to assess the success of a merger retrospectively. For example, assessing the merger at Case Study 5 is problematic because the staff who started the initiative have long since left and the reasons for the original merger are not specifically known, beyond that it was a vision of how information services should be in the future. Plans and procedures for monitoring a merger need to be made as soon as it is embarked upon, and amended as the organizational structure develops.

The third reason for difficulty in formulating assessment criteria is that mergers may be judged variously by different people. They may be initiated by senior officers of the university, pursuing a single issue such as economic efficiency and be deemed successful by financial managers but not perhaps by staff or users.

Although not necessarily aimed at assessing mergers there is evidence of user opinion, from questionnaires, faculty and liaison committees and verbal feedback. At Case Study 5 it was pressure from the heads of academic schools across the university – who wanted the disaggregated services to be more obviously accountable to the schools than when merged with the library – which caused the vice-chancellor to remove academic computing support from the information service. By contrast, the dissatisfaction with the merger at Case Study 6 was that it had not gone far enough. There the academics wanted even more merged liaison between the information service and the faculties, with one liaison person rather than separate library and computing representatives.

Student opinion is often more difficult to obtain because they are a transient population, not usually interested in management issues within universities. Indeed, at Case Study 1, the merger was even intended to be invisible to the students to avoid causing them disruption.

Although disaggregation or deconvergence may be seen as a sign that a model has failed, it is more constructive to see it in the context of a response to the institution's changing needs. The deconvergence at Case Study 5 may be interpreted as a positive response to the academic schools. The university is not reversing its strategic commitment to convergence; the combined library, systems support for network computing, MIS, and the now separate academic computing support all finally report to the same vice-chancellor. It is thought that the changes will be invisible to the students and that there will be no deterioration in the coordination of the service which is provided for them at the learning centre.

RECOMMENDATIONS FOR THE MERGER PROCESS

In both the literature and the case studies the merged services all give a different combination of reasons for their response to the convergence issue. Some are more merged than others, and most models continue to change and evolve. Thus it is difficult to produce a set of recommendations for models and processes that will suit everyone. Universities should adopt flexible models that can accommodate the limitations of resources, buildings, staffing structures, personalities, skills and institutional culture. The following recommendations have been drawn from the best practices observed in the case studies and the literature, to which I have added some project management concepts. They are intended as a framework of suggestions around which institutions can build their own plans. The principal stages, which will often overlap, are as follows:

1. **Define the objectives of the merger.**
   Typical objectives are:

   - to improve and develop services, particularly networked services to users
   - to maximize resources available beyond what is achievable if the services remain separate.

2. **Establish the desired benefits of the merger.**

   - What services is the proposed merged service to provide?
   - What economic results are required?
   - How will merger relate to the university's information strategy?
   - How will merger fit with the teaching and learning strategies of the university?

3. **Establish the scope of the merger.**

   - Which existing individual services are to be merged?

4. **Define the merger model.**
   Consider which of the following types of merger would be most suitable:

   - organizational
   - managerial
   - operational
   - physical.

   Consider possible staff restructuring with regard to:

   - team structures
   - management structures

- communication structures
- job specifications
- person specifications.

5. **Identify constraints.**

   Assess the resources available:

   - What funding is available – for example, for training and recruitment of staff?
   - Is the existing physical accommodation of the information services adequate or is there a need for new buildings or building alterations?
   - Is new equipment needed?

   Assess the cost of the process of implementation in terms of:

   - management time
   - staff time
   - start-up costs
   - funding any deficiencies in the above-mentioned resources.

   Assess the human resources – carry out a staff and skills audit to ascertain:

   - the personalities and skills mix within the merging services in order to establish which roles will need to be filled and what training and recruitment will need to take place
   - the leadership skills, vision and personalities of the directors of the existing services in the light of the requirements of the merger.

   Audit the culture of the organization to understand the behaviour of the different professional groups within their own environments, especially with regard to teamworking, management processes and decision-making. Chapter 9 suggests the application of systematic culture audit before management restructuring and intervention takes place. This process would help managers of different departments such as computing and library understand each other's organizational cultures and learn how they might work together. This would have been particularly appropriate for easing the merger at Case Study 4.

6. **Research other mergers.**

   Gather information about other institutions' experiences by:

   - visiting other universities
   - listening to the experience of directors and staff of merged services
   - studying the convergence literature.

7. **Decide whether merger is a necessary or appropriate way of achieving the objectives and the desired results.**
   In the light of knowledge collected through the above stages a merger may not be the best policy at the time. Therefore establish whether:

   - some of the aims of the merger can be achieved without merging – for example, by cooperation
   - existing problems, such as inadequate funding, can be solved or will remain and weaken the newly created service
   - there is sufficient support and vision from the university's senior officers to ensure that the merger will succeed.

8. **Prepare the institution.**
   This should be done before, during and after the merger to assess reaction to, and ensure support for, the changes. Methods of preparation observed from the case studies fall into two categories. First, there are informative methods such as meetings, presentations and Web or printed communications – for example, university newssheets and library bulletins. Second there is the participative approach through discussion groups and job shadowing. There are four main parties to be informed:

   - Promote the benefits of the merger to senior officers of the university to ensure their support.
   - Prepare the staff of the services that are to be merged:
     - in a consultative way about matters which they can influence
     - to promote, communicate and explain the merger, especially in situations where it is a *fait accompli*
     - to reassure them that appropriate training and support will be available for their new roles
     - to ensure that line managers understand and support the changes in order to be able to implement them.
   - Prepare service users by explaining the benefits and structure of the new information service: to academic staff whose resource allocation and service liaison arrangements may change, and to students to promote new services.
   - Prepare staff and student representative bodies such as trade unions and student unions. Consultation will be needed with the former, especially if contracts are to be changed. In some cases, trade union intervention will be a constraint.

9. **Establish an implementation structure.**

   - Appoint a senior manager to manage the process of change.

- Establish a working party or management committee whose individual members should be responsible for specific aspects of the merger process. These will usually report to a pro-vice-chancellor.
- Establish reporting procedures.
- Plan evaluation at key milestones.

10. Establish a schedule for implementation
Decide on an appropriate, realistic and accepted order and timescale for:

- a consultative and informative programme for university, staff and users
- a training programme for staff
- a recruitment programme
- the appointment of managers of new teams
- the structuring of new teams
- the movement of staff to new posts
- the movement of staff to different buildings
- changes to the financial structures of the merging departments.

11. Implement the merger.

12. Evaluate the merger process and outcome.

- Monitor the resourcing, financial management and service provision of the merged information services, taking into account the timescales established above.
- Listen to users and information services staff to establish the quality of the service.
- Ask whether the desired results are being achieved.

If the desired results are not being achieved, then the reasons need identifying, following which the process, and possibly the chosen model, need to be adjusted by reconsidering the above steps.

CONCLUSION

To impose the constraints of patterns and categories on the myriad operational and organizational responses to the convergence of university libraries and computer centres is rather contrived. The aim here has been to explore different levels of convergence in which there has been a genuine effort to provide some level of merged or coordinated service, and to highlight a number of considerations for those embarking on a merger. These are as follows:

- Mergers vary in terms of operational and managerial degree but first appearances of managerial and organizational structures can be misleading as to the merged operations of the information service.

- Mergers are determined and constrained by technical, economic, strategic and political factors and by physical location.
- The imperatives to merge are interrelated, and different players have different priorities.
- The most difficult aspect of merging is managing the staff, and most important to success are the personalities and flexibilities of this staff.
- Professional and cultural differences exist between computer centre and library staff but can be overcome by training, working together and appropriate recruitment.
- The vision and leadership of the directors of the service, backed by the university's senior officers are vital ingredients in the processes of merging and running a merged service.
- Planning, evaluation, and flexibility are essential in implementing and sustaining a merger.

REFERENCES

Allen, B. (1995), 'Academic information services: a library management perspective', *Library Trends*, **43**(4), 645–62.

Anonymous (1996), Liverpool John Moores Aldham Robarts Learning Resource Centre (1996), *deLiberations*, (6), http://www.lgu.ac.uk/deliberations/lrc/ljm.html

Bebbington, L. and Cronin, B. (1989), 'Courtship and competition on campus: the convergence of university libraries and computing centres', *Library Review*, **38**(2), 7–16.

Bluck, R. (1996), 'Organizing libraries for customers' in C. Pinder and M. Melling (eds), *Providing Customer-oriented Services in Academic Libraries*, London: Library Association Publishing, 87–104.

Brewer, G. (1998), 'Minotaur', *Ariadne*, (15), May, http://www.ariadne.ac.uk/

Clegg, S.M. (1995), 'The challenges for learning resources staff', unpublished paper presented at the Learning Resources Development Group Libtech seminar, September 1995.

Clegg, S.M. (1998), 'Converged enquiry/help desks: rhetoric or reality?', *Relay*, **45**, 7–10.

Collier, M. (1996), 'The context of convergence' in M. Oldroyd (ed.), *Staff Development in Academic Libraries: Present Practice and Future Challenges*. London: Library Association Publishing, 68–80.

Corrall, S. and Lester, R. (1996), 'Professors and professionals: on changing boundaries' in R. Cuthbert (ed.), *Working in Higher Education*, Buckingham: The Society for Research into Higher Education and Open University Press.

Dye, J. (1997), 'The development of the Rivermead Learning Centre – Anglia Polytechnic University', *deLiberations*, http://www.lgu.ac.uk/deliberations/lrc/anglia.html

Fleit, L.H. (1986), 'Choosing a chief information officer: the myth of the computer czar', *CAUSE/EFFECT*, **9**(3), 26–31.

Foster, A. (1995), 'The emergence of convergence', *Library Manager*, **11**, October, 12–13.

Garrod, P. (1996), 'Skills for the new professional', *Library Technology*, **1**(5), 99–100.

Garrod, P. (1998), 'SKIP: Skills for new information professionals', *Ariadne*, (11), http://www.ariadne.ac.uk/

Godwin, P. (1996), 'Managing convergence of academic support services in higher education: British Universities Film Video Council Conference, London, March 1996', *Audiovisual Librarian*, **22**(2), 124–25.

Harris, C. (1988), 'Academic information services at the University of Salford', *British Journal of Academic Librarianship*, **3**(3), 147–52.

Huntingford, J. (1998), 'The Impact of IMPEL', *Ariadne*, (13), http://www.ariadne.ac.uk/

Irving, A. (1998), 'Beyond Dearing: handling certainty uncertainly', *Relay*, **45**, 11–12.

John Fielden Consultancy (1993), *Supporting Expansion: A Report on Human Resource Management in Academic Libraries for the Joint Funding Councils' Libraries Review Group*, Bristol: HEFCE, July 1993 (revised September 1993).

Joint Funding Councils' Libraries Review Group (1993), *Report*, (Follett Report), Chair: Professor Sir Brian Follett, Bristol: HEFCE.

Joint Information Systems Committee (1995), *Guidelines for Developing an Information Strategy: A Report Prepared by Coopers & Lybrand and the JISC's Information Strategies Steering Group*, http://www.jisc.ac.uk/pub/infstrat

Lovecy, I. (1994), 'Convergence of libraries and computing services', *Library and Information Briefings*, **54**, 1–11.

Lovecy, I. (1995), 'Responses to "Convergence – an update"', *Relay*, **42**, 7.

Macartney, N. (1995), 'Convergence planning', *Library Association Record (Technology Supplement)*, **97**(8), 3.

National Committee of Inquiry into Higher Education (1997), *Report*, (Dearing Report), Chair: Sir Ron Dearing, London: HMSO.

Naylor, B. (1988), 'The convergence of the library and the computing service: the central issues', *British Journal of Academic Librarianship*, **3**(3), 172–86.

O'Riordan, G. (1997), 'Access to Network Resources: EDUCATE', a paper delivered at New Tricks 2 Conference: eLib and Telematics – Projects and Partnerships, University of Bournemouth, 27–28 August.

Priestley, J. (ed.) (1996), *Working Papers on University Library Staffing Structures*, London: SCONUL.

Pugh, L. (1997), *Convergence in Academic Support Services*, British Library RIC Report 54, London: British Library Research and Innovation Centre.

Ratcliffe, F. and Hartley, D. (1993), 'Library services', Letter, *The Times Higher Education Supplement*, 5 March.

Royan, B. (1994), 'Are you being merged? A survey of convergence in information service provision', *SCONUL Newsletter*, **1**, Spring, 17–20.

Sidgreaves, I. (1995), 'Convergence: an update', *Relay*, **42**, 3–6.

Smith, T. (1995), 'Responses to "Convergence – an update"', *Relay*, **42**, 7–8.

Stark, I. (1997), 'Down your way: University of Bath', *Ariadne*, (9), May, http://www.adriane.ac.uk/

Sutherland, P. (1992), *The Management of Integrated Learning Resources*, Brighton: Council of Polytechnic Librarians.

7   The change agent

Matt Holland

INTRODUCTION

The term 'change agent' is used in the library literature to encompass phenomena and events which drive change, such as new technologies or change in government policy through to individuals who lead change. This chapter focuses on change agents as people rather than events. It places change agents within the context of the diffusion of innovation and explores some of the possible roles which are proposed for change agents in communication and management literature.

Much of the theory related to change agents is underpinned by a two-step model of the communication of information. The two-step model was originally proposed by Katz and Lazarsfeld in 1955 to describe how media messages are diffused through opinion leaders. Although primitive, this model is still used by writers and researchers on innovation. It works in the following way. In step one innovations are promoted to opinion leaders who are likely to be receptive to new ideas. Once new ideas are accepted a second phase begins in which opinion leaders encourage others to adopt them. In the first phase change agents are active in promoting innovations, in the second phase the diffusion of new ideas becomes an integral part of the communication processes of opinion leaders.

Following the logic of this framework two types of change agent emerge: first, those who are 'made' – highly communicative individuals who are likely to take a leading role in any organization which they join; and, second, those who choose to take on the role, perhaps working on behalf of an agency whose objective is to promote an innovative product or a new behaviour. A third category is proposed for those whose role as change agent is emerging from an existing role. Information professionals might fall within this third category, since, as a result of developments in networked information and networked communication, they find themselves at the forefront of technological change within their organization. This is, of course, a generalization, as such individuals may also find themselves in either or both of the first two categories.

NATURE'S CHANGE AGENTS: A BRIEF REVIEW OF THE COMMUNICATION LITERATURE

The role of opinion leader or excellent communicator has long been identified in communication research. They are likely to be the innovators or early adopters in the cycle of innovation proposed by Rogers (1983). Broadly, the definitions offered combine the concept of the gatekeeper with the identification of key attributes and traits. Kurt Lewin proposed the gatekeeper concept in the 1940s and it has since been widely adopted. This simple idea describes a highly networked individual who controls the flow of information into and out of an organization. Adapted by Allen (1969) as the technological gatekeeper, the concept was revised by Shoemaker (1991) in an attempt to give it more depth.

Adams (1983) identified the boundary role person (BRP) who works as a link between an organization's internal and external environment. The key characteristic which he identified was a certain psychological, and perhaps physical, distance from their organization. The BRP is a representative of their organization and its agent of influence in the external environment. Tushman and Scanlan (1981) take a slightly different perspective. They identified the role of boundary spanners who are perceived internally as technically competent and, externally, as communication stars who have a specialized area of expertise.

Smith (1980) describes the intermediary role of the relay men who pass information from source to recipient using their expert knowledge to filter and process information. Liaison persons described by Farace and Danowski (1973) and cosmopolitanites described by Rogers combine good education, communication skills and intelligence, and become centres of communication inside and outside their organization. McClure (1978) talks of the information-rich employee who combines the traits of liaison person with the capability to acquire, process and utilize information to a high degree.

THE CHARACTERISTICS OF BOUNDARY-SPANNING INDIVIDUALS

The terms I have adopted to describe this group is boundary-spanning individuals – a term which reflects their most significant ability. A brief review of the literature suggests that such individuals are likely to have five characteristics in common.

1. They transfer information between the internal and external environments of their organizations. This combines with the ability to understand and interpret the local language of the source and represent that information in the language of the recipient.

2. They are able to interact with many groups, but do not belong exclusively to one group. They form ties transferring information between groups and individuals.
3. They are likely to be excellent communicators with extensive external contacts, to communicate frequently with others and be consulted often by colleagues. This combines with other qualities such as a good educational level and intelligence. Within a research-based organization like a university, they are likely to have published, give papers at conferences, attend conferences and have links with professional organizations.
4. They are likely to have a high status. Tushman and Scanlan (1981) suggest this is because that they are well favoured by colleagues and therefore likely to be promoted. Mintzberg suggests that this collection of skills is an essential part of a successful manager's make-up and linked to high performance and to promotion. However, high status need not imply any formal recognition such as a title.
5. They are likely to have a recognized area of expertise.

The task of the change agent is to seek out and contact boundary-spanning individuals. They are the conduit through which innovations will be adopted by the majority.

CHANGE AGENTS AND CHANGE ORGANIZATIONS

Rogers, in his pioneering book the *Diffusion of Innovations*, has a clear idea of the change agent working within a change organization. The change agent has the task of promoting a specific innovation or new behaviour. This model reflects the origins of diffusion research focusing on the promotion of innovation in the areas of agriculture and health by government agencies. From his synthesis of diffusion studies Rogers identified a seven-point process of change agent activity from an initial contact to the end of the agent–client relationship:

● to develop the need for change on the part of their clients
● to establish an information exchange relationship
● to diagnose their problems
● to create intent to change in their clients
● to translate this intention into action
● to stabilize the adoption of an innovation and to prevent discontinuities
● to achieve a terminal relationship.

In this context eLib projects, such as TAPin and Netskills, could be viewed as change agencies. Staff working within them are placed in the role of change agents following closely the model of change agent activity Rogers outlined. Rogers also summarizes behaviours and factors which researchers have found to be positively related to the adoption of change:

- the extent of change agent effort in contacting clients
- a client orientation rather than a change agency orientation
- the degree to which the diffusion programme relates to clients' needs
- the change agent's empathy with clients
- homophily (similarity) with clients
- credibility in clients' eyes
- the extent to which change agents work with opinion leaders
- increasing clients' ability to evaluate innovations.

THE CHANGE AGENT AS AN EMERGING ROLE

The change organization/change agent model has limitations, however, when it is applied to people already working within organizations. A comparison of the change agent/change agency model with that of an information professional in an emerging change agent role highlights some of the key differences (see Table 7.1).

There are dangers in associating too closely with the change agency/change agent model. Examples of these dangers might be: becoming too closely associated with a single innovation; the danger of failure or rejection of the innovation reflecting on other aspects of work; and the finite nature of the change agent–client relationship.

The emerging change agent should adopt behaviours that are likely to encourage and facilitate change but which are compatible with their existing role and skills.

CHANGE, UNCERTAINTY AND INFORMATION SEEKING

Communication scholars argue that all communication seeks to reduce uncertainty. Evidence from research (Farace *et al.*, 1978) suggests that both organizations and individuals increase their information-seeking in times of uncertainty. Other effects also noted are the greater use of external sources and a stronger preference for face-to-face communication. (Huber and Daft, 1987).

The degree of uncertainty is difficult to measure. However, complex innovations, such as networked communication and networked information, create significant levels of uncertainty for the individuals and organizations affected by them. A subjective measure proposed by Duncan (in Daft, 1995)

Table 7.1 Comparison of change agent role versus emerging role

Change agency/change agent model	Emerging role (information professional)
Simple organizational structure	Complex organization (for example, an academic library working within a university)
The change agent volunteers to participate and is likely to have a strong motivation and identification with the task	The information professional may have both a strong motivation and dedication to the existing or previous role but be uncomfortable or ambivalent about a change agent role
Single defined objective	Many objectives
The change agent has a finite relationship with the client	The information professional seeks an ongoing relationship with academics
Likely to promote a single innovation. Change agency has the advantage of selecting and refining the innovative product or behaviour	Many innovations and new behaviours stemming from developments in networked information and networked communications
There is certainty as to role, task and form of the change agent organization	The information professional operates under conditions of uncertainty, which affect role organizational structure and task
The change agent is selected on the basis of appropriate skills	The information professional is selected on the basis of the skills for their profession, which may or may not incline them towards the role of change agent

records the degree of uncertainty across two axes: simple–complex and stable–unstable. These technologies score highly on both. They have a large number of diverse elements (complex), and these elements change frequently and are unpredictable (unstable). *Information professionals are operating in conditions of uncertainty. This changes communication preferences and information seeking.*

Grosser, in a survey of the literature of human networks and information processing, concludes that there is evidence for 'an overwhelming preference for human as opposed to document- or computer-based information sources' (Grosser, 1991: 387).

Researchers suggest that the need for information changes for the decision-making process: impersonal sources create awareness, but personal sources are preferred for decision-making. Daft and Lengel (1984) suggest that the selection of communication media is linked to the degree of equivocality or the existence of multiple and conflicting interpretations of the evidence. The idea of equivocality is closely linked to that of uncertainty, where previous experience does not necessarily provide a guide to future actions. The authors suggest that, in equivocal situations, individuals are likely to choose the richest media – that is, the media that carries the most information – or face-to-face communication.

Face-to-face communication offers the opportunity to give immediate feedback, can convey multiple cues, such as tone of voice and facial expression, can be easily tailored to the immediate situation and allows variety in language. By comparison, progressively 'leaner' media might be a telephone conversation, a written personal message or a written report (Huber and Daft, 1987; Daft, 1995).

Other research reviewed in Robertson and Kassarjian (1991) suggests that interpersonal communication is sought in situations where other forms of information are unavailable or conflicting, or where they are seen as biased. Personal contact, where it draws on the experiences of peers who may enable the information-receiver to avoid extensive and expensive information-seeking on their own behalf, reduces anxiety. It is possible that, in a personal encounter, information will be presented in the form of a conclusion or decision or that a decision may emerge from dialogue with colleagues.

Several studies have tested the relationship between electronic media and face-to-face communication (McKenny *et al.*, 1992; Trevino *et al.*, 1990). They support the idea that individuals choose channels of communication based on the equivocality (ambiguous nature) of the task and furthermore suggest that, in equivocal situations, face-to-face communication is preferred over electronic communication.

Change agents should seek to emulate the preferred communication style of their client community. Research suggests that this is face-to-face interpersonal communication – a preference favoured even more highly under conditions of uncertainty.

INFORMATION SOURCES AND UNCERTAINTY

In their review of the literature on diffusion and technological innovation, Maguire and Kench (1984) argue that external sources are important in the innovation process but the degree to which external contacts are the source of innovation cannot be determined. Other research supports the idea of the significance of external sources. Innovative individuals tend to be characterized by the extent of external networks. Research in the management literature suggests that effective managers (boundary-spanning individuals) engage in scanning and probing focused searches. Scanning is a routine monitoring of the external environment. Probing focused searches result from a dissatisfaction with existing information and a conscious decision to discover new information, likely to come from external sources perhaps triggered by rapid technological change, where internal information will be inadequate and levels of uncertainty are high.

Evidence suggests a greater use of external sources during periods of uncertainty. Change agents may become the target of probing and focused searches. They will be more effective the more visible they are to their client community.

INFORMATION AND KNOW-HOW

Descriptions of the innovation process are underpinned by the assumption that signalling or passing on information is the most important factor in adoption. Attewell (1992) raises questions about the differences between information and know-how. His approach is to look at innovation in terms of a learning organization theory. Attewell suggests that organizations have knowledge barriers to innovations. Passing on information is not enough: barriers to knowledge have to be lowered in order for organizations to take on new ideas. Such barriers are lowered by acquiring know-how – skills that enable organizations to internalize innovations. The example offered is that of the computer industry: in cases where new service organizations appeared to develop and install products for clients, they carried the burden of know-how until the clients were able to take it on. Because they completed the same tasks many times over for different clients, they also learned faster and were more effective.

Know-how is the knowledge that makes the implementation of innovative ideas possible, bridging the gap between awareness and knowledge. Change agents take on the burden of knowledge until clients are able to accept their know-how. The successful exchange of know-how with individuals who are motivated and powerful within the organization leads to learning and, finally, to implementation.

Change agents need to be experts, prepared to take on the burden of holders of know-how on their clients' behalf.

UNCERTAINTY AND NETWORKS

Grannovetter's (1973, 1982) theory of the strength of ties provides a basis for understanding how links between individuals can lead to mass actions. He defines the strength of ties as a function of three factors:

1. time spent communicating
2. emotional intensity
3. intimacy.

Strong ties, which would score highly on Gannovetter's three measures, tend to exist between similar people who know each other well and who share the same knowledge. These ties are unlikely to be sources of new information. Weak ties, however, are bridges between different groups where members of each group are unlikely to be known to each other. Therefore weak ties carry new information between groups.

This paradox gives rise to the idea of the 'strength of weak ties' in conveying information between groups. The theory suggests that those with many weak ties are more likely to receive and convey new and novel information. The capacity to build 'weak' networks is well developed among boundary-spanning individuals, but is also a requirement for change agents to be able to influence across many groups.

Some research suggests that, under conditions of uncertainty, the use of weak and strong ties changes. Grannovetter (1982) suggests that people in insecure positions are more likely to resort to friendship (strong) ties as a means of reducing uncertainty. In their discussion of élites and outsiders Albrecht and Hall (1991) suggest that élite groups form to discuss new ideas as a tactic to reduce uncertainty. These groups, based on personal relationships, form a stable and trusting environment in which to discuss new ideas. The significance of these élite groups is that they are likely to have control over information and resources and be influential in the decision-making process.

Krackhardt (1992) proposes the existence of two types of group within organizations: advice networks centred around the expertise of key individuals and philo (friendship) networks based on trust, friendship and frequent communication. During routine changes, information flows through advice networks. In times of crisis, change or uncertainty advice is sought within the philo (friendship) network.

Albrecht and Hall draw a distinction between the outsider, the weak tie, who is the source of new information and the élite group which controls decision-making and has a large stake in the decision outcomes.

Change agents need to be outsiders with weak ties to many groups. They cannot become part of the closed group if they have no stake in the outcomes of the decision process.

NETWORKS AND COMMUNITIES

Monge and Contractor (1996) define communication networks as structures built on the basis of relationships between individuals, groups, organizations or societies. The network perspective allows an examination of the ties and links between individuals and of how their communication activity can lead to the mass dissemination of information and wholesale adoption.

Rogers and Kincaid (1981) describe the communication process as a sharing of information in order to arrive at a mutual understanding. Their convergence model envisages several iterations of question and response before mutual understanding is achieved. This model better fits the ideas of communicating across (electronic) networks which frequently, although not always, take the form of an iterative exchange of information.

Ideas of what constitutes community are also changing. In their review of the literature on virtual communities Fischer *et al.* (1996) suggest a continuum from communities, linked by social relationships and a sense of belonging created by face-to-face communication and shared space, to those linked by a sense of shared identity. The latter would encompass the idea of virtual communities. Cohen departs from the concept of community expressed as structure and physical place and advances the idea of the symbolic construction of community:

> The symbols of community are mental constructs: they provide people with the means to make meaning. In doing so, they also provide them with the means to express the particular meanings the community has for them. (Cohen, 1985: 19)

Contractor and Eisenberg (1990) suggest that there is evidence to support the theory that adopting communication technology changes communication networks. They suggest that it increases communication between employees and managers, increases the volume of communication and the diversity of 'strong ties', and helps reduce uncertainty by adding additional channels of communication (multiplexity).

New ideas about networks and communities provide evidence of the potential power that resides in the change agent role. Change agents are able to use the capacity of networks to distribute information, and digital networks add an extra dimension to this, reducing barriers of time, space and distance. A redefinition of the nature of communication as an iterative process is sympathetic to the exchange of information across networks. A redrawing of the definition of communities allows the concept of communities existing within digital networks or physically disparate communities connected by digital networks.

In this context networks are the weak ties which connect one to many. Individuals may be linked to more than one network. Information provided to one individual may feed into many networks. Information delivered into different networks will reach many individuals.

Looser definitions of community, based on research interests, academic disciplines, work groups or personal interests, equate with friendship groups, and perhaps with élite decision-making groups which translate information into action.

Obviously this is a simplistic interpretation. There exists a significant area of research devoted to theories directed at understanding information exchange that is not discussed here. Nor can electronic communication fully emulate the immediacy of face-to-face contact which is so important in the decision to adopt change. However, communication networks and communities, both virtual and real, have a magnifying and unpredictable effect on the distribution of information. New communication technologies increase the volume of information, the diversity of channels and possibly the efficiency of the communication process. The power of an individual change agent may seem limited, but this power can be significantly increased by appropriate exploitation of networks.

(Digital) networks are powerful tools at the disposal of change agents. Change agents need to exploit their potential as well as recognize their limitations.

BEING A CHANGE AGENT: BEHAVIOURS THAT ARE LIKELY TO LEAD TO SUCCESS

The intention of this chapter has been both to extend and refine an understanding of the role of the change agent. To have value, however, theory must influence practice and practice should be informed by theory. For information professionals experiencing uncertainty and change and who are placed in the role of promoting innovative technologies, some approaches are likely to be more effective than others. The analogy of doing and being, borrowed from advice given to those who enter other cultures, is useful here. Whoever we are (being), changing our own behaviour (doing) will make our actions more appropriate and communication more effective. The analogy between information professionals and *being* change agents is profoundly unhelpful if no advice on *doing* is offered. The following summary suggests behaviours likely to engender change in others.

● Change agents are experts. They have know-how to pass on to clients and act as a reservoir of knowledge from which clients can draw.
● Change agents understand the communication networks of their client group. They seek to identify boundary-spanning individuals who are influential in the distribution and use of information.
● Change agents emulate the communication patterns of boundary-spanning individuals. There is a significant body of research suggesting that these individuals prefer interpersonal communication and most favour face-to-face contact. This preference is reinforced during periods of uncertainty.
● Change agents are visible. Change agents, who are visible to their client community, are likely to be targeted by information-seeking boundary-spanning individuals and others. This behaviour increases during periods of uncertainty.
● Change agents are outsiders. Research suggests that, during periods of change and uncertainty when information-seeking increases, élite groups

prefer to discuss this within their immediate circle. The change agent needs to be accessible to many groups, but not necessarily a member of any. There is some evidence to suggest also that, in times of uncertainty, people prefer to seek information outside their immediate circle.

● Change agents should exploit networks. These can have a powerful amplifying effect on the distribution of information.

REFERENCES

Adams, J.S. (1983), 'The structure and dynamics of behavior in organizational boundary roles', in M.D. Dunnette (ed.), *Handbook of Industrial and Organizational Psychology*, New York: John Wiley & Sons, 1175–1200.

Albrecht, T.L. and Hall, B. (1991), 'Relational and content differences between outsiders in innovation networks', *Human Communication Research*, **17**(4), 535–61.

Allen, T.J. (1969), 'Information needs and uses', *Annual Review of Information Science and Technology*, **4**, 2–29.

Attewell, P. (1992), 'Technology diffusion and organizational learning: the case of business computing', in M.D. Cohen and L.S. Sproull (eds), *Organizational Learning*, London: Sage.

Cohen, A.P. (1985), *The Symbolic Construction of Community*, London: Methuen.

Contractor, N.S. and Eisenberg, E.M. (1990), 'Communication networks and new media in organizations', in J. Fulk and C. Steinfield (eds), *Organizations and Communication Technology*, Newbury Park, CA: Sage.

Daft, R.L. (1995), *Organization theory and design*, Minneapolis, MN: West Publishing Company.

Daft, R.L. and Lengel, R.H. (1984), 'Information richness: a new approach to managerial information processing and information design', in B. Shaw and L.L. Cummings (eds), *Research in Organizational Behavior*, Greenwich, NY: JAI. 191–233.

Farace, R.V. and Danowski, J.A. (1973), *Analyzing Human Communication Networks in Organizations*, Michigan: Michigan State University, Department of Communications.

Farace, R.V., Taylor, J.A. and Stewart, J.P. (1978), 'Criteria for evaluation of organizational communication effectiveness: review and synthesis', in B.D. Ruben (ed.), *Communication Yearbook 2*, New Brunswick, NJ: Transaction Books, 271–93.

Fischer, E., Bristor, J. and Gainer, B. (1996), 'Creating or escaping community? An explanatory study of Internet consumers' behaviors', in K.P. Corfman and J.G.

Lynch (eds), *Advances in Consumer Research*, Provo, UT: Association of Consumer Research, 178–82.

Grannovetter, M. (1973), 'The strength of weak ties', *American Journal of Sociology*, **78**(6), 1360–80.

Grannovetter, M. (1982), 'The strength of weak ties: a network theory revisited', in P.V. Marsden and N. Lin (eds), *Social Structure and Network Analysis*, London: Sage.

Grosser, K. (1991), 'Human networks in organizational information processing', in M.E. Williams (ed.), *Annual Review of Information Science and Technology*, **26**, Medford, NJ: Learned Information.

Huber, G.P. and Daft, R.L. (1987), 'The information environments of organizations', in F. Jablin, L.L. Putnam, K.H. Roberts and L.W. Porter (eds), *Handbook of Organizational Communication: An Interdisciplinary Perspective*, Newbury Park, CA: Sage.

Krackhardt, D. (1992), 'The strength of strong ties: the importance of philos in organizations', in N. Nohria and R.G. Eccles, *Networks and Organizations*, Boston, MA.: Harvard Business School, 216–39.

McClure, C.R. (1978), 'The information rich employee and information for decision making: review and comments', *Information and Processing Management*, **14**, 381–94.

Maguire, C. and Kench, R. (1984), 'The introduction and difussion of new technological innovation in industry: an information research perspective', in B. Dervin and M.J. Voigt (eds), *Progress in Communication Sciences IV*, Norwood, NJ: Ablex, 163–99.

McKenny, J.L., Zack, M.H. and Doherty, V.S. (1992), 'Complementary communication media: a comparison of electronic mail and face to face communication in a programming team', in N. Nohria and R.G. Eccles (eds), *Networks and Organizations*, Boston, MA.: Harvard Business School, 262–87.

Monge, P.R. and Contractor, N.S. (1996), 'Communication networks', in A. Kuper and J. Kuper (eds), *The Social Science Encyclopedia*, (2nd edn), London: Routledge, 108–109.

Robertson, T.S. and Kassarjian, H.K. (eds) (1991), *Handbook of Consumer Behavior*, Englewood Cliffs, NJ: Prentice-Hall.

Rogers, E.M. (1983), *Diffusion of Innovations*, (3rd edn), New York: Free Press.

Rogers, E.M. (1995), *Diffusion of Innovations*, (4th edn), New York: Free Press.

Rogers, E.M. and Kincaid, D.L. (1981), *Communication Networks: Towards a new Paradigm for Research*, New York: Free Press.

Shoemaker, P.J, (1991), *Communication Concepts 3: Gatekeeping*, Newbury Park, CA: Sage.

Smith, A., (1980), *Goodbye Gutenberg: The Newspaper Revolution of the 1980s*, Oxford: Oxford University Press.

116

Trevino, L.K., Lengel, R.H., Bodensteiner, W., Gerloff, E.A. and Muir, N.K. (1990), 'The richness imperative and cognitive style: the role of individual differences in media choice behaviour', *Management Communication Quarterly*, **4**(2), 176–97.

Tushman, M.L. and Scanlan, T.J. (1981), 'Boundary spanning individuals: their role in information transfer and their antecedents', *Academy of Management Journal*, **24**(2), 289–305.

8 Identifying and working with stakeholder perspectives

Rob Lloyd-Owen

INTRODUCTION

This chapter is based on the experiences of a project manager responsible for the evaluation of a JISC-funded Electronic Libraries Programme project, Project Phoenix, during the period February 1996 to July 1997. A review of a paper entitled 'Changing the culture: the people factor in electronic libraries' (Bell, 1998), struck a sympathetic chord with the editors of this book and, accordingly, this chapter illustrates some of the human issues and themes actually encountered whilst exploring the potential applications for on-demand publishing (ODP) technologies. The Phoenix consortium members from three new UK universities: De Montfort University (DMU), South Bank University (SBU) and the University of Huddersfield (UH) were interested in exploiting networked academic information in this context.

As project manager working within the library community, whilst lecturing in a higher education (HE) institution on a part-time basis and having recently been a Masters student (MSc Innovation Studies), I had a unique personal perspective on the perceptions of three primary stakeholder groups impacted upon by the project: students, academics and academic support staff (IT, library staff, computer services and others). Whilst much of the material in this chapter is drawn from project reports and presentations (Phoenix, 1997a), the views expressed here are mine and should not be taken to represent the official views of any of the universities involved in Project Phoenix.

THE PROJECT PHOENIX BACKGROUND

RESEARCH OBJECTIVES

The project sought, as its overall aim, to conduct research and integrate technologies which would enable course support materials to be delivered to students on demand. The key objectives of the research were:

119

1. to research and integrate emerging electronic publishing and distribution technologies to deliver course support materials to students on demand
2. to develop and establish procedures, using document and copyright management software which collate and store materials which can be prepackaged or delivered to screen and printed on demand
3. to evaluate the impact of these technologies on the educational process.

ODP processes, tools and techniques were investigated in an attempt to improve the flow of course support materials to students as text. An effective introduction to the development of ODP can be found in Akeroyd (1994). Two different, but complementary, approaches were taken by the partners. DMU developed a system for screen delivery via the Web, offering students the choice to read materials on-screen, print pages, reserve a library copy or purchase a bookshop copy. SBU developed a system for the preparation and delivery of course packs preprinted on demand. Bell's review (1998) described these differing systems as '"just-in-time" and "just-in-case"'. These approaches built on work previously undertaken at DMU and SBU. The UH leads the evaluation activities by testing the transferability of the operational models.

TECHNOLOGIES INVESTIGATED

The technologies investigated by, and the operational experiences arising from, Project Phoenix have been reported (Lloyd-Owen, 1997), including how to obtain the tools, documentation, and support for installing and using them. A variety of reports exist at the Phoenix archives website in Adobe Acrobat portable document format (PDF) (Phoenix, 1997b). The Phoenix operational report also presented the future vision of an integrated ODP system which could be expected when the various pieces of the technological jigsaw outlined are drawn together into a coordinated whole. The report concluded that:

> The electronic library has arrived, but more as a concept than a totally integrated technological system. As an ideal, the electronic library (one source, with universal access to everything, by anyone anywhere) cannot fail, but we as people might fail to realize it.
>
> It is through the process of people sharing ideas that Data becomes Information, Knowledge becomes Understanding and with time may, we hope, become Wisdom. An electronic library must be designed for people by people thinking and acting for each other's benefit. Exploit the technology, learn to use it – serve the ideal of the electronic library. (Lloyd-Owen, 1997)

EVALUATION OBJECTIVES

Evaluation should form an integral part of any development programme and

Project Phoenix, like all eLib projects, was encouraged to carry out effective evaluation at all stages in order to make available to the wider HE community the learning from its successes and failures. The Tavistock Institute provided a very comprehensive documented evaluation framework (Tavistock, 1996a) and training guidelines for eLib project personnel to enable them to become aware of the range and application of available evaluation techniques. Evaluation was seen by the Tavistock Institute as an integral part of a continuous development cycle involving a triangular loop of activities: action, evaluation and decision-making.

Project Phoenix had three evaluation objectives for the prototypes:

1. evaluation of their operation and technical effectiveness
2. evaluation of user reactions to them and to their end-products
3. evaluation of their potential impact on HE generally.

Several evaluative techniques were used, but this chapter concentrates on the findings from the focus groups which were used to obtain the views, impressions and feedback from the various stakeholders on whom the prototypes would impact.

STAKEHOLDERS AND FOCUS GROUPS

Project Phoenix operated with definitions for stakeholders and focus groups refined by Tavistock (1996b). Stakeholders can be recognized as belonging to one of three groups: first, those whose support and cooperation is necessary for the project to succeed; second, the intended users or beneficiaries of the project outcomes; and, third, those who are expected to use or act on the evaluation findings.

Focus groups are a particular type of group in terms of purpose, size, composition and procedures. Their purpose is to obtain information of a qualitative nature from a predetermined and limited number of people. Typically they comprise seven to ten participants sharing certain characteristics relating to the topic of the focus group and a skilled interviewer/facilitator who seeks to promote self-disclosure among the participants through open-ended questions within a permissive environment. The process itself involves a sharing of ideas, perceptions, feelings and attitudes by group members and group members influencing each other through the social situation. Normally a number of groups are run to form a series (Krueger, 1994).

Morgan (1997) considers it appropriate to use focus groups in the following circumstances: when there is a communication gap in understanding, opinion or perception; when investigating complex behaviours and motivations; when the researcher wants to understand diversity; or when a friendly respectful research method is needed. Focus groups are inappropriate when they imply commitments that can't be kept; if the participants are not comfortable with one another; when the topic is not appropriate for the participants; and when a project requires statistical data.

Greenbaum (1998) identifies the following as appropriate uses for focus groups: new product development studies; positioning studies; habit and usage studies; packaging assessments; attitude studies; advertising/copy evaluations; promotion evaluations; idea generation; and employee attitude and motivation studies. The following were considered to be abuses of focus groups: use as a cheap alternative to quantitative research; use for the production of data they are not intended to generate (for example, estimating sales of a new product or determining the optimal price of a product or service); holding more sessions than are necessary to achieve the research objectives; holding groups in more locations than is necessary; or taking the technique too seriously.

There are differing opinions on the right and proper use and methods of running focus groups. I concur with Vaughn who suggests that 'A common misconception is that focus group interviews are primarily used for gauging consumer reaction to a product or marketing technique ...' and goes on to state strongly that '... focus group interviews are a versatile tool that can be used alone or with other methods (qualitative or quantitative) to bring an improved depth of understanding to research in education and psychology' (Vaughn *et al.*, 1996: 33).

FOCUS GROUP METHODOLOGY AND APPROACH

A focus group design day resulted in agreement amongst consortium members that three key areas needed to be addressed at focus groups:

1. the documenting of stakeholder views on the delivery of course support materials to students, focusing firstly on current provision and then the Phoenix prototypes. (The primary stakeholders were targeted to be academics, students and academic support staff.)
2. identification of the benefits and limitations of on-demand approaches and products
3. identification of stakeholders' views on pricing, in terms of what is acceptable.

Six focus groups were run at each of the universities – DMU, SBU and the UH. They were run with independent groups from three stakeholder communities: students, from a range of schools and courses; academics, from a range of schools; and academic support staff, from schools and support units such as the library, computing services and learning resource centres. Two focus groups ran for each set of stakeholders, each one concentrating on a different prototype and its outputs, the pre-assembled course reader system being developed at SBU and the Course Book Web Server being developed by DMU. The participants were informed about the purpose of the focus group in the recruitment literature:

> Before the Project commits the University to the development and deployment of OD systems, it is vital to understand and document the views of users and providers. Project Phoenix wants to document these views through the use of focus groups.

The following agenda was used to manage the discussions for each of the six groups at each university:

1. Introduction – why?
2. Existing services – participants' experience of their strengths and weaknesses
3. Presentation of an alternative delivery method
4. What participants like/don't like about this and its implications
5. What still needs addressing in terms of access to learning materials
6. Review of session

Sample course readers and a prototype demonstration were used during the focus groups to support the presentation in agenda item three.

RESULTS AND OUTCOMES OF THE FOCUS GROUPS

EVALUATION REPORTS

Individual reports were constructed from an analysis of individual responses to focusing questions. The analysis involved clustering individual comments under themes in hexagons (see Figure 8.1). After all the focus groups had been run, separate confidential reports were produced for each institution. Following this, an overall report synthesized from all three institution reports was made available for public consumption using a similar method of clustering. The reports were constructed under the main themes and the comments woven together, respecting the verbal integrity of the views of the focus group participants. Participants knew that they had been heard because they were able to recognize their own words in print, although non-participants would be unable to identify who actually said what.

OBSERVATIONS ON RUNNING THE FOCUS GROUPS

In the preparation and running of the focus groups I was supported by an external consultant who had experience of social research and investigation of client needs in both academic and public libraries. At evaluation planning sessions, Tavistock representatives had suggested that project members were more than capable of running focus groups. However, the project team agreed

Student Interface

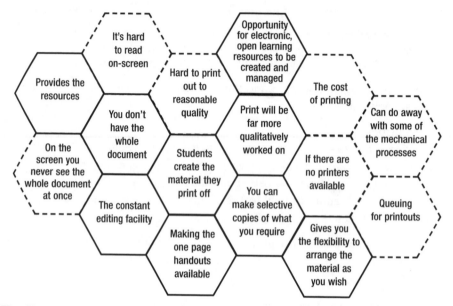

Key: Hexagons with a solid border represent positive views – dotted lines negative views. The original diagrams on the Web are in colour.
The report and the focus group comments (as pages of hexagons) are available at the website (Phoenix, 1997b).

Figure 8.1   Sample hexagon clusters of focus group participants' comments

that it was more appropriate for someone external to facilitate and report on them. This proved to be a crucial decision, and I was grateful to the consortium for providing the support to allow an external consultant for several reasons, including the following:

1. At the focus group design stage it is all too easy to restrict the debate which identifies the key issues and agrees a focus. It must be remembered that focus group activity is not likely to provide specific answers to the research questions posed – more, directional information to the issues requiring further exploration.
2. The *alternative delivery methods* prototypes were presented at the focus groups by myself. The presence of an external referee prevented my prejudices contaminating the views of focus group participants.
3. At a focus group a presenter can be drawn into debate and defence of the solutions proposed instead of objectively listening to the feedback from participants. Focus groups are about documenting the diversity and range of views, not about reaching consensus.

4. Little debate was allowed at focus groups. The *I am Right You are Wrong* (De Bono, 1991) type of debate was avoided. What we were seeking to collect were the views of stakeholders about the existing provision and the proposed alternatives.

5. It can be quite a shock to a novice facilitator to discover the gaps that can exist between and within different communities of individual stakeholders. These gaps can occur in their views and perceptions about technologies and concepts, and are especially sobering when they relate to something that the researcher feels is quite obvious because of its familiarity, such as an electronic library, digital printing, scan, store and print or even eLib.

6. The facilitator was also able to protect those stakeholders who were absent from being cited as the causes of the problems, when those in a specific stakeholder focus group decided the faults and failure lay with others. The strategy was to focus on constructive criticism not moaning.

At the focus groups the facilitator recorded the participants' own words on flipcharts with no censorship or editing. It is interesting to note, at meetings, how much editing is done by the person with the pen!

FINDINGS FROM THE FOCUS GROUPS

CONCLUSIONS ABOUT THE CURRENT SITUATION

The existing services were felt to be fairly comprehensive but insufficient. Resourcing was a key issue to help respond to the rapid increase in student numbers, which was creating additional demand, and to finance the development of access through new technology.

CONCLUSIONS ABOUT COURSE READERS

Course readers can provide an effective and assured source of core reading material for students. Academics can use them as an aid to supplement and enhance their contact with students, resulting in an improved educational process. However, this approach cannot be exploited to its full potential whilst copyright charges remain prohibitively expensive and until the universities develop the design and production skills and resources necessary to do it professionally. Potentially this technology could provide local and distance access to core material which can be readily updated. Equally, the system could have the capacity for a very wide range of material for each course.

CONCLUSIONS ABOUT THE WORLD WIDE WEB APPROACH

In principle the Web approach to providing core text-based material has a great deal of merit in providing a medium which gives assured access to material which is up-to-date when the student requires it. However, the capital and revenue costs to bring this into reality may be beyond the funding capacities of the universities, and no fully blown system has yet been tested. Moreover, this approach does not have the convenience of a book and not everyone is competent to use IT equipment.

It also requires the full cooperation of academics to create the core text and keep it up-to-date as well as a technical infrastructure of people with publishing and IT skills to help it function. There was a significant concern expressed at all three campuses that this approach was being promoted as a way to save money without an understanding of the technical and educational implications of taking such a course of action. Use of the Web, to be successful, needs to be appropriately resourced, and the opportunities and risks it offers the educational process should be carefully considered.

EDUCATIONAL IMPLICATIONS

The place of the library service in the educational process of each university was a source of many comments. Current provision was failing to cope with peak demands for core texts due to the increased number of students and the development of course work assessment to supplement examinations. Course readers and Web technology could assist in ensuring that everyone has access to the core texts, but academics have a key, and new, role to play in the creation of this material. Academics were not only concerned that they would not be given the time and support to carry out this new work, but also about copyright over their own work. Some academics expressed concern about the implications for their role and the risk of losing live contact with students. Other academics, especially those experienced in developing and using course readers, enjoyed the opportunity it offered to develop a more effective teaching strategy in which students ask questions and have read the appropriate core texts before lectures or seminars.

The Web approach also raised corporate threats and opportunities. Where subjects or specialisms could be serviced nationally or internationally from one centre of excellence, certain universities may become redundant or others may take over the whole system. The question to be addressed educationally is the nature and value of the relationship between the academic and the student. In the opinion of many respondents, the rapid expansion of higher education has already had a significant impact on this relationship, and on the quality of the education provided. Web technology offers radical opportunities for distance learning and student-directed learning, leading academics to ask 'What kind of university do we want to be?' and 'What do we want our graduates to have when they leave us?'.

MANAGING THE PROCESS

The new technologies, and especially the Web approach, require an infrastructure and an implementation strategy that needs to be very skilfully managed. At two of the universities the senior management stance was felt to be primarily directed towards cost-cutting: courses were packaged and put on the Web, without an understanding of the implied learning processes and cultural–structural issues that would need to be addressed. The current system, respondents felt, seems to value productivity rather than innovation in teaching and leads to a view that core texts are education in themselves, rather than simply information. There was general scepticism that, in the present financial climate, the Web approach could be adequately resourced to be truly accessible and solve the problem of providing core texts on demand. The librarians were already feeling overworked and underresourced and did not see the Web as providing a cheaper operation, given that it could not replace the need for books. Concern was also expressed at the competence of the universities to service complex technology, given the difficulty they had in keeping the photocopiers going.

Finally, there was the whole area of corporate management. At present, the universities have not agreed common standards across faculties and there is no integrated network in existence in any of the three institutions. Schools are very decentralized and there is no institution-wide strategy for information provision and learning support. Respondents even felt that senior management did not know how to put strategy into action effectively and there was fear that management would abdicate responsibility after the pilot stage.

SUMMARY OF THE MAIN FINDINGS

1. The existing provision is quite comprehensive but has become inadequate because of an inability to cope with peak demand for core texts. Pressure on funding has also limited the range of journals available and has caused library staff to feel overstretched in providing a satisfactory level of service.
2. Text-based information is currently provided in the form of books, journals, lecturer's handouts, course readers and CD-ROMs. The Web technology is in the early piloting stage at DMU.
3. Photocopying is widely used by both academics and students, but the suitability, capacity and reliability of the machines was often felt to be inadequate.

4. Academics felt that they needed more time and appropriate technical support to produce good-quality handouts and course readers.

5. Where they are provided, students value the availability of PCs, but felt that there were not enough of them.

6. Those with experience of course readers found them to be a very useful resource, provided that something can be done to obtain copyright permissions at an affordable price.

7. Course readers provide a portable packaging of core texts that students could supplement with their own reading.

8. Course readers can be used effectively to enhance the educational process by obliging academics to review their teaching in producing them, and then supplementing what is said and discussed in lectures and seminars.

9. The Web approach could provide a medium which gives assured access to material which is up-to-date, both on site and from a distance.

10. To be implemented successfully the Web approach needs significant capital and revenue expenditure, a radical training strategy and the development of agreed operating systems and production standards across the whole institution.

11. The Web approach still lacks the portability of a book and requires the full cooperation of academics to create texts and keep them up-to-date.

12. The issues of data security, risk of viruses and back-up provision if the system crashes need to be considered.

13. Both academics and academic support staff felt that both course readers and Web technology would result in students failing to develop independent research skills.

14. There were serious doubts expressed about the capacity of the institutions to manage the complexity of an integrated Web system.

15. Educationally the course reader and Web could create greater distance between academics and students, especially in a cost climate where information starts to be considered as education.

16. The Web, in particular, has a potential that obliges each university to question its role, its marketplace, its educational purpose and values.

17. Neither of these technologies currently replaces the need for books.

DISCUSSION AND IMPLICATIONS OF THE FOCUS GROUP FINDINGS

DISCUSSION OF FINDINGS BY CONSORTIUM MEMBERS AND OTHERS

After dissemination of the reports a meeting was held to discuss the findings (Phoenix, 1997b). Present were consortium members, eLib, JISC and Tavistock representatives and the focus group facilitator. The key issues arising were summarized as follows.

1. Even a few people attending focus groups can confirm one's suspicions. No one was surprised by the findings, but the information gleaned would provide a rich source to provoke future debate, specifically regarding ODP and more generally about the impact of technology on teaching and learning.
2. All the stakeholders had misunderstandings and misperceptions about the technology and what it was going to be used for, and each stakeholder group had its own focus of concerns. The data emphasizes the differing perceptions of the stakeholders.
3. The data collected provided a useful benchmark of current perceptions of academics and academic support staff, which could be used to anticipate what might happen if consortium members went ahead with the prototypes and would certainly provide a useful reference for later evaluations as developments continued.
4. Copyright is a significant problem.
5. There are huge resource issues in attempting an innovation such as this on an institution-wide basis: major economic costs of infrastructure; value and recognition of academic value for materials production; implications of passing costs on to the students; importance of access to quality resources and support. If the system does not function adequately users will give up no matter how good is its potential.
6. The academic voice was strongest, and students were underrepresented. At all three institutions it proved difficult to recruit students.
7. The academics were perceived to have the most genuine concerns about the whole issue of educational development, including the fear that delivery of information was being seen as a substitute for education.
8. Concern was expressed about the importance and need for an overall institutional strategy for educational and technology development. There was a perceived need to bring the different stakeholders together to collaborate, and to raise these points with senior management.
9. Whilst those who were informed about the use of course readers were able to comment positively on their potential, many people were still confused about the potential of the Web approach.
10. It was felt that most of the issues would need to be dealt with locally – especially infrastructure and resource investment – and that recognition of this fact was a national issue. There is no universal panacea. The people issues also need to be addressed locally if the technology is to be exploited to its maximum benefit and the culture moved forward constructively, without uncertainty and fear of change.

129

11. The report highlighted academic concerns about management, development and the support for technology applications and how to integrate these into courses. These concerns were also strongly bound up with issues of power, control and ownership of the curriculum and the educational development process, in a time of rapid change and a movement to mass university education.

IMPLICATIONS FOR CHANGE AGENTS

If change agents choose to use focus groups they will need to make sure that they have sufficient support from a facilitator who is sufficiently independent to be able to see and hear all of the perspectives of the various stakeholders involved. Each stakeholder group will have its bias and will not necessarily see or understand the differing perceptions of other stakeholders, especially when the agent is seeking to introduce a fresh innovation. Focus groups provide change agents with a useful and economical research method both in terms of time and expense, as well as a means of understanding stakeholder perspectives of current reality. Even if you know where you want to go, if you don't know how far from your goal those you have to take with you are, you may never be able to manage your way there. Change agents can use focus groups to build trust and commitment from their key stakeholders, because as they describe their 'current reality' and their voices are recorded and reported, their views are heard and honoured even if they, as individuals, cannot be identified.

Focus groups do not solve problems but they can usefully help in terms of directions to explore and indicators on how stakeholders might like the future to evolve. Change agents should seek to keep existing and traditional educational delivery modes in operation whilst ensuring that those less keen to embrace change are exposed to new methods and exemplars, and at the same time providing adequate technical support until the strange becomes familiar. As there is no single model across the HE sector which will yield solutions, it is vital to understand the culture of the host organization in which the agent is seeking to bring about change.

In particular, change agents must avoid being seduced by the technology. If they are clear about their purpose most people will embrace a technology if its exploitation enhances and furthers that purpose. They will vigorously resist it if they see it as promoting technology for technology's sake. Often, seeking to deploy a technology can have far-reaching consequences as in Project Phoenix, where attempting to alter and make the delivery of text to students more efficient challenged the existing paradigms of academics, librarians and students. Particularly in the new model of the electronic library, the question is 'Who is to control the modes of working?'. Ultimately, technological adoption is hindered because humans are tactile: although information technology is certainly 'high tech', it is not 'high touch' as Naisbitt (1994) argued in his book, *Global Paradox* – hence the reader's usual preference for a book rather than a computer screen.

Change agents need to ensure that the organizational context within which they are operating is one with: effective leadership; the capacity for managing change; champions for the change required; good teamworking; good exemplars to build on; a culture of cooperation and collaboration; support for risk-taking; willingness to learn from mistakes and encouragement of mutual trust and respect amongst the stakeholders. Thus for information technologies, such as ODP, to become fully exploited they must be: user-led, not technology-driven; purpose- not cost-driven; creative and humanistic; designed *with*, not *for*, users; consistent with library ideals within an electronic context.

INVOLVING STAKEHOLDERS IN INITIATING AND SUSTAINING CHANGE

STAKEHOLDER PERSPECTIVES

Readers from any of the stakeholder groups mentioned in this chapter may well recognize the problems alluded to, particularly those arising from differences in perspective between themselves and the other stakeholders with whom they interact in an academic environment. These differences manifest themselves in the way individuals think, communicate, use language, conceptualize, listen to one another and feel about themselves, their work and each other.

During Project Phoenix, and since its completion, I have sought out alternative ways of working with stakeholders. A number of cultural change models were explored including Beer (1979, 1985), De Bono (1992), Fritz (1994c), Garratt (1994) and Senge (1990). Only Fritz and a recently encountered approach from Weisbord and Janoff (1995) will be discussed in more detail. The introduction to a New Economic Foundation's text entitled *Participation Works* begins with the following statement: '"Consultation" and "participation" are fashionable words. Our institutions are starting to appreciate that lack of accountability breeds a lack of legitimacy and trust' (New Economic Foundation, 1998).

In *Pedagogy of the Oppressed* Freire (1996) describes the opposing theories of cultural action antidialogics and dialogics. Antidialogics is an instrument of oppression characterized by conquest, 'divide and rule' and cultural invasion. By contrast, dialogical action is characterized by cooperation, unity, organization and cultural synthesis. Perhaps a simpler way of explaining this is by using one of the seven habits of highly effective people, 'Seek to understand – before you seek to be understood' (Covey, 1992). Thus we can build trust and commitment by giving stakeholders a voice, listening to them and giving them feedback so that

131

they know they have been heard. We should work towards cultural synthesis, not cultural invasion.

> When you listen to somebody else, whether you like it or not, what they say becomes a part of you. ... The common pool is created, where people begin suspending their own opinions and listening to other peoples' ... people begin to recognise that this common pool is more important than their separate pools. (Bohm, quoted in Weisbord and Janoff, 1995: 15)

Project Phoenix team members were acutely aware of the gap between academics' views and government and centralized university policy over issues of planning and resourcing, as evidenced by some of the comments in the 'Main findings' section. What I was seeking was ways of *working with* stakeholders to develop solutions as opposed to the old service provider notion of *doing things to* or *for* their customers.

SOLVING PROBLEMS OR CREATING THE FUTURE

Many of us in academic circles pride ourselves on our excellent research and problem-solving skills. Recently, creativity and creative problem-solving have become more common elements in undergraduate and graduate study. Important new perspectives on the distinctions between problem-solving (including creative problem-solving) and creating have been drawn (Fritz, 1994a) – in particular, that problem-solving is an activity directed at trying to remove, deal with or overcome something that already exists, whilst 'creating' is one targeted at attempting to bring something into existence which currently does not exist.

Fritz (1994c) describes the need to exploit structural tension which provides the energy for creating solutions which bring into being an imagined future. He also explains how to diagnose and unlock the structural conflict in organizations, which leads them into being reactive and merely responding to external events, rather than being proactive. He and his associates have developed structural consulting techniques which seek to design organizational structures so that organizational goals are congruent with structural tendencies. The need for this is echoed in the following quote: 'Cultural change is as much a result of structural change as a promoter – effective cultural change rarely happens without simultaneous changes in structures.' (Tavistock, 1996c)

Understanding these structural issues can be helpful to change agents, many of whom will have experienced the frustrations of seeing situations remain the same regardless of any effects to bring about change. In seeking to bring into being an imagined future one is trying to reduce the uncertainty and risk associated with the future by actively developing solutions where one can exert some control. Fritz's books (1994a, 1994b, 1994c) give simple and clear strategies which help with creating the future.

FUTURE SEARCH: A TOOL FOR INITIATING AND IMPLEMENTING CHANGE

Change agents operating in the roles described elsewhere in this book and Project Phoenix team members would probably empathize with the following statement:

> As a society we have painted ourselves into a technological corner. We have more ways to do things than ever before. Yet a lot of what matters to us is not getting done, despite the large sums we spend on public and corporate business. (Weisbord and Janoff, 1995: xii)

The more we know and learn, the more we realize there is to know and learn. We may feel impotent, we may become cynical and frustrated, wishing we could achieve some of our goals. We may often feel that they – whoever *they* are – could make things happen if they would only listen to us. But I suspect *they* feel just as overwhelmed by the scale, complexity and uncertainty associated with trying to implement technological change. Those of us who believe we are technologically literate need to remember that many stakeholders are not and have no wish to become so. They may not see the situation as we do.

I see innovation as 'the initiation and implementation of change' (Gill, 1995) – an undertaking that is not without problems as noted by Machiavelli. We need to seek methods of working *with* stakeholders to build sustainable futures, through participative processes that unlock the potential for change and succeed in initiating and implementing it. I believe that Future Search offers change agents such a method.

A Future Search conference adopts a whole systems approach by gathering all the stakeholders together in a room for about 16 hours over three days. In the process participants come to grips with each others' current reality and, by means of a shared encounter, deal with the chaos, uncertainty and complexity we normally avoid – the critical element here being the *sharing*. Importantly, the Future Search neither replaces nor is a substitute for rational planning. It is '… an umbrella for building commitment … allows people to work far enough through the dynamic issues that stand in the way of implementing anything – dreams and schemes, systems and projects, visions and dreams' (Weisbord and Janoff, 1995: 3). The uses of Future Search, according to Weisbord, fall into three categories: first, Future Search processes encourage stakeholders to create a shared future vision for their organization or community; second, Future Search conferences enable all stakeholders to discover shared intentions and take responsibility for their own plans; and, third, these events can help people implement a shared vision that already exists.

A Future Search conference often comprises 60–70 people and has as its purpose joint action towards a desired future for a community, organization or issue. Participants undertake five simple tasks: review the past; explore the present; create ideal future scenarios; identify common ground; and make action plans. Work on the past and future is done by mixed groups of stakeholders. Work on the present is done by individual stakeholder groups who will have similar perspectives on the issues. An event usually takes place over three days and includes two nights. There is plenty of evidence to support the effectiveness of the methodology in the form of case studies and reports (Weisbord *et al.*, 1992).

This chapter has sought to share my experiences during a particular project with those who may be about to embark on the perilous road to innovation. The final section of this chapter, in focusing on involving stakeholders initiating and sustaining change, has sought to bring to the reader's attention methods and knowledge which I would have wished to have known about before embarking on the project described, because both creating the future and searching for a better future are better alternatives than just waiting for things to change on their own.

REFERENCES

Akeroyd, J. (1994), *Digital Books? On Demand Printing and Publishing*, London: Library Information Technology Centre.

Bell, A. (1998), 'Changing the culture: the people factor in electronic libraries', (Report of a conference paper by R. Lloyd-Owen), *Relay*, (45), 18–19.

Beer S. (1979), *The Heart of Enterprise*, Chichester: Wiley.

Beer S. (1985), *Diagnosing the System: For Organizations*, Chichester: Wiley.

Covey, S.R. (1992), *The Seven Habits of Highly Effective People: Powerful Lessons in Personal Change*, London: Simon & Schuster.

De Bono, E. (1991), *I am Right You are Wrong*, London: Penguin.

De Bono, E. (1992), *Handbook for the Positive Revolution*, London: Penguin.

Freire, P. (1996), *Pedagogy of the Oppressed*, (new rev. edn – 1st edn 1973), London: Penguin.

Fritz, R. (1994a), *The Path of Least Resistance*, London: Butterworth-Heinemann.

Fritz, R. (1994b), *Creating*, London: Butterworth-Heinemann.

Fritz, R. (1994c), *Corporate Tides: Redesigning the Organisation*, London: Butterworth-Heinemann.

Garratt, B. (1994), *The Learning Organisation: And the Need for Directors Who Think*, London: HarperCollins.

Gill, H. (1995), Comment during a lecture given as part of the Innovation Module of a Masters degree in Innovation Studies at the University of Huddersfield.

Greenbaum, T.L. (1998), *The Handbook for Focus Group Research*, (2nd edn), London: Sage.

Krueger, R.A. (1994), *Focus Groups: A Practical Guide for Applied Research*, (2nd edn), London: Sage.

Lloyd-Owen, R. (1997), 'On demand publishing – researching its application to some library problems: Project Phoenix', *Library and Information Briefings* (74).

Morgan, D. L. (1997), *The Focus Group Guidebook. The Focus Group Kit 1*, London: Sage.

Naisbitt, J. (1994), *Global Paradox: The Bigger the World Economy, the More Powerful its Smallest Players*, London: Brealey.

New Economic Foundation (1998), *Participation Works: 21 Techniques of Community Participation for the 21st Century*, London: New Economic Foundation.

Phoenix (1997a), Phoenix Archive Site, http://hud.ac.uk/schools/phoenix/pages/homepage.htm (This site also contains links to both De Montfort University and South Bank University documentation not contained within it.)

Phoenix (1997b), Phoenix Archive Documents, http://hud.ac.uk/schools/phoenix/pages/documents.htm (All the public documents created as part of Project Phoenix are available in portable document file (PDF) format from here.)

Senge, P.M. (1990), *The Fifth Discipline: The Art and Practice of the Learning Organisation*, London: Doubleday.

Tavistock Institute (1996a), *Evaluation of the Electronic Libraries Programme: Evaluation Framework for eLib*, London: Tavistock Institute.

Tavistock Institute (1996b), *Training Workshop June 1996 for ELib Managers*, London: Tavistock Institute.

Tavistock Institute (1996c), *Policy Mapping Study – The Set-up, Operation and Content of the Electronic Libraries Programme*, London: Tavistock Institute.

Vaughn S. *et al.* (1996), *Focus Group Interviews in Education and Psychology*, London: Sage.

Weisbord, M.R. *et al.* (1992), *Discovering Common Ground*, San Francisco, CA: Berret-Koehler.

Weisbord, M.R. and Janoff, S. (1995), *Future Search: An Action Guide to Finding Common Ground in Organizations and Communities*, San Francisco, CA: Berret-Koehler.

9 Organizational culture: assessment, audit and change

Bruce Reid and Helen Williams

INTRODUCTION

The recurring theme of this book is that cultural factors are of great importance in the successful organizational exploitation of networked information. This chapter will be devoted to a review of relevant literature on organizational culture and of methods of studying, assessing and changing it. It will particularly emphasize applications to the LIS environment and especially the electronic library. There are many hundreds of definitions of culture which are most helpful and illuminating within their appropriate context. For the layperson an acceptable definition might be 'a set of common patterns of behaviour associated with particular group/s of people'. For ethnographers this is too loose and externalized and they would require 'the acquired knowledge that people use to interpret experience and generate social behavior' (Spradley, 1979: 5). One important reason for the difference between these definitions is the level of description and analysis that would lie behind an understanding at that defined level: in the former, superficial; in the latter, in-depth. This distinction becomes important in selecting tools that help in understanding culture in organizations since, in practical terms, the returns are proportional to the investment of time, resource and effort. The concept of organizational culture is a metaphor from wider society and is itself the object of a multiplicity of definitions. Skyrme (1994) has counted 160! In the management context the metaphor is applied with varying emphases, but with an underlying consistency that makes it possible to devise an enumerative and ostensive definition derived from some of the principal writers on the subject which will serve as a working tool (Fletcher and Jones, 1992; Harrison, 1993; Shaughnessy, 1988; Skyrme, 1994; Wilkins, 1983).

Organizational culture is a pattern of:

- beliefs, values, principles, rituals, myths, sentiments, assumptions, attitudes, meanings, givens, ways of seeing the world.

The components of this pattern are:

137

- shared, implicit, taken for granted, customary.

These shared pattern components influence:

- behaviours of individuals
- behaviours of groups
- how decisions are made
- who makes decisions
- how rewards are distributed
- who is promoted
- how people are treated
- how the organization responds to its environment.

It is generally agreed that organizational culture is not the same as organizational climate or management style, although it may include basic assumptions that the organization has 'invented, discovered or developed in learning to cope with its environment'. (Shaughnessy, 1988: 6). The whole concept may also be encapsulated by the phrases 'the rules of the game' or 'the way we do things around here'.

Organizational culture and its management have been given some attention in the LIS literature, mainly by academic and public librarians. However, the examples used in this literature are more frequently from business or from the commercial sector of the information industry than from LIS themselves. Shaughnessy (1988: 6) summarizes the two predominant views in the literature: the first is that many successful executives have obtained a quick and beneficial culture change in their organizations without close study or understanding; the second is that culture must be understood before it can be managed. Drawing on work done on resistance to computers in an academic library (Albritton and Sievert, 1987), he concludes that awareness of a library's culture and proposals to change may be essential prerequisites to the successful implementation of new technology and concomitant changed work practices. Malinconico (1984), himself a public librarian, uses the examples of AT&T and OCLC to illustrate strong organizational culture. He attributes to the origins of the bibliographic utility OCLC in Columbus, Ohio much of the credit for its achieving culture. Thus a local ambience created by the presence of the Battelle Memorial Institute, the Engineering School of Ohio State University and Chemical Abstracts Service (coupled with the clarity of direction provided by its director) produced a practical results-oriented and client-oriented organizational ethos. He further argues that US public libraries, which have a tradition of delegating many responsibilities to branches, have had culturally-induced problems with centrally automated catalogues. In an interesting exploration of the interface between information activities and organizational culture Norton (1994) illustrates the potential for culture dissonance between the task-based and person cultures with the example of librarians in law firms.

ORGANIZATIONAL CULTURE AUDIT

The study of organizational culture has led management theorists to seek valid ways of measuring and comparing it. Since the 1970s one widely accepted method, the organizational culture audit, has been employed by managers and management consultants in business and commercial environments as well as in the public sector, notably government departments. If it has been used in LIS environments, it does not seem to have entered the published literature. Other chapters in this book have descibed such factors as mass access, the changing needs of learners, the potential and convergence of new technology and underresourcing that have led to substantial re-engineering in HEIs. In such a context it could be argued that the need for measuring organizational culture is greatest as an essential prerequisite for any organizational change in order to ensure optimum implementation and as a 'before and after' measure of success or failure. In the case of encouraging networked electronic information use, where culture change is such a critical factor to success, culture audit should prove to be an invaluable tool.

Specific tools available to managers use various methodologies but all are based on employee perceptions of aspects of their organization. These may be tested by reactions to details such as: task variety or task significance; to actual and preferred expectations in terms of, for example, motivation or conflict resolution; or to detailed scenarios. Specific tools are discussed below.

Our intention is to review the history and literature of the technique, examine some published case studies, and suggest some guidelines for its application to the electronic library situation. Harrison (1993) claims that the concepts involved in auditing organizational culture were developed jointly by himself and Charles Handy in the summer of 1970. The published literature confirms this. Handy (1978) subsequently published his version of the organizational culture model in *The Gods of Management*. A substantial stimulus to US business interest in organizational culture audit was provided in the late 1970s and early 1980s by economic turbulence which caused major changes in the structure and orientation of individual companies, and by the markedly different but highly successful culture of prototypical Japanese companies. These factors provided a new perspective on behaviour previously taken for granted in US companies and led to the realization that, in order to compete effectively, companies would need to pay attention to their organizational culture. First, cultures whose work and reward assumptions are appropriate to their business need to be developed.

139

Second, in the face of change, it is essential to understand the existing organizational culture in order to influence or redirect it. Culture audit was developed in response to this need. Several tools are currently available, all primarily designed for the business environment and all based to varying degrees on the research literature of such relevant areas as motivation theory and occupational health.

There are a number of problems inherent in the execution of any culture audit. The most important is that many shared assumptions are never articulated in general terms but only implied in many concrete examples. For instance, employees in an organization may think it is 'better' in some way than its apparent peers, but find this difficult to justify concisely. However, stories elicited about approved behaviours and working arrangements may well reveal assumptions of, say, a strong service ethic or an egalitarian ethos. There is also the question of how representative of the organization an audit is and the need, in large organizations, to uncover subcultures whose shared values may be markedly different from one another. Most tools attempt to take these potential difficulties into account.

APPLICATIONS OF CULTURE AUDIT

Some of the more obvious applications of culture audit are to reduce absenteeism, reduce stress and reduce staff turnover. These are clearly related problems in the sense that a reduction in one is likely to result in a reduction in the others, but the achievement of improvement in any one of them through changes indicated by a culture audit can mean large savings and increases in cost-effectiveness. Other specific purposes to which it can be put include the following:

- To form a framework within which to undertake job redesign. The gap between existing and ideal situations revealed in the data can be used as a benchmark for collaboration between shopfloor, supervisory and management staff in redesign.
- To compare cultural perceptions between different sections or functions in an organization.
- To measure the impact of projects aimed at changing organizational culture. The tool can be used to assess current culture and then, at a later date, after intervention aimed at change, reapplied to ascertain whether the desired change has been achieved.
- To tailor training to suit staff employed within an organization of a particular culture.
- To discover whether staff within an organization believe that its culture is consonant with its publicly projected values.

- In teambuilding to offer a basis for assessing the differences between where a team is and where it wants to be, and for making agreements about changing ways of working together.

In an interesting and well documented application of cultural audit in the public sector Colville and Packman (1996) investigated how successful the attempts of senior management had been in securing desired cultural change in HM Customs and Excise. The desired change was based on a requirement 'for an organizational form that can cope with dynamic and complex environments', and this had been seen to entail 'a shift away from managing through the "book" to one of managing through "people" ... by treating them as professionals who add value to the organization by exercising their skills and initiative'. Interestingly, the audit was based on the contention that, at some point, any attempt at changing culture must go further than merely changing attitudes to work (although that might be a prerequisite) to changing behaviour in the desired direction. Furthermore, the researchers began with the hypothesis (based on their observation) that working practices had changed to a greater extent than had attitudes and that this fact had not been adequately detected by surveys of attitudes and morale carried out by external consultants in 1991 and 1992. This is an important factor that should be taken into account by anyone evaluating, as fit for their purpose, any of the tools reviewed in this chapter.

Before the audit could be attempted it was obviously necessary to obtain agreement from senior managers on what reported behaviours would count as valid indicators of desired cultural change and these were forthcoming in the form of three clusters/categories:

- **Participation and initiative.**
  - involvement in planning processes
  - taking own course of action from local knowledge, especially where this went against perceived orthodoxy
  - extent to which the above decisions were used as learning experience, especially when they were perceived to have gone wrong.
- **Communications**
  - flexibility of channels
  - contact with opposite numbers elsewhere without using the bureaucratic chain
  - informal language.
- **People**
  - respect for the individual
  - personal development activity
  - recognition of individual's contributions
  - service delivery to 'customers'.

The methodology of the audit comprised 80 individual semi-structured interviews of approximately one hour with people drawn from the three junior grades, supported by four group interviews with working teams (for example, an anti-smuggling team) which lasted over two hours. The latter were recorded, transcribed and analysed using the same categories as for the individual interviews. Some 600 examples of behaviour were recorded in all: most under 'Participation and initiative', then under 'People', and least under 'Communications'. Examples of behaviours running counter to desired ones made up 20 per cent of the total. The findings showed that the culture shift in terms of people's behaviour was greater than the change in their attitudes.

Apart from a number of practical issues of utility to HM Customs and Excise, the authors conclude more generally that 'we could not arrive at a satisfactory way of deciding how much change had taken place' and that 'auditing change during a time of change is particularly difficult' (Colville and Packman, 1996: 31).

SOME APPROACHES TO CULTURE AUDIT

This is not an area of methodology where consensus should be expected. Whilst not necessarily agreeing with Peters (1993) that consultancy in organizational culture is licensed theft, the conscientious reviewer must endorse the conclusion of Team Technology that:

> There is no standard formula for changing the culture of an organization – there are a variety of tools and techniques, and you need to select the one most appropriate for your situation. You also need to identify the critical success factors that are unique to your particular environment. (Team Technology, 1997: 3)

There are many variant forms of the culture audit – some of them promoted by individual management consultancies – but the underlying principles are very similar and are well exemplified by the Organizational Culture Inventory (OCI) (Cooke and Lafferty, 1987) from Human Synergistics. The OCI claims to provide a 'statistically valid and reliable measurement of the embedded beliefs, values and behaviours that shape a given organization's culture' (Cooke and Lafferty, 1987: 1). It is administered as a survey questionnaire using 96 statements to which respondents' reactions are graded and

> … measures twelve distinct thinking and behavioural patterns or 'styles' that members of an organization might adopt in carrying out their work and interacting with others. The composite scores for each style are then plotted on a circumplex [*sic*] creating a visual profile of the organization's current culture. (Cooke and Lafferty, 1987: 1–2)

Most methodologies make use of typologies of culture, attitude, and behaviour; base their measurement on individual responses to hypothetical statements about the organization; distinguish between the way things are and the way the respondent would like them to be; profile the culture by aggregating scores; and allow for the detection of variation within subcultures. It is intended here to deal only with the two most important current instruments and two alternative developing approaches of steadily increasing importance.

FLETCHER'S CULTURAL AUDIT (FCA)

The most important current (and still evolving) UK instrument is Professor Ben C. Fletcher's *Business Audit: An Individual and Organizational Tool* (Fletcher, 1997; also 1991). Fletcher's research instrument (fully explained in Fletcher and Jones (1992) on which most of this section is based) is securely rooted in relevant pre-existing research. Its questions are designed to elicit responses whose significance is based on the body of research evidence in the areas of job design, motivation theory, goal-setting, and occupational stress. To take job design as an example, research has shown that there are five characteristics of jobs which are beneficial both to the individual and to the organization. These are:

- skill variety – the degree to which a job requires a variety of different activities involving different skills
- task identity – the degree to which a job may be seen as entire in itself rather than a fragment of something bigger
- task significance – its impact or importance
- autonomy – the freedom to decide ways of working
- feedback – the amount of information the individual receives about the quality or effectiveness of his or her work

An approach based only on the considerations above, however, would not take into account the differences in individuals with respect to needs and aspirations. To incorporate this, previous research into modelling the 'Person–Environment Fit' (Van Harrison, 1978) has been drawn on to score the individual's perception of their own position and of their preferred or ideal. Finally personality factors are acknowledged through measures of elements of self-esteem and perceived control which, although they do not represent all areas of personality, have been shown to moderate relationships between work features and outcomes.

The measurement method of the instrument is not norm-based and does not require comparison with other organizations: what it reveals are variations within the organization and changes in culture through time if, for example, the audit is repeated after an intervention such as training. Earlier editions of the instrument measured on a five-point scale for each response element:

- the respondent's perception of their own situation (M-score)

- their perception of the situation of others in the organization (O-score)
- their ideal situation (I-score)

Later editions have omitted the O-score.

The use of the FCA can be tailored to the needs of individual organizations, but its primary outcomes will be to provide:

- data on current staff perceptions of organizational culture and by how much, and in what ways, it deviates from their ideal
- a measure of how receptive the organization is to change and the introduction of new ideas, techniques, procedures and so on
- a profile of discrepancies in culture within the organization
- an assessment of the effectiveness of interventions or new initiatives
- monitoring of the change process.

Since the FCA uses types and dimensions as a way of differentiating organizational culture, it has been possible, with increasing experience of its use, to distinguish organizations in terms of four general descriptive bipolar types:

1. **Homogeneous versus heterogeneous culture.** A homogeneous culture may produce similar audit profiles in a wide range of departments. This may make it easy to manage major organizational shifts, policy implementations and change, but may be inappropriate in an organization with a range of different functions.
2. **Enriched versus managed culture.** An enriched culture will have numerous jobs high in, for example, autonomy, variety and feedback and occurs in organizations that give individuals greater responsibility and take advantage of individual talent. It is less easy to direct and may not be appropriate to some organizations or at some times.
3. **Developing versus stationary culture.** A developing culture has an active, motivated workforce with a high level of demands and responsiveness to change, but also highly marketable staff. A more stationary culture will probably display less 'fire-fighting' and more strategic planning.
4. **Balanced versus dissonant culture.** A balanced structure is one in which individual job demands and the financial, technical, and social resources available to meet the demand are in balance, whether demands are high or low. Management structure and communications are clear, and workers' expectations are being met. This makes for stability but not necessarily for a proactive approach or for responsiveness to change.

HARRISON'S DIAGNOSING ORGANIZATIONAL CULTURE (DOC)

The best known US instrument (Harrison 1992, 1993) is norm-based and provides tabulated scores which may be used as a basis for comparison with both individual and organizational scores. Norms have been compiled for a variety of groups of different nationalities, and professional users of the instrument are requested to provide copies of their answer sheets to the author to add to a database of comparative organizational–culture profiles intended to assist research into how different national cultures affect organizational cultures. DOC is based wholly on the concept of four archetypal organizational cultures which are characterized as follows:

1. **The power culture: based on strength.** The organization is based on an inequality of access to resources – for example, money, privileges, job security, working conditions – and the ability to control others' access to these. People are motivated by rewards and punishments and by the wish to be associated with a strong leader.

    At its best, leadership is based on strength, justice and the leaders' paternalistic benevolence. The leaders exercise power according to their understanding of what is good for the organization and all its people.

    At its worst, there is a tendency towards rule by fear, with the leaders, their friends and protégées abusing their power for personal advantage.

    The power culture is very appropriate to entrepreneurial and start-up situations in which leaders have the vision, intelligence and will to manage the business and have a personal relationship with loyal followers.

    As size increases, power-oriented organizations become inefficient, fearful and confused and, unless there are effective structures and systems, control becomes difficult.

2. **The role culture: based on structure.** Structures and systems give protection to subordinates and stability to the organization. Duties and rewards are carefully defined. Key values are order, dependability, rationality and consistency.

    At its best, it provides stability, justice, and efficient performance. People can spend less time looking after their own interests and more energy on their work.

    The weakness of the role culture is a relative inability to adapt to rapid change because of excessive control and limits on discretion and autonomy to innovate outside the rules.

3. **The achievement culture: based on competence.** The main rewards and satisfactions are intrinsic to the work itself or to the context in which it is done. People are self-motivated. There is a clear mission. Communication channels are open, organization is egalitarian, and failure is viewed as a learning experience, rather than a sign of personal inadequacy. Contributions are freely given in response to a shared purpose.

145

At its worst, the achievement-oriented organization is underorganized and relies on high motivation to overcome its deficiencies in structures, systems and planning. People's needs are subordinate to the organization's mission and its needs. This may lead to burn-out and disillusionment.

4. **The support culture: based on relationships.** The organization is based on mutual trust between the individual and the organization. People help one another beyond the formal demands of their jobs, enjoy spending time together, and communicate not only about work but about personal concerns. People know that the organization will look after them when they need it and reciprocate by caring for the organization's facilities, resources, output and reputation. They also avoid confrontation, sometimes to the point of leaving important matters unresolved.

Other weaknesses include overvaluation of consensus, causing inability to move decisively and ignoring of differences in skill and ability in the interests of 'equal treatment'.

The assumption behind DOC is that a dynamic and creative tension between elements of each of these culture types is needed for the optimal functioning of any particular organization, and that diagnosing the 'mix' in an individual organization is the first step towards improving it.

The instrument itself consists of 15 incomplete statements about the organization, each followed by four optional clauses to complete them. The respondent is asked to rank these four clauses, each of which corresponds to one of the archetypal cultures, in order of its dominance as a view within the organization's culture. He or she also has to carry out a second ranking according to personally most preferred options. The statements cover such areas as: priority-setting; career success; task assignment; decision-making processes; motivation; conflict and so on. The tabulated scores reveal mismatches between personal and organizational culture as well as differences between subcultures. Similarities in preferred culture between respondents set against agreed mismatching with existing culture may suggest common ground for planning the direction that change should take.

ETHNOGRAPHY AND THE SCENARIO-ASSISTED CULTURE AUDIT (SACA)

There is continuing disagreement about the validity of using quantitative and qualitative methods to assess culture. Proponents of the latter claim that standard off-the-peg questionnaires sterilize culture into bland overgeneralizations, whilst others maintain that the theoretical construct of culture has become habitually associated with qualitative methodologies only because of the historical roots in anthropology of those researchers who have turned their attention to it.

Whichever view is taken of this debate, however, the fact remains that the most frequently used qualitative method to assess organizational culture is the ethnographic study and that this technique has a number of serious deficiencies and disadvantages for this purpose, which are enumerated below.

'Ethnography is the work of describing a culture' (Spradley, 1979: 3). Spradley also makes clear that the goal of ethnography is to grasp the native's point of view, to which end the investigator must learn the language of the group studied and frame questions so as to reduce the tendency of informants (not subjects or respondents, note) to translate into the vernacular of the researcher. The intention with an organization would be to use a disciplined and skilled method to build up an understanding of how its members give meaning to their environment. This would normally require time-consuming observation of the organization and interviews with many of its members – what Schwartzman calls 'the various ways that researchers have developed for learning about the cultures and structures of organizations from the inside out' (Schwartzman, 1993: 4). The main advantages are:

● the in-depth data that can be obtained
● the potential for speculative investigation into processes and areas that little is known about
● the use of the organization's own terminology and concepts to describe itself.

The main disadvantages in using ethnographies in this context are:

● they are extremely time-consuming and consequently not very timely
● they require a high degree of expertise and must be conducted by outsiders
● because of the foregoing they are very expensive
● most ethnographers follow an ethical code which requires that 'these [the informants'] interests must be considered first' (Spradley, 1979: 35) – a factor that may not always meet the needs of management.

Hale (1991) attempts to realize the advantages of ethnographic methods whilst avoiding their disadvantages by combining them with customized surveys in his Scenario-assisted Culture Audit (SACA) methodology. This is a refinement of earlier culture audit tools and warrants further consideration for adaptation to the exploration of networked information cultures. Hale acknowledges the depth and richness of ethnographic reports, but points out 'that they do not provide descriptive statistics which quantify how widely or intensely each cultural perception is shared by sub-groups within the organization' (Hale, 1991: 46). This also makes them unsuitable for measuring the impact of programmes intended to change organizational culture or to judge the effectiveness of a culture. He gives some weight to ethnographers' doubts that 'any survey instrument designed by researchers prior to their encounter with a culture can capture the particular

147

frames of reference contained in the unique culture of that organization' (ibid.: 49) but attempts to meet this objection in his methodology.

The SACA is based on the assumption that culturally plausible scenarios written especially for the specific organization 'have the potential to tap into culture specific frames of reference' and, in so doing, audit culture more deeply, accurately and significantly. There are two stages of data collection. In the first, ethnographic interviews of 1–2 hours are conducted with a small selected sample of staff, and internal documentation such as organizational charts, performance appraisal systems, organizational policy manuals and promotional materials is examined. The interviews serve both as a means of collecting cultural information needed to create culturally relevant scenarios and as data for an ethnographic report back to the organization. In the second, the SACA is created and administered to all or a large representative sample of the organization. The survey consists of a series of plausible situations that might occur in the organization and is designed to elicit the respondent's perception of how members of the organization would behave in each of these context-rich scenarios. The respondent is asked to select which of two plausible reactions is likelier to take place and also state their degree of certainty that their selection represents what actually happens in the organization. An example, set in a printing company, is as follows:

> Suppose that a bomb went off in the press room. Even though none of the employees were physically injured, there was a great deal of emotional trauma and several employees were emotionally shaken. Immediately after the explosion, the press foreman calls the corporate headquarters to report the incident. The corporate staff would be most likely to ask which question first?
> 1 How much damage was done and how soon can you have the press operating again?
> 2 Was anyone hurt? How are our employees handling the trauma?
> (Hale 1991: 234)

SACA data is statistically manipulable, and scores from the methodology have tested positively for reliability and validity.

CULTURE AUDIT AND NETWORKED INFORMATION

The most extensive general reviews of the literature on cultural and organizational change in the HE electronic library environment have been provided by the IMPEL project team (Edwards *et al.*, 1993; Day *et al.*, 1996). From these and other interim reporting (Huntingford, 1998) it emerges that information technology continues to be the major catalyst for change, but also that:

> ... in such a dynamic and uncertain environment policy makers may struggle to

manage and predict change effectively. ... IMPEL2 has found examples of a 'cultural lag' in which the most rapidly changing part of an institution ... forges ahead leaving the rest of the organization struggling to cope with the changes left in its wake. (Huntingford, 1998: 3).

Clearly, an enormous amount of change is being reported as LIS organizations modify their shape and orientation under the influence of that most persuasive influence of all – the accelerating growth in availability of networked information and communication. If change towards a network-oriented culture may be regarded as a continuum on which the present position of particular organizations (or their components) may be plotted at various points (as the IMPEL evidence suggests) then it must be of considerable interest to individual organizations to gain an awareness of where on that continuum they presently lie. However, so far, little attention appears to have been given to audit techniques as a means of achieving this or of first understanding then guiding and facilitating a change in orientation.

A number of appropriate potential applications of culture audit, particularly of the scenario-assisted kind, suggest themselves:

● Identification of cultural perceptions in advance of technological change. This allows support and training to be designed appropriately and avoids expensive non-use of new systems/services.
● Identification of cultural differences between sections, departments, or role groups and management of potential conflict or dissonance between them. This has a clear application to the whole convergence/merger issue discussed in Chapter 6. It may also be regarded as an important tool for teambuilding, since it allows identification of areas of agreement for preferred change to provide common ground for new ways of working together.
● Job redesign resulting from a re-evaluation of work ends and work means. Changing professional and para-professional roles in LIS is just one example where cultural information might enhance, as well as facilitate, change.
● Stress reduction by increasing support or reducing constraints. Examples in the networked environment would be provision of training, new or enhanced equipment or connectivity, or time for exploration/innovation.
● Intervention assessment. Successive audits of a networked environment to determine the impact of planned programmes.

NETWORK-ORIENTED CULTURE: MARKS, SIGNS, AND TOKENS

The TAPin project sought to identify changes in attitude, behaviour, and culture through several of its survey instruments and case study evidence collection protocols. These activities were primarily directed at assessing the impact of the TAPin intervention of planned support on the six consortium universities, and much of the data related to perceptions of individual members of these institutions. However, as far as the organizational culture of the six university libraries is concerned, some evidence was collected by non-participant observation of the physical library environment. Chapter 14 mentions the concept of the access library culture as a research instrument (p. 231), and its definition for purposes of the project is fully explained in the TAPin Second Annual Report 1997. In brief, 'an institution with an access culture was defined as one which embraced networked information and was changed or transformed in the process' (Newall *et al.*, 1997: 19). Examples of the kind of evidence that may be used to diagnose an institution as network-oriented or not are:

- accessibility and identification of points of access to networks
- screen-based guidance to networked resources (for example, Web pages) and degree of integration with the OPAC
- presence at key locations (foyer, enquiry points and so on) of signs and print guidance to networked resources
- tone and register of treatment of networked resources in printed and verbal presentation (positive or negative content analysis)
- visible acknowledgement of remote users
- published guides which integrate networked resources with other formats
- visible examples of networked resources linked with passwords, help, training and contacts

These are examples only, but provide ample scope for an amateur scriptwriter/ information professional to draft a scenario-based audit.

Networked information makes change in an organization's culture inevitable, but it does not make it easy. Facilitating it is likely to yield substantial organizational dividends and understanding it is the first step. Indeed, perhaps what we need is action research, as Eidet seems to suggest.

> If you want to shape or change the culture, you must develop a conscious attitude towards it. Go into it – experience it, understand it and participate in it. Create new heroes and new rituals, and change your workplace from a place to be into a place to learn. (Eidet, 1993: 20)

A number of the major considerations for wider research into networked information use in the future are dealt with in Chapter 15. Existing culture audit tools are useful in establishing the nature of existing culture, but have limitations in suggesting preferred ways forward in the context of rapid and radical technological change. Ethnographic work can provide a deeper understanding of why organizational and individual interaction with networks is as it is and what various stakeholders want in the future. This provides knowledge of the new situation for which cultural audits can be adapted, recalibrated or recast to capture new realities.

REFERENCES

Albritton, R. and Sievert, M.E. (1987), 'Investigating resistance to computers (computers anxiety) in an academic library', paper presented at ALA Library Research Round Table, 28 June 1987.

Bell, A. (1998), 'Changing the culture: the people factor in electronic libraries', (Report on a conference paper by R. Lloyd-Owen), *Relay*, (45), 18–19.

Colville, I. and Packman, C. (1996), 'Auditing cultural change', *Public Money and Management*, July–September, 27–32.

Cooke, R.A. and Lafferty, J.C. (1987), *Measuring Organizational Change – Organizational Culture Inventory*, Human Synergistics, http://www.hsnz.co.nz/Products/oci.htm

Day, J.M. *et al.* (1996), 'Higher education, teaching, learning and the electronic library: a review of the literature for the IMPEL2 project: monitoring organizational and cultural change', *New Review of Academic Librarianship*, **2**, 131–204.

Edwards, C. *et al.* (1993), 'Key areas in the management of change in higher education libraries in the 1990s: relevance of the IMPEL Project', *British Journal of Academic Librarianship*, **8**(3), 139–77.

Eidet, R.E. (1993), 'The organizational culture of public libraries – a Mafia network?', *Scandinavian Public Library Quarterly*, **26**(2), 14–20.

Fletcher, B.C. (1991), *The Cultural Audit: An Individual and Organizational Investigation*, London: PSI Publications.

Fletcher, B.C. (1997), *Business Audit: An Individual and Organizational Tool*, Imagination Technology Global Limited (available only from Professor Fletcher or Bob Stead at the University of Hertfordshire).

Fletcher, B.C. and Jones, F. (1992), 'Measuring organizational culture: the cultural audit', *Managerial Auditing Journal*, **7**(6), 30–36.

Hale, E.B. (1991), *Assessment of Organizational Culture via the Scenario-assisted Culture Audit Methodology*, Ph.D dissertation, Provo, UT: Brigham Young University.

Handy, C. (1978), *The Gods of Management*, London: Souvenir Press.

Harrison, R. (1972), 'Understanding your organization's character', *Harvard Business Review*, **50**(3), May–June, 119–28.

Harrison, R. (1993), *Diagnosing Organizational Culture: Trainer's Manual*, San Francisco, CA: Pfeiffer.

Harrison, R. and Stokes, H. (1992), Diagnosing Organizational Culture, San Francisco, CA: Pfeiffer.

Huntingford, J. (1998), 'The impact of IMPEL', Ariadne, **13**, 3.

Malinconico, S.M. (1984), 'Managing organizational culture', Library Journal, **109**, 15 April, 792.

Newall, L. et al. (1997), TAPin: Training and Awareness Programme in Networks: Second Annual Report, Birmingham: University of Central England, Centre for Information Research and Training.

Norton, B. (1994), 'Organizational cultures and their relevance to information organization', Aslib Proceedings, **46**(6), 173–76.

Peters, T. (1993), Crazy Ways, Crazy Days, London: BBC Video.

Shaughnessy, T.W. (1988), 'Organizational culture in libraries: some management perspectives', Journal of Library Administration, **9**(3), 5–10.

Schwartzman, H.B. (1993), Ethnography in Organizations, Newbury Park, CA: Sage.

Skyrme, D.J. (1994), 'When information management encounters organisational culture', Records Management Bulletin, (64), 3–5.

Spradley, J.P. (1979), The Ethnographic Interview, Fort Worth, TX: Harcourt Brace Jovanovich.

Team Technology (1997) 'Organizational team building', http://www.teamtechnology.co.uk/tt/t-articl/tb-org.htm, Effecting successful cultural change, p. 3.

Van Harrison, R. (1978), 'Person environment fit and job stress', in C.L. Cooper and R.L. Payne (eds), Stress at Work, Chichester: Wiley.

Wilkins, A.L. (1983), 'The culture audit; a tool for understanding organizations', Organizational Dynamics, Autumn, 24–38.

10 The special library environment

Sharon Penfold

THE NATURE OF THE BEAST

The traditional nature of special libraries has been based on 'in-depth knowledge of print and electronic information resources in specialised subject areas and the design and management of information services that meet the strategic information needs of the individual or group being served' (Special Libraries Association, 1996). The emphasis is very much on access to that specialized information rather than archives or holdings. Marketing, promotion and a strongly proactive approach have long been part of the range of skills required by the information professionals concerned. In the connected world, these same information professionals have been urged throughout the 1990s to exploit the network technologies within their parent organizations in ways to most benefit their customers – in other words, to:

- understand the business needs for information services;
- understand how IT can help us improve our services;
- influence IT, both directly and via end-users, to ensure the infrastructure reflects the information service needs. (Swain, 1993: 34).

The downside of electronic, networked technologies is their effect on the known world and stable infrastructures:

> ... they demand unprecedented and often unwelcome collaboration, invite unrelenting change, threaten to introduce unmanageable costs, and make time and place irrelevant. The disorientation they bring is virtually complete. (Council on Library and Information Resources, 1998: 7).

Balancing the challenges, advantages and implications of the technologies is just one of a wide-ranging set of issues and areas that information specialists must understand and deal with. In principle at least these are the same, whether their host environment is academic, public, government or otherwise. The extent to which they affect the library and the implications for librarians' personalities, technical abilities and communications skills are another matter.

153

Special libraries and librarians (also referred to as information units, information services, information managers and so on) tend to be on the receiving end of a more direct and immediate impact from events in the outside commercial world. This is so whether the library is a one-person unit in a voluntary organization or a lavishly funded team in a management consultancy.

As well as keeping up-to-date with the technologies and their potential for enhancing services, it is also vital that they understand what future predictions and innovations will mean – as far in advance as possible. Negotiating and evaluating the broad sweep of claims for the future encompasses all extremes:

> ... a typical business by the year 2000 will have more than 40% of the workforce involved in collecting, analyzing, synthesizing, structuring, storing or retrieving information. (St Clair, 1994: xiii)

> By 2025, sovereign individuals will be competing in cyberspace – the world's largest economy – in a realm without physical existence ... most ... will be information-poor. (Cawkell, 1998: 56)

> Laying out papers on the desk is a way of arranging our thoughts and helps us read across multiple surfaces ... the paperless regime may ... be less efficient than the litter strewn playpen. (Watson, 1998: 56)

Most predictions tended to ignore the Year 2000 issue which at the time of writing some expected to result in a major 'discontinuity', causing a fundamental backlash against the commercial use of IT (Manchester, 1998: 19). This is an excellent demonstration of the crucial multi-level approach in special libraries. The direct technological implications for their services resulting from any Year 2000 non-compliance have to be resolved. At the same time, the information manager also has to step back to evaluate the wider organizational impact and direction for the issue, planning for as many alternative outcomes to the 'Millennium bomb' as can be foreseen and simultaneously providing appropriate support and guidance to the organization and to any Year 2000 initiatives under way.

THE HOST ENVIRONMENT

The emphases and driving forces in business, industry and the economy as a whole have equally fundamental effects on the libraries and information services within each sector. Globalization, for example, has seen major pharmaceuticals corporations merging separate information units into a single, transnational service. Downsizing, automation and lean organizations, combined with frameworks (or fads) such as business process re-engineering, have resulted in an emphasis on:

● short-term, immediate needs

- business benefits
- cost and value analysis.

Hidden, altruistic, educational benefits are not sufficient to justify existence. The contribution that the special library makes to the operational mission of the organization must be made evident. The library must be proven – and seen – to be as dynamic and vital as all other functions. Guy St Clair, expert in organizational politics, following his early work on one-person libraries, points out that the information services department has to 'anticipate rather than react to' the corporate mission. Another part of the equation is perception – ensuring that all those individuals and departments who need to know the precise value of the library are continually made aware of it. This applies to those who hold the purse strings and those who control the internal politics as well as to those who can directly benefit from the information services.

With the advent of teleworking and hot-desking and of virtual and network organizations, flexible working is a current reality. Successful examples are widespread, from a Swedish car manufacturer to the major UK tele-communications companies. As a result, immediate (if not sooner) reliable end-user access to up-to-date information is even more of a driving force for information units. The implications for information services are in terms of:

- desktop delivery (technologies, interfaces, training and support)
- context-driven and timely information, with proactivity reaching further and wider
- flexibility and responsiveness, whatever the geographical, time and format requirements.

Learning organizations and knowledge management are well and truly part of the corporate vocabulary, thoroughly covered by the management literature. The opportunity that this offers to the information unit is discussed under 'Business approaches' (page 162), but the many forms of knowledge (from customer records and financial data to competitor analysis and market research) have led inevitably to information overload. Although over-hyped, overload will continue to play a key role in the immediate future, potentially paralysing teams and companies faced with too much data, too many sources and too little time. One important underlying factor for the information profession to resolve is that the 'mass introduction of information technology has confused the issues of information management and information provision' (Owens *et al.*, 1996: 50). Quality, accuracy, currency – all the basic measurements applied by information professionals – are easily lost in the confusion. Overriding the numerous problems and disadvantages are the considerable opportunities and advantages opening up to special libraries and information workers. On the human side, the essentials for information specialists within these new structures are:

- teamworking, across functions, departments and countries
- awareness of the basic human need for social interface and exchange
- supporting and encouraging that informal interaction, whether through a physical library/meeting point or a virtual discussion room.

Further organizational and management problem areas for the twenty-first century include the psychological, emotional, legal and motivational aspects and employer–employee relations. All pose problems and issues that will be resolved as we work towards a future where:

> ... as technology becomes more pervasive and invisible, and the emphasis is upon knowing, learning, thinking and sharing rather than just communicating, attitudes, interests and motives will assume greater significance [leading to] a shifting community of 'micro units', 'molecular entities', autonomous and self-managing teams and individual gurus who could be located almost anywhere. (Coulson-Thomas, 1997: 83)

PROFESSIONAL COMPETENCES

As far as the profession goes, special librarians have been faced with claims ranging from:

> ... as organisations sort out their technology and cultural issues they will then realise the true value of information skills – and information specialists are going to get rich very soon. (TFPL, 1998)

to the pessimistic:

> ... despite being at the vanguard of the information revolution in the early 1970s ... [librarians] never appreciated the importance of their emerging role nor exploited their technological lead or privileged position. (Jackson, 1992: 342)

to the more realistic:

> The information specialist's job is changing, but it will be a long time yet until it is gone. People have far too much to do these days and by searching and finding information they are creating even more work for themselves. (Dieckmann, 1998a: 21)

The demands of the parent organization and its sector certainly call for a combination of services and skills that is, in many ways, quite different from that required in public and academic settings. Common principles, aims and approaches include:

- cost-effectiveness

- performance measurement
- quality and reliability
- user-friendliness.

Equally, services are based on the same core technologies, skills and applications – all requiring an appropriately educated and developed professional.

Information managers in the special library environment must be:

> ... a team leader, a facilitator, must be able to monitor programs and evaluate programs and services, and must be willing to train. And at the same time, the manager is required to balance management skills, professional skills and interpersonal skills. It's a tall order, but there's no choice. (Lawes, 1994: 9)

Many elements not traditionally sought or developed in the profession are encompassed or extended: extreme time limitations; political involvement; commercial presentation of services; a consultancy approach; leadership and vision. Professionals are effectively skilling-up, building up management and technological abilities, whilst simultaneously deskilling as technology partially replaces or alters their role – as online search intermediaries or cataloguers for instance. Core competences for this sector of the information profession are thoroughly dealt with by the US Special Libraries Association. It suggests that the special librarian:

- Uses appropriate business and management approaches to communicate the importance of information services to senior management
- Develops specialized information products for use inside or outside the organization or by individual clients
- Continually improves information services in response to the changing needs

Whereas personal accomplishments include:

- Is committed to service excellence
- Sees the big picture
- Looks for partnerships and alliances
- Creates an environment of mutual respect and trust
(Special Libraries Association, 1996)

Some rather more fundamental suggestions for librarians attempting to help corporations 'derive the missing benefit from I.T.' can also not be faulted:

- Give up trying to control: enable instead
- Proselytize the new future
- Use your influence with the digit-heads who are building the Superhighway
- Digitise everything that moves, then add information value to it
- Wear 'hype' deflectors at all times. (Withey, 1994: 49–50)

Finally, combine the above competences and advice with a positive message for the profession which is equally valid:

There is a future but not as we know it. We ... have the skills, knowledge and experience that the intelligent organisation needs. All we have to do is get on and do it! (Nunn, 1994: 6).

CHANGE MANAGEMENT

The question, then, is how? On a personal level, information professionals need to be 'flexible and positive in a time of continuing change' (Special Libraries Association, 1996). From an organizational perspective, change management is another subject area in its own right, well covered in business bookshops. The crucial success factors are recognized as:

- commitment from senior management
- nature and intensity of resistance to change
- culture of the organization
- knowledge and skill of the 'change agents' – those who help to execute the change (Conner, 1998).

There is a fundamental conflict in that change 'is often a random process which outwits the predictions of rational, intelligent and orderly people' and we are advised to 'avoid the belief that change falls into steps or categories and perceive change as an incremental process of flow' (Atkinson, 1998: 181).

However to cope with it – to manage change and successfully transform activities, functions and organizations – some form of logical methodology has to be applied. To bring the two apparently opposite extremes together, a musical metaphor is often used – various instruments and activities brought together as an orchestra, creating and, at the same time, evolving a special sound. Certainly there is a toolkit of methods available to those leading, managing and undergoing change. Flexibility in their application and development is crucial. The key building-block takes the form of strategic management, within the information service and at the highest organizational levels.

STRATEGY

The foundation for successful change in the special library environment – especially when introducing a technology or approach that is totally foreign (for example, an intranet and end-user searching, where all information searching has previously been done by information staff using traditional online hosts) must be a review of the information service's current position. Otherwise:

... there is a danger that current technical solutions relate to problems that will soon no longer be relevant. It is easier to solve existing visible problems than to create a framework for more effective working, particularly when the move is away from structure towards greater flexibility. (Cropley, 1998: 30)

Once the whole picture has been ascertained, or updated, it is then possible to see where a new technology fits in, what the implications are and how to approach them. More importantly, such preparation and planning may justify to the parent organization the initial (and future) investment in the special library as a whole – as well as in specific new services.

Strong evidence of the value of this approach is seen in Zurich Reinsurance's strategic information plan and subsequent developments, which aimed to solve an 'info-famine' and create a responsible 'information culture'. The work started in 1995 when 'the level of understanding about information usage and the tools available were not sufficiently advanced to support end-user information services'. The Information Centre established as a result is now making a 'significant contribution to meeting the company's strategic objectives and helping it to succeed in a changing marketplace'. More importantly, the strategy and services steadily progress towards end-user access and information-sharing across the company (Dyson, 1998: *passim*).

Communicating with the hierarchy and the wider organization in meaningful business terms is often half the battle in special libraries. Proving that the information service is adding value to the organization, knows what the wider strategy is, understands where it fits in and is constantly looking to the future puts the service on a very different footing. Such recognition is frequently painful to win, and takes equal effort to maintain. However, ensuring that the information unit's strategies and plans are regularly reviewed, updated and expanded where necessary is essential; ideally, it should be part of the parent's business planning process if it isn't already.

REVIEW

The first stage investigates what is currently done, using one method or a combination. The depth and extent of the analysis depends partly on the degree of the service's integration into the organization's business planning system, how much integration has already taken place, how long ago and whether it is continuing on an ongoing basis. Useful frameworks are:

- **SWOT (Strengths, Weaknesses, Opportunities and Threats)**. This addresses the questions: Where is the service particularly strong (and weak)? How could it develop? What are the dangers (such as a rival company being especially strong on competitive intelligence)?
- **PEST (Political, Environment, Social and Technological)**. This identifies

the trends in these categories affecting services, the unit, the company, the profession and the sector. For example, computing skills shortages would fall under the 'Social' heading and the Year 2000 issue would fall under 'Technological'.

Both need to look at:

- the macro-environment – the outside world in general;
- our own industry environment – library and information services;
- and the corporate or internal environment. (Corrall, 1994: 10)

PEST and SWOT can also be used on a specific project basis, preferably once the entire service and organization have been covered. Examples might be:

- **Information audits/information mapping** – based on what information the organization has; where it is located; who uses it; how it is maintained; how new information is acquired; how much time and money it absorbs.
- **Existing plans and strategies** – general business and departmental, as well as those specific to information and/or the library unit. What references are there to information needs and future developments? Where have existing information services been missed, or where is the potential to develop services to underpin broader aims within the organization? What corporate initiatives are under way, or planned – and where can the library fit in?

ANALYSIS

Following the review, the services are investigated. Why are services provided? Who for? What do users actually need? This leads to the production of summaries or statements along the following lines:

- **Vision and mission.** Where is the service heading? What is its overall purpose? How does it then fit with any other organizational visions and missions?
- **Aims and objectives.** What are the general goals? How are they then quantified?
- **Critical success factors.** What are the key efforts, areas of activity and conditions necessary to achieve the goals?
- **The information customer.** What are the customer's requirements (taking into account both pragmatic, real-life needs and 'blue-skies' desires – should the resources be available to fulfil them)?
- **Benchmarking.** This comprises a comparison of services and processes against other information units and across other sectors.

Establishing, or further developing, this clear picture of why services exist and what is required (again using appropriate business methods and terminology) reveals what is currently of value and where the library needs developing, leading naturally on to the next stage.

PLANNING AND IMPLEMENTATION

This is arguably the most complex part of the process, establishing what must be provided, what is possible and how. However, in the real world, particularly with the speed of change and technological advances, it is a matter of 'adopt – then adapt'. Flexibility is another key word.

The *strategic plan* builds on the foundation provided by the earlier steps, covering targets, tasks, priorities, project champions (where appropriate) and timescales. A *tactical plan*, covering the current year's projects may also be helpful (developing into full project management methods if necessary). A useful mnemonic in the planning context is SMART: Specific, Measurable, Achievable, Realistic, Timetabled.

Other areas to be incorporated into the process are:

- **Service levels.** What services, to whom and at what performance requirements?
- **Staff development.** What training or other form of development is needed to provide the 'team' (whether an individual in the case of a one-person library – or as many professional/administrative staff as are involved in providing the information services) with the necessary skills? How can these be cascaded through the team (and wider organization if relevant)?
- **Communications.** Building and consolidating the library's credibility and influence is a constant process in itself. The focus is on team participation and relationships – again, both within the service and the entire business. Obtaining feedback on plans, service levels, statements and suchlike is useful both in developing and refining them further, and in sending very clear messages to senior management about the information unit's capability and value. Finally, well presented and succinct annual reports are an essential.

MAINTAINING MOMENTUM

- **Marketing and promotion** – market research, customer satisfaction surveys, training and publicity. All should be carried out on an ongoing basis, promoting new services and ways of using existing ones. Useful and/or interesting information, should be constantly disseminated, from examples of how competitors are using technology to news about library personnel. Targeted training sessions (for departments, for individuals obviously needing assistance but not asking for it, for specific subject areas) should be held. A proactive stance is essential: it is time-consuming and easy to get wrong, but the impression created and the rise in the use of services should be well worthwhile.

- **Strategic corporate involvement.** If not already regarded as such, the library should be established as an internal consultant on matters involving information management and dissemination, from databases to intranets, knowledge management to websites.
- **Continuous evaluation and improvements.** This should comprise ongoing reviews and revisions, measuring results, identifying problems, starting the planning cycle once more.
- **Scenario planning or 'futuring'.** This should take forward such initial work as opportunities and threats analysis, combining facts and perceptions. 'Multiple futures – alternative images, projections or visions' can stimulate thinking about changes and make views of the future more positive, as well as supporting strategic planning (Corrall, 1998).
- **Cost analysis and financial management.** Budgets and proposals should be made rock-solid and hidden costs and evidence of business benefits should be assessed. This is not the most professionally stimulating task, but such management information will prove the unit's value to the organization and, more importantly, that of the information services provided.

BUSINESS APPROACHES

Having gained the necessary depth of organizational understanding through establishing strategic foundations for the information service, it is possible then to develop and take advantage of a wide range of services and programmes within the parent company. Some of these, or similar, techniques, may already be under way either throughout the organization as a whole, or in individual departments. If any are currently in place on a wider scale, and the special library is not an active participant, then some form of involvement is imperative as soon as feasible. The minimum could be just ensuring that progress updates from those concerned are obtained regularly. Making the library part of the communications loop at least provides an initial foothold, and the opportunity to put forward useful information or suggestions. The information manager's knowledge of the company and its politics will indicate whether most will be achieved initially through a 'softly, softly' approach or a more proactive stance. There will certainly be various contributions that information professionals can make throughout such corporate initiatives – with the potential to be at the forefront.

KNOWLEDGE MANAGEMENT

Businesses are undoubtedly in the midst of a 'knowledge boom', aiming towards 'systematic leveraging of information and expertise to improve organisational innovation, responsiveness, productivity and competency' (Wharton, 1998: 7). Learning organizations, corporate memory, information resources management, intellectual capital – whatever the terminology or phrasing – chief executives recognize that knowledge management will be key to competitive advantage, profits and success.

It is, unfortunately, all too easy to overemphasize specific aspects and ignore the whole picture – the financial worth of the intellectual capital for instance, or the stimulating gadgets and facilities offered by the technologies. Information staff should be in a strong position to step back, uncovering where this is happening, providing guidance on the full range of feasible benefits and advising on other areas which could be developed to balance or contribute to an organization-wide approach. The central skills of librarianship could easily be promoted in the context of knowledge management to ensure that internal documents are well indexed, organized and maintained. This is perhaps even more the case in electronic form, because of the implications of version control, legal admissibility and archiving.

Current emphasis is certainly on the technologies and their capabilities, but these provide only the infrastructure to achieve knowledge management. There are more than enough technological difficulties in laying down those basic foundations – including the implications for training and support where the end-users are concerned – but this is purely the start of the process.

One possible obstacle is that major changes in employment have seen careers move from one end of the spectrum (a working life spent in one organization) to the other (contract and more flexible working). So 'the carriers of corporate memory are eliminated' (Megill, 1997: 6). This factor is combined with further loss of knowledge through the proliferation of documents and innumerable copies of originals. Unnecessary duplication of the same data is often made worse through desktop access to networked services and the Internet. The natural instinct not to share information is a further barrier. Consciously or not, the maxim of 'information is power' rules – particularly in aggressively commercial and financial sectors.

Making knowledge management a reality depends as much on overcoming these human elements as on supplying the technologies and establishing document management strategies. Employees must see and understand the importance of knowledge and information in the corporate strategy. The common rules of motivation apply: 'recognise and reward the value and knowledge of each member of staff and allow them scope to maximise their contribution for the benefit of themselves, their co-workers, the shareholders and the company's customers' (Allday, 1998: 50). Ultimately, knowledge management, although still viewed as a fad, may yet metamorphose into 'knowledge leadership'. This is based on a dynamic mixture of leadership and people management skills with knowledge creation and innovation (Skyrme, 1997: 26).

Information professionals have the option to be involved to the degree that they choose.

INFORMATION TECHNOLOGY AND ENTERPRISE INFORMATION MANAGEMENT

Concepts centred around the phrase 'information management' are appearing ever more frequently in the computing arena. Free-circulation journals such as *Information Age, Document World* and *Information Strategy* review the technologies and standards necessary to collate and access organizations' internal information resources. These publications cover such subjects as information management strategies, enterprise resource planning or enterprise management, but from a software engineering and computer hardware viewpoint. Typically, discussion will concentrate on document workflow or customer databases, focusing on 'business knowledge' but paying little attention to external resources or traditional information services. However, the overenthusiastic adoption of these theories by an organization's computing services can lead to significant conflict with its information unit. In smaller companies especially, there can be the very real threat of a merger of the two functions or even a shortsighted replacement of the library by the computing department. More positively, the international pharmaceuticals company SmithKline Beecham has successfully established its transnational Scientific Information Group under the banner of Computer and Information Sciences (Dieckmann, 1998b). The ideal, whatever the size or nature of the parent organization, is to ensure that information specialists work with the IT staff, building up the softer aspects of information work to make the whole greater than the parts. Cross-functional working is increasingly encouraged in the business environment, and information professionals can potentially contribute much to the technologists' systems – for example:

- indexing, searching
- archiving, records management
- legal implications of electronic documents
- user-friendly interfaces and training.

One current area of growing interest for both parties is that of information security standards. A draft of the British Standards Institution's BS7799 on Information Security Management is now available. Its value for information professionals lies in the fact that it covers all forms of information, viewing the 'information and the systems and networks that support it' as 'important business assets' (British Standards Institution, 1998: 1). The principal factors are confidentiality, integrity and availability, which all underlie the work of any special library. Implementation of such standards could offer a useful opportunity to bring the work of the library and the IT departments together.

On a wider scale, these areas are in turn encompassed by the UK government's work in analysing and encouraging the use of information and communication technologies (ICTs). The Department of Trade and Industry (DTI) views these as 'a major determinant of competitive advantage as we move into the 21st Century' (Spectrum, 1998). Practical support schemes, targeted at small and medium-sized companies in particular, are intended to open up the full range of possible business benefits from effective use of ICTs. Once more, this is an opening for the information manager to alert the organization's management to the schemes and/or to become part of their application.

A pragmatic and constructive approach to information management across organizations is provided by Wilson who defines the subject as 'the efficient and effective exploitation of the data, information and knowledge resources available to the organisation' (Wilson, 1997: 23), whilst stressing that this 'requires a multi-disciplinary team, working within a clearly understood strategic vision and planning framework' (ibid.: 24). This statement takes an information technology and business data (or management information) perspective rather than that of library services, but the contents include a 'Seven Levels of Information Management' framework to assess organizations, the final level being 'The Knowledge Net'. This takes us another step closer to integrating and coordinating all of the relevant specialisms, skills and requirements.

IT TRAINING

Using (or ensuring involvement in) internal computer training sessions further helps to market and promote the information service. There are many variables determining how feasible this is over the long or short term – for example, in terms of computing development/plans, whether external trainers are brought in to run company-wide courses, and how supportive and open relations with computing staff are. Offering an information skills component to form at least an element of any relevant courses, or to integrate library services sessions with the IT department's schedule, can contribute towards establishing constructive partnerships with that IT department.

THE INTERNET AND EDI

Rising usage of the Internet, electronic commerce and electronic data interchange (EDI) offers yet more potential openings. However, the Internet does constitute another key flashpoint for territorial battles, particularly intranets and tailored gateways to Internet resources. The stimulating nature of the technologies involved and the massive potential to develop (apparently) low-cost services can only prove highly attractive to any computing department worth the name. Again, the two sides could achieve far more by jointly developing and supporting Internet technologies, contributing significantly to the organization in business terms.

End-user access to the Internet trebled in just over a year according to one business information resources survey, whereas online and CD-ROM services have failed to achieve anything like this level of desktop penetration. The same survey found that business librarians now expect Internet services to 'change the nature of their work, but not to reduce their role' (Smith, 1998: 5–21)

More widely, the implications and role of the Internet in business and production operations, especially electronic commerce and EDI, could stimulate a further need for the training and support capabilities of information staff (for example, searching principles, history of the Internet). This may be basic, but it is another chance to spread the information unit's skills and reputation through the organization.

DESKTOP DELIVERY

Perhaps closer to the traditional functions of a special library is the proactive delivery of news and information. One aim is to infiltrate publications and updates throughout the wider organization – perhaps targeting tips and pointers for valuable information sources at specific departments, publicizing company-wide information developments or highlighting projects that have benefited from information services. All can be published in electronic or print formats – or both if this will better suit the marketplace. In addition, dedicated information services newsletters offer advantages which include setting the service's identity and capabilities, publicizing network services and encouraging feedback.

Tailored delivery of information and promotion of the use of desktop services extends traditional mechanisms of current awareness bulletins and selective dissemination of information. The requirements are regular, timely, high-quality updates, with an emphasis on user-friendly and professional presentation, and ideally flexible enough to be incorporated into internal databases and other IT applications.

CORPORATE INITIATIVES

Organizations tend to have many initiatives under way or planned, all emphasizing communications and dissemination of information. Investors in People (IIP), total quality management (TQM), BS5750 (the UK quality systems standard) and BPR (business process re-engineering) are excellent examples. The information manager needs to ensure that their service provides the initiative with whatever support is feasible. This may take the form of online searches to ascertain benchmarks and locate case studies of similar oganizations, and possibly news briefings on the standards involved, taken from a combination of websites, print and other electronic resources. Building that support into the scheme is valuable in itself for publicity and political reasons, but special libraries can benefit directly from the methodology being adopted, even to the extent of winning funds and support for new services or technology to support the aims of the project.

THE PHYSICAL ENVIRONMENT

Fundamental change in the size, layout and nature of the work environment is another inevitable factor which affects special libraries. British Telecom is amongst organizations that have noted a constant rise in the proportion of communal space required to encourage informal communications and compensate for the loss of dedicated, personal workstations. Increased working away from the organization and working on the move can mean a greater risk of isolation, unless offices and processes are specifically designed to encourage staff and work groups to gather, or to meet by chance, to improve interaction.

For library and information units more specifically, physical arrangements partly determine the end activity – for example, OPACs are, by nature, aimed at a single user; group use is uncomfortable in traditional line-ups and layouts. Information units can take advantage of these factors, particularly if offices or buildings are being redesigned (or should be). Hewlett Packard and Unipart offer examples of how large corporations can radically alter their information services and working environments. Both these companies have UK sites which offer attractive, supportive, open-plan layouts:

- Hewlett Packard (Bristol) has integrated its library area with a 'coffee house', encouraging individuals and groups (plus coffee) into the information services area and vice versa.
- Unipart (Midlands) has located its information area on the ground floor by the entrance and the Internet/IT development section.

Such set-ups clearly reflect the list of factors provided in Chapter 9, p. 150, to ascertain whether an institution is network-oriented.

PROFESSIONAL DEVELOPMENT

Sensitivity to the many issues and reactions involved in change underlies all of the above. The personal development implications for information workers over and above their core professional competences lie in the areas of:

- technological capabilities – in particular, keeping up-to-date, and possibly considering formal IT qualifications and training such as MCP (Microsoft Certified Professional)
- business and management understanding and skills
- marketing, communications and interpersonal abilities
- awareness of competition from other occupations (and creating appropriate coping strategies – for example, partnerships, coordination, integration)

The latter has fundamental implications in terms of career development, since it was predicted in 1989 that:

> ... library and information workers will not be the only professional specialists to identify and pursue the possibilities and opportunities which will open up in what has hitherto been largely their own professional field. (Saunders, 1989: 14)

From the information sector perspective job titles such as 'Information Officer' have long been somewhat misleadingly used in such areas as marketing, the media and pharmaceuticals. Within organizations there seems to be an increasing number of battles for ownership of information-related initiatives – relating to internal data as well as commercial external services. Computing, marketing (customer/membership data) and accounts departments are the most obvious sources of this potential conflict – all wanting to make full use of internal information and wanting to offer it in a reliable, speedy, flexible and user-friendly fashion, at the staff member's point of work (desktop, laptop, meetings).

Other departments may start developing an interest in, or isolated access to, tailored external information sources. Desktop delivery, particularly in the lucrative business information market (law, news, economics), has been steadily developing throughout the 1990s, frequently promoted directly by the supplier to the end-user.

Inevitably a combination of separate, non-integrated sources and projects can result in basic problems of overlap, underuse, confusion, lack of access and a waste of organizational financial resources. The information professional's life can easily become bogged down with political negotiations and conflict. Alternatively, the door is open (or can be forced!) for that information professional to bring the services together and support their use, ensuring that the company obtains full business benefit.

Competition from technology, network and solutions providers is equally now very evident, and can only continue to head towards formidable levels. The sales executives for these vendors possess the same range of commercial skills that information professionals now require:

> ... concept-sellers, highly technology-literate with an ability to grasp the specific needs of individual clients and to communicate with widely diverse audiences within any one client organisation. ...

> ... a hybrid with breadth and depth of skills is a valuable commodity. (Thew, 1998: 36)

SUMMARY

In the special library environment there is usually a constant pressure, overt or otherwise, to prove the value of its staff, services and existence. Pitfalls include jumping on bandwagons, such as knowledge management, yet failing to justify the costs or measure the business benefits. Equally, there is the danger of failing to become involved in initiatives where information skills are paramount – possibly due to internal politics or to focusing so entirely on providing a good-quality service that the opportunity passes by unnoticed.

Even if a commercial approach is not demanded, whether the information unit is based in a charity or a global pharmaceuticals corporation, justifying current expenditure and future investment is considerably more straightforward and very much less stressful if the business already appreciates the unit's contributions and strengths. Political, communication and strategic skills are at least as important as core information and technology competences. Supplying high-quality, relevant and timely information through a user-friendly, reliable network to well trained and supported users may be professionally fulfilling, but is in itself pointless. The organization must see consistent, clear evidence of the impact on existing business functions as a minimum, but preferably also on its profits and on future business developments. The final complicating factor is that, whilst 66 per cent of companies apparently see information management as a 'boardroom item' and a business-critical issue, IT departments believe that they have the most clearly defined role and greatest responsibility for information – as do finance and marketing departments (Anonymous, 1998). Although all have parts to play, perhaps the library and information sector is being offered the opportunity to:

● take control of organizational information strategies

- coordinate and drive the technologies
- promote business use and benefits.

Overall, 'we need to embrace innovation, eschew modesty and display ... "constructive arrogance". Our approach to meeting the needs of the early twenty-first century requires us to be positive, participative and professional' (Heery and Morgan, 1996: 147).

REFERENCES

Allday, D. (1998), *Spinning Straw into Gold. Managing Intellectual Capital Effectively*, London: Institute of Management.

Anonymous (1998), 'Information management moves into the boardroom', *Inform*, (204), May, 2.

Atkinson, P. (1998), *The Iceberg Agenda. Mastering Corporate Potential*, London: B.T. Batsford.

British Standards Institution (1998), 98/682025. *Revision of BS 7799: Part 1. Code of Practice for Information Security Management*, London: British Standards Institution.

Cawkell, T. (1998), 'The Information Age – for better or for worse', *Journal of Information Science*, **24**(1), 56–58.

Conner, D. (1998), 'Jack be nimble – the four pointers to change management success', in *National Conference, Institute of Personnel and Development*, October 1998.

Corrall, S. (1994), *Strategic Planning for Library and Information Services*, London: Aslib.

Corrall, S. (1998), 'Scenario planning. A strategic management tool for the future', *Managing Information*, **5**(9), November, 34–35, 37.

Coulson-Thomas, C. (1997), *The Future of the Organization. Achieving Excellence through Business Transformation*. London: Kogan Page.

Council on Library and Information Resources (1998), 'CLIR and AAU to publish book on the transformation of academic information resources', *CLIR Issues*, (3), May–June, 3, 7–8.

Cropley, J. (1998), 'Knowledge management: a dilemma', *Business Information Review*, **15**(1), March, 27–34.

Dieckmann, H. (1998a), 'BP International', *Managing Information*, **5**(5), June, 20–21.

Dieckmann, H. (1998b), 'SmithKline Beecham', *Managing Information*, **5**(7), September, 20–22.

Dyson, C. (1998), 'A strategic plan for information at Zurich Reinsurance', *Managing Information*, **5**(9), November, 30–32.

Heery, M. and Morgan, S. (1996), *Practical Strategies for the Modern Academic Library*, London: Aslib.

Jackson, A.E. (1992), 'A retail opportunity in the contemporary information market', *Aslib Proceedings*, **44**(10), October, 341–49.

Lawes, A. (1994), in G. St Clair, *Power and Influence. Enhancing Information Services Within the Organization*, London: Bowker Saur.

Manchester, P. (1998), 'Practical benefits – and problems', *Financial Times Supplement. Managing Information: 50 years of I.T.*, 3 June, 19.

Megill, K.A. (1997), *The Corporate Memory: Information Management in the Electronic Age*. London, Bowker Saur.

Nunn, H. (1994), 'Introduction', in HERTIS, *The Value of Information to the Intelligent Organisation*. Hatfield: University of Hertfordshire Press.

Owens, I., Wilson, T. and Abell, A. (1996), *Information and Business Performance. A Study of Information Systems and Services in High Performing Companies*, London, Bowker Saur.

St Clair, G. (1994), *Power and Influence. Enhancing Information Services Within the Organization*, London, Bowker Saur.

Saunders, W. (1989), *Towards a Unified Professional Organization for Library and Information Science and Services*, London, Library Association.

Skyrme, D.J. (1997), 'Knowledge management: oxymoron or dynamic duo', *Managing Information*, **4**(7), 24–26.

Smith, G. (1998), 'Annual business information resources survey, 1998', *Business Information Review*, **15**(1), March, 5–21.

Special Libraries Association (1996), *Competencies for Special Librarians of the 21st Century*, http://www.sla.org/

Spectrum Strategy Consultants (1998), *Moving into the Information Age – An International Benchmarking Study 1998*, London: Department of Trade and Industry, http://www.isi.gov.uk/isi/bench/

Swain, S. (1993), 'Networked information services in support of pharmaceutical research', in *Computers in Libraries International 93*, Proceedings of the Seventh Annual Computers in Libraries International Conference, London, February 1993, London, Meckler.

Thew, D. (1998), 'Taking your career in hand: the need for creativity and vision', *Business Information Review*, **15**(1), March, 35–39.

TFPL (1998), 'The eighth european business information conference – EBIC'98 – report, http://www.tfpl.com/

Watson, I. (1998), 'The information society', *Managing Information*, **5**(5), June, 56.

Wharton, A. (1998), 'Common knowledge', *Document World*, October–November, 7.

Wilson, M. (1997), *The Information Edge. Successful Management Using Information Technology*, London, Pitman Publishing.

Withey, R. (1994), 'Inside the virtual corporation' in HERTIS, *The Value of Information to the Intelligent Organisation*, Hatfield: University of Hertfordshire Press, 43–51.

FURTHER READING

Biddiscombe, R. (1996), *The End-user Revolution. CD-ROM, Internet and the Changing Role of the Information Professional*. London: Library Association Publishing.

Boddy, D. and Gunson, N. (1996), *Organizations in the Network Age*, London: Routledge.

Clegg, A. (1998), 'The technophile office', *Management Today*, April, 94–101.

Confederation of British Industry (1998), *Knowledge Management. A Real Business Guide*, London: Caspian Publishing.

Coote, H. and Batchelor, B. (1997), *How to Market your Library Service Effectively*, (2nd edn), London: Aslib.

Davenport, T.H. and Prusak, L. (1998), *Working Knowledge: How Organizations Manage What They Know*. Boston, MA: Harvard Business School Press.

Guns, B. (1996), *The Faster Learning Organization*, San Francisco, CA: Jossey-Bass.

Macdonald, J. (1997), *Calling a Halt to Mindless Change*, New York, AMACOM.

Ramsden, A. (1998), *ELINOR: Electronic Library Project*, London, Bowker Saur.

Roberts, S.A. (1998), *Financial and Cost Management for Libraries and Information Services*, (2nd edn), London, Bowker Saur.

Woodfill Park, M. (1998), *InfoThink. Practical Strategies for Using Information in Business*, Lanham, MD: Scarecrow Press.

11 The TAPin model

Kay Flatten

INTRODUCTION

The importance and use of models in information science has increased with the explosion in the availability and use of electronic information. TAPin was an eLib project which developed, implemented and evaluated a model for use by librarians when supporting academics in a networked environment. It was based upon models developed by Barry (1995, 1997) and Finlay and Finlay (1996) which provided an understanding of the relationships between 'learning/knowledge', 'motivation/attitude' and 'time/use' in the take-up and use of networked information systems by academics and librarians. The TAPin project is outlined in the Introduction to this book and further discussed in Chapters 12 and 13.

The TAPin model consists of a development component with the one-off phases of assessment and training and the continued phases of support, promotion, finance and management, plus a delivery component with the basics of who, what, where, how and when of networked information support provision. Each of these components and phases is explained in this chapter.

Hints for adapting the TAPin model to other organizations are also provided, along with comments from people who developed or received the support. The chapter gives a sound basis for understanding the need for using planned interventions, such as models, when managing change, and then offers a tried and tested model for others to adopt and adapt to meet their own needs.

DEFINING A MODEL FOR CULTURE CHANGE

A social engineering model represents relationships among groups of people and their actions, adding a logical structure to what otherwise evades observation, recording and purposive intervention. Modelling helps define important group roles and actions which produce an outcome. Providing support to academics in their uses of networked information was the outcome of the TAPin model developed for the Electronic Libraries Programme.

This social model represented a plan to follow during uncertain times. Networked information provision changed rapidly on campuses during the late 1990s. The TAPin model met the needs of both the libraries and learning resource centres as well as the personal needs of academics and information workers.

Designing and executing a social model gives an organization time for requisite learning and change. New processes and procedures inevitably evolve during times of change. A model affords systematic growth, which might be disruptive and divisive if left to chance developments. The universities which used the TAPin model shared in a common effort to provide computing and information services across recently installed networks to keep ahead of user demand. The TAPin model focused the actions of academics and librarians while their managers were coming to terms with the blurring of lines between existing areas of work and responsibility. Academic and library staff were learning essential skills for future teaching and learning environments. Designing and executing the TAPin model provided these universities with time for learning and managerial change in the context of a new networked environment.

The personal needs of workers is another reason to follow a model. Workers take comfort in habitual patterns and behaviours, because they have developed confidence and expertise through these experiences. During times of change the usual habits and behaviours come under threat because they may appear devalued in light of newer ways to work. Below are some examples of the thoughts or words which might be directed at someone adopting new ways of working without the support of a model or other planned intervention. An appropriate relevant changed behaviour should be mentally inserted in the square brackets.

'What does he think he is doing?'
'[Relevant changed behaviour] is not what she was hired to do.'
'Who is going to be left with the regular work while he is doing [relevant changed behaviour]?
'She is just trying to get in with management by [relevant changed behaviour].'

This externally directed thinking is damaging to morale in the workplace as are perceived threats to a worker's confidence. Those workers who are internally, rather than externally, driven may harbour thoughts such as:

'I'm not sure where [relevant changed behaviour] is leading, so I'll ignore it.'

'If I try to work in this [relevant changed behaviour] way I will expose my weaknesses.'

'I can't put trust in [relevant changed behaviour], which I don't understand. Others depend on my in-depth knowledge.'

'This [relevant changed behaviour] is going to take over and I am going to be out of it and lose respect.'

'This [relevant changed behaviour] is rubbish and I will ignore it, or run it down.'

Both internally and externally motivated workers benefit by having a model to follow during change. The assessment element of the TAPin model uncovered great apprehension amongst the librarians who were struggling to understand the implications of information sources on the Internet. Academics also distrusted information on the Web and spoke disparagingly about e-mail, discussion lists, and using the Web in their teaching. However, an assessment of the TAPin model's impact found these opinions had changed after 30 months of working through the model.

The TAPin model encompassed elements from other social engineering models. These models represented the interactions of humans with training and information technology. They were taken from the information science field with specific application to academic settings.

MODELLING THE UNIQUE ASPECTS OF THE DIGITAL INFORMATION EXPLOSION

The Venn diagram for modelling increased relevance in information retrieval. Figure 11.1 shows the most basic representation of Boolean logic.

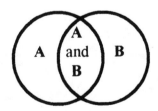

Figure 11.1   The Venn diagram of the Boolean operator AND

Information modelling has expanded to cover complex interrelations used in information retrieval. These operators and logical sequences now power search engines which crawl and trawl the Internet daily. *Library and Information Science Abstracts* indexes the term *models*, and the number of articles retrieved using this term grew from 24 in 1990 to 46 in 1997. The convergence of computing and information science has encouraged the development of information models. More recently, sociologists have developed models of the culture change process. Several of these form the bases of the TAPin model.

Christine Barry (1995, 1997) used modelling techniques to illustrate the impact of IT on information activity in academic research. Her model found the increase in information and the complexity of the technology affected information skills training. Electronic skills training needed elements not present in traditional library skills education and depended on perceptions of the amount of time required and the motivation to learn. Figure 11.2 illustrates Barry's information skills model. This model illustrates the following categories of information skills resulting from factors increasing the amount of information and the complexity of the delivery systems:

A. judging information by evaluation of quality, filtering of excess, and focusing on specifics

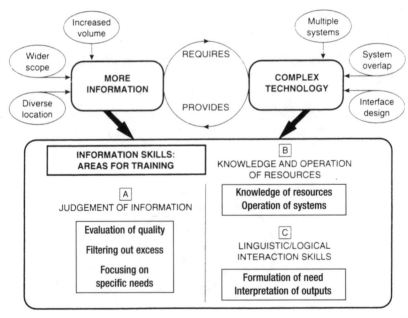

Source: Barry (1997: 27).

Figure 11.2   Information skills for dealing with increasing information and complex technology

B. knowing how resources and systems operate
C. using interactive skills to formulate an information need and to interpret outputs.

Barry challenged the traditional library training model:

> ... a stand up lecture, whilst perfectly adequate for library instruction, has limited efficacy in teaching operation of IT resources. Users learn better by doing and that requires sufficient resources, for example individual terminal access in training sessions, and open access to computers with Internet connections for ongoing use. (Barry, 1997: 236)

She also highlighted the human factors affecting the uptake of digital information by academics in her second model, illustrated in Figure 11.3. This model shows the complex interrelationship between perception, motivation and learning, as well as the dependency of all three on the time available to learn and use IT (Barry, 1995).

This model shows the following links:

● Motivation is needed before a commitment is made to learn more about the systems (including finding time). This usually takes the form of a specific motivating event, such as the need to do a particular task (letter 'a' in Figure 11.3).
● Motivation is needed to give up valuable time to learn how to use the systems (letter 'b').
● Motivation to use depends on a specific motivating event and also relies on perception of the advantages of the system to the individual. They need to know what it can do before they see an application for it (letter 'c').
● This creates a paradox in that to perceive the advantages of the systems

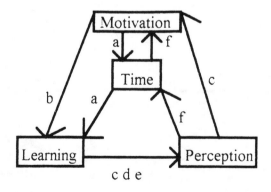

Source: **Barry (1995: 129).**

Figure 11.3   Factors affecting the take-up and use of IT-assisted information systems

requires putting some effort into learning about them, but motivation to learn in the absence of perception of system advantages tends to be low (letter 'd').

- The more academics learn about a system, the more likely they are to realize the inherent possibilities, and the more prepared they are to invest time and effort in learning how to operate the system (letter 'e').

- The allocation of time to learn depends on perceptions of the amount of time required and motivation to prioritize this above other activities (letter 'f') (Ibid.: 128–29).

All these findings were important to the delivery of the TAPin model of support to academics.

Another model helped in understanding how the librarians themselves would develop and deliver their Internet support to academics. Karen and Thomas Finlay (1996) studied the relationship between the tendency for librarians to be innovative and their knowledge, use and attitudes to the Internet. Their model, represented in Figure 11.4, was developed and tested in Canada. The strongest positive relationship was 'knowledge' causing 'Internet use' (γ-coefficient =.74, t = 18.4). Knowledge also influenced attitudes towards the Internet (γ-coefficient =.43, t = 14.3). Innovativeness similarly had an effect on attitude towards the Internet (γ-coefficient =.15, t = 5.3), but not on usage (ibid.: 77).

Having a high level of knowledge about the Internet was clearly the driving force in attitudes towards, and use of, the Internet. Knowledge also appeared to be a necessary prerequisite for varied and frequent use. Positive attitudes to the Internet led to its greater use when knowledge levels were also high. Feeling good overall about the Internet, therefore, appeared to enhance the propensity to acquire knowledge, which in turn positively influenced its use (ibid.: 80).

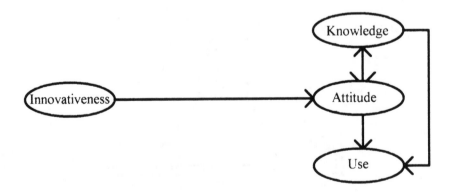

Adapted from Finlay and Finlay (1996: 79).

Figure 11.4   A simplified version of the model for librarian use of the Internet

Two other findings from this study were also useful when developing the TAPin model.

1. The knowledge, which motivated use, was not acquired through training. Librarians used books, academic articles, magazine articles, and word-of-mouth through conversations with peers at work and at conferences.
2. Librarians with high innovativeness tended to hold more positive attitudes towards the Internet and, when combined with knowledge, were frequent Internet users (ibid.: 80).

The fact that attendance at training programmes was not found to be a significant factor in increased use of the Internet may be a reflection of the effectiveness of such training during 1995–96. It may also indicate that such training was not available for librarians in a format that they could fit into their work schedules. The TAPin model tested these further by structuring training specifically to librarian needs. In addition, TAPin librarians were seconded from their normal work for training away from their workplace, thereby facilitating and formalizing their attendance.

THE TAPin MODEL

TAPin carried the concepts from the previous models further by focusing on the delivery of information skills and the support of network use. It incorporated the following points from the previous models:

- Academics benefit from help dealing with the increased quantity of information, specifically with:
  - evaluation of quality
  - filtering out excess
  - focusing on relevance.
- Variability in IT at the point of delivery calls for in-office support on end-user machines.
- Librarians need training on networked resources and operation of systems.
- Academics and librarians need to work together to formulate need and interpret output.
- Perceptions held by academics about lack of time inhibit their motivation to take up support; therefore support needs to be delivered in their own offices by prearranged appointments.
- Knowledge empowers librarians for the delivery side of the model; therefore, their training is first priority.
- The selection of academic staff to receive support needs to take into account

the academic's attitude and innovativeness. Delivery of the model to those who are unmotivated towards the use of computers and electronic information leads to failure.

Education, law and life science subject librarians and their managers designed and implemented the TAPin model to support academics with computer networked information. Academic library and resource centre managers shaped the development side of the model working with eLib funds and the staff in the Centre for Information Research and Training at the University of Central England. The delivery side of the model was agreed by the librarians after reviewing the barriers to culture change highlighted during assessment.

The following academic year the librarians supported their academic colleagues in accordance with the model. The *Impact Study* (Flatten *et al.*, 1998) reported on the model's effectiveness in changing academic staff perceptions of computer networked information, and their understanding of the changing roles of information services in higher education. Chapter 12 in this book reports on the impact of the model on the libraries and librarians.

Figure 11.5 illustrates the two halves of the model and the components of each. The development activities occur first, with those elements pictured within the box as ongoing activities, while those outside the box are one-off, sequential events.

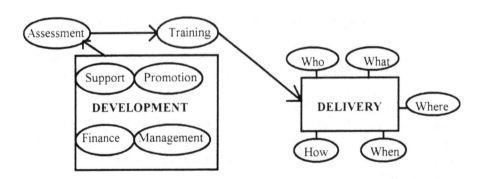

Figure 11.5   The TAPin model for network information support by librarians

ASSESSMENT

This is frequently referred to as user information needs analysis. This developmental task involved assessing the librarians' training needs and the academic staff information needs, as well as seeking the opinions of both groups about IT and networked information. An audit of the physical provision of computer network access for librarians and academic staff was important – specifically to find out what network access and facilities were on office desktops and in homes and what network tools were available to use. The needs analysis revealed that IT training fails academics when it is offered in fixed classes of several hours' duration in locations away from the office, and on hardware and software different from the academics' own. The support was often a waste of time because it was either too basic or failed to provide the skills staff needed. Academic staff expressed a wish for training and support of high relevance and on their own configured computers at the moment of need. Basically they wanted a 'colleague down the corridor' to answer their questions when they encountered difficulties. Librarians said that they wanted training in the use of networks – specifically, search engines, HTML, quality assessment, FTP, e-mail, Adobe Acrobat, image capture, bookmark management and metadata tagging – before they would attempt to support their academic colleagues.

Computer technicians within subject departments and librarians were also contacted. They answered questions on network geography and access for their departments and libraries and also provided percentage data for academic staff on librarian hardware and network access and the applications and software they used. The subject departments were single sites; however, the libraries and resource centres were multi-sited. Connection to campus networks with global access varied among subject departments and between universities although sites were in the process of being connected. A common standard enabling academics and librarians to use networks and communicate effectively, regardless of hardware platform and network topology, was desired but in 1996 this was not feasible, nor was dial-in access from outside. However, certain minimum requirements were found to be essential for librarian support of academics. The following specification was deemed necessary for both academics and librarians to execute the model:

- a Windows-based operating system
- netscape or comparable browser
- e-mail account
- 486 or higher specified PC.

Packages for FTP, Usenet newsgroups, graphics viewer, telnet, compression utilities and video viewers were also felt to be desirable.

181

TRAINING

A librarians' training programme was set up with over 40 hours of group work in a networked computing lab with Netskills (1998) or other consultant trainers. The training of the information workers was one of the first activities in executing the model. This built confidence and morale during a time of apprehension about the future and change. Early training helped those who would be executing the delivery side of the model to take ownership of it. Training took place over half or full days at one of the six universities. There was a training session each month for four months and a follow-up on Adobe Acrobat and Metadata tags during the delivery stage. The components of the TAPin training programme were as follows:

- Internet use skills including:
  - file transfer skills
  - configuring Netscape
  - capturing and manipulating images
  - caching, proxy servers, bookmarks
  - creating Web demonstrations with PowerPoint.
  Similar online training is available through TONIC (1997).
- Methods of end-user support:
  - means of developing effective learning
  - developing awareness of the impact of networks on approaches to teaching and learning
  - planning support and training sessions
  - reviewing the skills required in support and presenting
  - planning a small group presentation.
  Similar training is available through EduLib (1998).
- Document delivery and indexing:
  - Adobe Acrobat
  - Metadata tags.

SUPPORT

Once trained, librarians did not necessarily immediately begin to work with unfamiliar resources and access tools: they still had to perform most of their usual tasks in traditional ways. It would have been very easy to slip back into 'only' managing printed holdings and in-house support. Most of the librarians did slowly take on the new forms of support. To keep the issue of culture change and the execution of the model on their desktops, various support activities were organized. These included circulating a monthly printed bulletin describing TAPin activity at all six participating universities during the execution of the model. This had the dual advantages of recognizing the achievements of some TAPin librarians, while providing ideas and inspiration to others. The model was always put on the agenda at management meetings where, once again, work in progress was reported and problems or concerns aired. A closed discussion list, TAPin-all, was used to communicate with members of the group executing the model. Although this list was not heavily used, it made sure that everyone received the same information, and librarians read the messages even if they did not send to the list. Librarians received the hardware and software described as essential in the assessment. Gradually, over the execution of the development and delivery sides of the model, their own network access improved as it did for the academic staff they supported. Further training and 'exchange of experience' days were held to maintain the sense of camaraderie and commitment. Librarians were given extra IT assistance when requested and were able to buy books for their personal reference libraries. When they had developed Web pages in their subject areas, these were written as links into other university pages.

PROMOTION

Awareness-raising is the first step in change. The model used this fact in several ways:

- Campus newsletters carried short articles about the early stages of the model, giving the process visibility and recognition locally.
- Talks were given at professional meetings which covered the barriers identified in the assessment. This gave the process visibility and recognition, both within the UK and internationally. Monthly activity reports informed others what was happening.
- Articles were published in the professional literature.
- Web pages were written and linked to libraries' and resource centres' websites.
- Librarians and their managers worked to publicize their support.

FINANCE

Activity follows money, and culture change behaviours needed financial support from the outset. Each library subject site was provided with a laptop computer with projection tablet running Windows 3.1 and, Netscape 2.0, WinZip 6.3, Microsoft Office including PowerPoint 4.0, HTML Assist, and LView Pro. Other resource expenses were requested by each university according to need. Three universities wanted BIDS before model delivery. The training programme required £6000. Expenses for training and social gatherings included: consultant fees, travel for librarians and consultants, room rentals, postage and hospitality. Dissemination activity was also expensive; the activity reports were sent to 125 people. However, by far the largest expense was paying for the librarians to have one day per week free to work on model activity. Some library and learning resource centre managers split this between two librarians freeing up a half day for each. Others offered the experience broadly and allowed any librarian who wished to attend training or develop support activities to do so during their work time. It is impossible to offer a figure for financing the model because each organization will have differing needs; however, the broad areas to finance are staff time, IT, training and dissemination.

MANAGEMENT

Whereas the delivery side of the model depends heavily on the librarians and the academics, the development side is the responsibility of library and learning resource centre managers. Management styles vary and various approaches will be successful. The TAPin model used a four-tier management structure.

The first tier was the funding source – in this case, the Joint Information Services Committee and the Higher Education Funding Councils through the eLib programme. In a local execution of the model this would be the university directorate.

The second tier was the Steering Group comprising senior managers in the six university LIS. This was the group that shaped the development plan and monitored its progress. They allowed the librarians time and equipment to design and implement the delivery side of the model. They opened doors of opportunity and solved problems. Their time and commitment extended to their own adoption of networked information skills and behaviours.

The TAPin project staff constituted the third tier. These comprised 2.5 FTE (full-time equivalent) staff during the development stage and 1.5 FTE during the delivery stage – necessary when working with a six-university consortium and a national IT initiative. It should be borne in mind that TAPin had to develop the model and report the lessons learned back to the HE community and this would not be a requirement for a local execution of the model. Nevertheless, it is advised that execution of the model be delegated to one or more staff with clerical support.

The fourth and most critical tier was the librarians who underwent the training, designed the delivery side of the model and executed it for one academic year. The success of the model depends on how well managers support this level with release time, IT access/hardware/software, training, and the possibility of promotional gain through performance evaluations.

The delivery side of the model followed the completion of the assessment and training. The components which make up the support are described below.

Who

The librarians targeted academic staff who expressed an interest in training or who perceived themselves as already skilled in using networks. They, in turn, agreed to target responsive persons known to be keen, whether skilled or not. This decision was prompted by the belief that those resistant to IT would not be as receptive to change, and if librarians could develop a core of 'champions' within subject departments they might have a greater influence on the culture change and the promotion of a positive image for the library in the networked campus. It was also decided to target staff who had Internet access and an Intel 486 or Pentium processor desktop computer. These three elements – network access, processor speed and, most importantly, staff member attitude – provided the ingredients necessary to deliver effective support.

What

The librarians taught the techniques of searching networks for information and the ability to discriminate between the various search engines and how best to search using each. Search engines vary in effectiveness for specific subject areas. Next, the librarians provided a selection of URLs and CD-ROMs which were known to be close to the individual staff's information need. These Web pages and database sources were evaluated to assure quality and, as academics often brought URLs to the attention of the librarians, both worked to evaluate such sites – adding value to resources. The librarians also included evaluated URLs in their own subject gateway Web pages which were often linked to their universities' information service websites. They also raised current awareness in departmental 'hot topics' – for example, carrying out initiatives to inform staff working on research teams what was on networks.

Where

Within departments support was given through staff computers, so the access pathways were the same for the end-user academics whether they were learning about, or using, the networks. This caused problems for librarians because machines varied and were often configured differently, and there was little the librarians and learning centre managers could do to resolve these differences. Unfortunately, librarians were acting as agents in the change process in technical settings that were neither standard nor ideal and they had to create their own coping strategies.

How

Because the nature of hypertext and client server networks risk staff losing their way or spending too much time on networks, the librarians were committed to help staff by guiding them quickly to relevant information. To save time librarians prepared in advance of the support visit by:

- confirming the information needs specific to the staff member
- establishing the availability of Intel 486 or Pentium processors and Netscape 2.0 browsers on the academics' desktops
- preparing back-up support either in the form of paper guides or stored files on computer notebooks.

During the support session librarians and academic staff concentrated on the information needs using various resources, most of which were accessed via Netscape and the Web. In some cases librarians introduced the staff members to Netscape, the Web, search engines and basic search strategies. In other cases the time was spent on subject specific resources and gateways. After these sessions, librarians e-mailed the academics to assess the success of, and degree of satisfaction with, the training and resources. A few other URLs which were felt to be relevant were also sent in these follow-up communications. These e-mail messages also served as the beginnings of e-mail enquiry services, allowing staff to contact the librarians at the moment of need.

This TAPin model, although structured and planned, was individually tailored and all teaching and support was informal. The familiarity of staff members' own machines and offices, and the conversational opportunities which one-to-one settings provided, made the training non-threatening, supportive and reciprocal.

When

TAPin librarians spent two months compiling lists of staff to target and familiarizing themselves with staff information needs. Next they collected URLs and talked to selected colleagues about the value and worth of various resources. In so doing, they identified a community of those who provide products, services, or are professional associations important in their subject areas. They then prepared generic documentation such as paper guides, Web pages and checklists based upon the most commonly used networked resources. When they felt confident, they telephoned staff and arranged the visits while confirming staff IT desktop access. The one-to-one visits took the remaining six months of the academic year.

ADAPTING THE TAPin MODEL

As stated before, social engineering models represent relationships among groups of people and their actions. The groups and actions used in developing the TAPin model were unique to each partner university, although elements of the TAPin model can apply to other universities, and even other organizations, once adapted.

The diagnostic tools used to gather data in the development side of the model will need editing to fit local needs (TAPin, 1997). This can be achieved in various ways:

- Librarian training might become part of in-house courses offered through existing staff development offices on campuses.
- The support given during the execution of the model will need to fit within existing structures. For example, models can become regular features in currently published newsletters and the TAPin-all electronic discussion list might be adapted to become distributed e-mail lists for academics and librarians in subject areas.
- Marketing departments welcome new ideas and innovative developments, and may be willing to promote the model if the processes for producing the text and photographs are agreed. To do this, they will require agreed timescales and target audience contact details for dissemination.

Adapting the financial support for the model may be the foremost hurdle to overcome. In this age of devolved budgets it may be possible to charge subject departments for the networked information support provided to their staff. Absorbing needs into existing departments, as discussed above for training and promotion, controls costs and avoids duplication of effort across campuses. The greatest financial costs will be the purchasing of time for librarians to attend training and deliver support. It might be possible to decrease the number of print journals in favour of electronic journals in the subject areas where support is provided, and to use these savings for extra staff.

The management element of the development side of the model will require extensive adaptation. TAPin was an eLib project and, as such, fitted the management structure of the eLib Programme. Most academic libraries and learning resource centres will want to assign the day-to-day management of the model to one member of staff with senior management overseeing long-term progress. Management meetings within libraries and between libraries and subject departments need to include the model as regular agenda items.

Adapting the delivery side of the TAPin model is best done by consensus of those who will be delivering the support. The 'who, what, where, how, when' elements will naturally evolve once assessment data are reviewed and the development side of the model is in place. Distributing results of assessments prior to meetings of subject librarians is advised. At these meetings it is possible to provide the delivery elements as they were executed by the TAPin librarians, then to allow open discussions as to how these could be adapted locally. Results from these meetings will form frameworks providing librarians with clear guidelines for delivering networked information support.

COMMENTS ABOUT THE TAPin MODEL

Comments from those who developed, delivered and received the TAPin model of networked information support highlighted the value added by its use. The academics who received one-to-one support in their offices were generally positive about the model. For instance, commenting on the type of support received, one said, 'The librarian with whom I deal keeps me informed about developments in the electronic journal field. Consequently I feel he can help me, previously I felt I had to do much of this for myself.' Another remark by another academic indicated that they were beginning to regard electronic data as their first information source: 'I'm beginning to use the library's list of journals to establish whether there is an electronic form of the article I am interested in.'

Their comments about support from the library validated the appropriateness and effectiveness of the model.

> I think there is more support available and it is easier to access than we sometimes think. The interview with [a TAPin librarian] and her understanding of my needs were surprisingly positive.

> I think academics are becoming increasingly aware of the need to seek support (as I have done) but there is still a large amount of resistance. Seeking advice through the TAPin model helped me optimise my literature searching etc. and I would recommend such a model.

Other comments included factors such as 'greater awareness of [the] variety of library support services' and 'I am now more aware of facilities which I was not aware of before, both in the library and those I can access from my office'. This awareness of support acknowledged the training aspects of the model, which cascaded from librarians to academics.

Many of the comments mentioned this increased awareness and confidence in using networked information. One academic said that the TAPin model gave 'valuable training that I hope will continue, and useful interactions with the science librarian. I feel that I need to continue my training as there are still enormous gaps in my awareness.' The academic viewpoint can be summarized by the following comment from a respondent from an education department:

> ... a major change within the university itself is the move from libraries to learning resource centres, [it is] so difficult to be sure what is attributable to the TAPin model and what to other changes. [Such as] greater access, [and] much enhanced IT facilities for students. But, quality of service and face to face dealings remain high and critical.

The model had its greatest impact at strategic levels and in libraries. Much of this feedback can be found in Chapter 12, but a few comments from library heads and deputy heads are given below.

> The TAPin model had an indirect impact on perceptions of the library. It operated at an organic level which percolated through to the development of overall LIS strategy. (Comment by a strategic manager)

> ... the TAPin model had an influence on the creation of subject pages and the raising of status for librarians. (Comment by a strategic manager)

> [The TAPin model showed that] we have a role in networked information. ... [showed] we have a lead over schools. ... [showed] we can work with academics to develop their skills ... [showed] we have a competence in the area of information that complements theirs. (Comment by a manager)

The systems librarians and subject department IT technicians were involved in installing new software for use with the TAPin model. One such librarian commented, 'I would envisage the TAPin model has helped to change staff perceptions in departments.' One subject department IT technician said, 'From a personal viewpoint the TAPin model had little effect. On a more institutional level it is difficult to separate the influence of TAPin from the growing general web awareness in society.' The role of the librarian was variously perceived as coordinator, trainer and consultant in electronic sources of information. As one respondent said 'librarians are now recognised as sources of expertise in networked information resources'. However, not all opinions were positive about the libraries' change of role in teaching and learning using networked information. Academics were honest about their practices, as reflected by this comment:

> When information is required in a hurry academics will turn to the method with which they are most familiar. Many will not use IT when in a hurry but will turn to books. Time is the main constraint. I would be more inclined to turn to IT now I have received instruction. Again time is important in training – people will not seek out support if they are busy.

Another academic pointed out negative changes with this comment: 'I am saddened by the university's exploitation of the library through independent learning. Students have been getting less and less teaching and the library has become home/refuge/youth club and prime source of advice.'

Nevertheless, with or without the TAPin model, academics generally acknowledged that networked information will continue to be an expanding field in the future. This was summarized by one respondent who stated, 'The availability of Internet facilities to myself and students will probably impact my teaching'.

REFERENCES

Barry, C.A. (1995), 'Critical issues in evaluating the impact of IT on information activity in academic research: developing a qualitative research solution', *Library and Information Science Research*, **17**(2), 107–34.

Barry, C.A. (1997), 'Information skills for an electronic world: training doctoral research students', *Journal of Information Science*, **23**(3), 225–38.

EduLib (1998), http://www.hull.ac.uk/edulib/

Flatten, K. *et al.* (1998), *TAPin: The Impact Study*, Birmingham: University of Central England, http://www.uce.ac.uk/TAPin/publications/impact.htm

Finlay, K. and Finlay, T. (1996), 'The relative roles of knowledge and innovativeness is determining librarians' attitudes toward and use of the Internet: a structural equation modelling approach', *Library Quarterly*, **66**(1), 59–83.

Netskills (1998), http://www.netskills.ac.uk/

TAPin (1997), Diagnostic tools, http://www.uce.ac.uk/TAPin/publications/append.htm

TONIC (1997), http://www.netskills.ac.uk/TONIC/

12 The impact of the TAPin project on LIS staff

Helen Williams and Bruce Reid

INTRODUCTION

The subsidiary aims of the TAPin Electronic Libraries (eLib) project were to enhance 'the network competencies of targeted library and academic staff' and research the 'IT cultures within individual institutions of specific academic disciplines and in the library, in order to identify potential barriers to effective skills developments' (Flatten, 1996: 2). Some library and information service (LIS) staff involved in the project have explained its role and the impact in their own institutions and their own professional activity (Mulvaney, 1997; Stant, 1997). A full description of the participants and aims of the project can be found in the published reports on the project (Flatten, 1996; Newall *et al.*, 1997; Flatten, 1998). The TAPin project is not the only example of one-to-one support in the exploitation of networked information being offered to academic staff. Aileen Wade (1996), for example, describes the services offered to academic staff at Sheffield Hallam University, which include 'training sessions in a convenient location, often in their offices'.

At the end of the TAPin project, an open-ended questionnaire (see Figure 12.1) was distributed to 21 LIS staff involved in the delivery of the TAPin model of planned support for academic staff in their use of networked information, to examine the overall impact of the project on them. The recipients had been named by academic staff as having provided one-to-one training or support in the exploitation of networked resources. In addition, at the end of the project a focus group consisting of the senior LIS managers at the partner institutions was held to elicit the views of those most closely involved, on its effect and on the model's potential to establish guidelines for future LIS activity.

LIS CULTURE

Early findings of the TAPin project emphasized the significance of the planned

191

Personal Questions

1. What impact has TAPin had on your developing awareness and use of networked resources? (DK)
2. Do you think that the skills, and/or awareness you have developed has improved your interaction with academic staff? (Y/N/DK)
3. Has the development work in TAPin changed your view of the future for libraries and librarians? (Y/N/DK)
4. Has it improved your own view of your skill, roles or competencies? (Y/N/DK)
5. What other benefits (other than improved use of network resources) has TAPin brought you (e.g., technical skills, ability to install software, fix IT problems, etc.)? (DK)
6. Will you carry on TAPin-type activities after the project has finished? (Y/N/DK)
7. In what way does your subject specialist knowledge affect your ability to provide networked information support? (DK)
8. How would you say this subject specialist knowledge affects your own skills in networked information? (DK)
9. Has TAPin work brought you into, or increased, your contact with sections of the university other than academic staff (e.g., computing)? (Y/N/DK) If yes, have roles overlapped? (Y/N/DK) Has there been collaboration or conflict or DK?

LIS Questions

10. Has TAPin's impact spread beyond you to other colleagues? (Y/N/DK)
11. Has the LIS gained strategic or operational benefits from TAPin? (Y/N/DK)
12. Where would we have been if we had not had the benefit of TAPin time and resources and training? (DK)
13. Has it changed academic staff perceptions of their role? (Y/N/DK)
14. Has it changed academic staff perceptions of their own competence? (Y/N/DK)
15. Has it changed academic staff perceptions of your role? (Y/N/DK)
16. Has this had an impact on information skills work with students? (Y/N/DK)
17. Has there been an increase in demand for information skills work? (Y/N/DK)
18. How far has the model provided a methodology for developing future collaboration with academic staff? (DK)
19. Have there been structural/operational changes within your LIS as a result of TAPin? (Y/N/DK)
20. How do you see the future of librarian support of subject specialist knowledge in the networked information rich campus? (Please answer for one only)
    (Diminished because/Growing because/Unchanged because/DK)

Resource Questions:

Please estimate how often you use the following resources:

Search engines	Database hosts	Current awareness
e-mail	CD-ROMs	Document delivery
Discussion lists	BIDS	e-journals
WWW	NISS	
CIS/OPACs	BUBL	

Figure 12.1 TAPin LIS impact questionnaire

programme of training delivered to LIS staff in the process of altering LIS culture. They also showed that 'Time pressures and belief in traditional information seeking behaviours were the two cultural barriers to change' (Flatten, 1996: 37). Later TAPin reports stated that librarians

    ... needed to recognise the important role they played in changing the cultures, of not only their library and information services, but of their institutions as a whole. They were gateways to the wider information available to academics and seldom recognised their roles as agents for change. (Newall *et al.*, 1997)

The interim TAPin evaluation results included an examination, in a case study format, of the widely varying cultures of the LIS of five of the six partner institutions in terms of *access versus holdings*. Assumptions made in the Case study 1 library were that: 'users had expertise or at least the ability to acquire expertise' and that 'users would be physically present in the library'. In Case study 2 there was an 'assumption of a print culture' and a perception among LIS staff of 'general Internet awareness as taking place outside the library'. In the Case study 5 library, the researcher noted that students 'were not independent end-users because they did not know where to get access to the Web and they were not trained in the skills of Internet retrieval'. A contrast in the cultures identified was evident in other libraries. In Case study 3, there was a 'familiar theme of the user being unable to identify and get access to networked resources. The recognition of this need was refreshing but had not led to action.' This contrast was even more noticeable elsewhere. In the Case study 4 library one librarian commented, 'I see myself as a change agent' and another that 'Our skills as communicators were more important than our location'.

THE IMPACT OF TAPin ON LIS STAFF

Of the 21 questionnaires distributed to the LIS staff involved in TAPin, 15 usable responses were received – nine from new universities and six from old. Seven of the respondents were male and eight female. The TAPin subject areas were all represented, including three librarians with subject responsibility for the control area of business studies. Apart from these, subject responsibility was represented by four respondents in education, three in law and five in life sciences.

All respondents commented on the effect of the TAPin project on their own awareness and use of networked resources (Question 1). Assessments of the personal impact ranged from 'None' and 'Difficult to judge' to 'A great deal' and 'Phenomenal'. Some practical advantages mentioned included the fulfilment of training needs and the speedier provision of hardware and software. Other comments included:

> At times, it has been very inconvenient to do TAPin work, but it has enabled us to leap-frog ahead in our professional development. In a changing academic environment, it has provided interest and excitement at work, and therefore increased enthusiasm.

and the following list:

> Collaborative work with colleagues, peer support, confidence-building, networks of

links and resources, networked resources for learning materials, web-page expertise, expansion of subject area.

The importance of appropriate training in increasing librarians' confidence levels had been described in earlier reports: 'Librarians need training on network skills in order to feel confident in skill transfer to staff' (Flatten, 1996: 38). This point was also mentioned by one respondent: 'TAPin, by an initial increase of confidence, has encouraged greater exploration of networked resources.'

Two-thirds of respondents – particularly those from new universities – thought that their developing skills and awareness had improved relationships with academic staff (Question 2). Some of those reported an enhancement of their status and recognition of skills among academic staff: 'I have been able to make suggestions about resourcing their modules electronically and to offer training to students which is embedded in modules. This has given me a much stronger foothold in the school.' Again, the way TAPin raised LIS staff confidence was noted: 'TAPin training helped my confidence in discussing access to networks, software and other IT issues with staff.' However, others felt that their relationship with academic staff had changed little – 'No more than I hope they would in the course of technological change' – although, in most cases, this was because they felt that their relationship was already good.

Respondents were split equally between those who found that their views of the future for libraries changed in the light of their involvement in the TAPin project, and those who did not (Question 3). Several emphasized the role of traditional library skills:

> ... there will always be a role for libraries to help filter and evaluate the mass of information out there.

> The dissemination of knowledge has gone through so many changes in the last 20 years but the enduring feature of libraries/librarians is the ability to add value. As long as we can do this there is still a need for our skills.

> Librarians are able to exploit their traditional skills in exploiting electronic resources. I already expected that teaching skills were required for librarians and that the electronic road was ahead of us.

Those whose views had changed little already held the view that electronic resources would be important – for example, 'My views had already extended to virtual libraries before TAPin began'. One respondent noted the potential for librarians to play a guiding role in future developments: 'With the knowledge we've gained, we are able to steer the development in an appropriate direction for local circumstances.'

Most respondents, particularly in the new universities, thought that the TAPin project had provided them with the opportunity to enhance their own skills/competencies, and the importance of the training in increasing confidence was emphasized (Question 4). Comments included:

> TAPin helped to speed up the process of gaining new competencies and skills particularly with the Internet so I do feel more confident in this area, but I would have had to develop those skills anyway.

> My own retrieval skills have developed. Carrying out the academic training has enabled me to realise more of my potential as an HEI librarian, and because of the new confidence, has enabled me to play a more pro-active role.

> I feel much happier now when dealing with electronic resources. This has paid dividends in developing a training role. I'm sure that my general level of skill and competency with IT is higher.

Skills enhanced through participation in the TAPin project included:

> Useful skills evaluation of sources, dissemination, skills training, liaison, expertise in electronic resources, expertise in search strategies.

One respondent found that the TAPin project enhanced knowledge in a more general way: 'It makes me realise how little I know or understand the individual academic.'

Most of the perceived benefits of the TAPin project concerned either improved technical skills or the development of links and collaboration with other LIS professionals (Question 5):

> TAPin has brought an awareness of professional colleagues working within similar environments. This professional contact will continue after the project.

> My technical skills improved particularly with exploiting the Showman in support of my teaching. The main benefit to me personally was meeting other librarians from local institutions and sharing each others' experiences.

> [It] certainly improved my technical skills. I am now seen as the local expert in all things computing.

> Some technical skills, contacts with people in local universities, closer collaboration with colleagues.

However, one respondent entered a caveat to the generally positive attitude to improving technical skills:

> Made me more convinced than ever that information specialists should concentrate on delivering relevant information and network/technical problems other than simple ones should be left to 'techie specialists'.

On the whole, the sharing of experiences in a fast-changing field was one of the most valuable outcomes of the TAPin project, and provided another boost to the confidence of participating staff.

Almost all respondents expected to continue TAPin-type activities after the end of the project, although some also commented that activities would be on a smaller scale (Question 6). One or two commented that this type of activity had already been part of their work: 'We'll be going on as usual, when new staff arrive or new services are introduced.' Specific plans included an open day and cooperation with learning resources teams, as well as general support for academic staff:

> Collaborating with academic staff, we are providing networked and hard copy information retrieval guidance to students. The training of academics which we undertook was well received. When time permits, further concentrated training will be undertaken. However, another positive influence on academic willingness for further training is the influx of more library-orientated academics with responsibility for research in their department.

Questions 7 and 8 concerned the interrelationship between subject specialist knowledge and networked information skills, including the support provided to others. Some respondents considered their information skills to be much more significant than their subject specialist knowledge:

> I am a generalist rather than a subject specialist. I have to apply my skills to all disciplines. Gives me a very broad overview but not in depth.

> [Subject knowledge] helps weed out the bad from the good. I am not a subject specialist, but an information specialist. Awareness of resources is not the same as using the resources: they are all merely tools, to be handed on to those who can best use them – the staff and students.

> Difficult to say as I have changed subject specialty so many times. My professional skills in finding information using a range of resources are more important I think. These enable me to transfer from one medium to another and take a holistic view rather than concentrating on networked resources alone.

In response to Question 8 some of those surveyed commented on the value of subject specialist knowledge in evaluating the usefulness of resources, although generally admitting that it is secondary in importance to the traditional information expertise of LIS staff:

> The subject specialist knowledge drives the skills, but is not the only factor in acquiring them. It is important, for example, to be able to offer support to staff/students in other subject areas.

> Knowledge of sources available, their content and how to search them.

> My subject knowledge is vital in this regard – you need to be able to assess a database or information source.

> Improves refining techniques in searching and information evaluation skills.

Most respondents, especially in the new universities, reported contact and collaboration with other services, such as learning support and technical staff

(Question 9). No conflict was reported. Some respondents commented that this collaboration had already existed for some time – for example, 'TAPin has not caused this – it was there already' – and one mentioned the general benefits of closer involvement in IT strategy: 'Excellent collaborative work involved in computing, with technicians and strategic developers of IT within own university.'

Overall, the participants' assessment of the TAPin experience was positive, the greatest single benefit mentioned being increased confidence as a result of the enhanced skills and the shared experience afforded by the project. This is consistent with the findings reported at an earlier stage of the project (Flatten, 1996). The comment on the importance of LIS staff skills as communicators, recorded during the visit to the Case Study 4 library, is also borne out by the importance given to information skills by participants in the project. The focus group perception was that TAPin was only one of a number of influences driving the increased exploitation of networked resources, and that the model had a valuable place among the strategies adopted by LIS staff to cope with the changes.

THE TAPin IMPACT ON LIS

The LIS staff were asked 11 questions about their perceptions of the impact of TAPin on their own LIS, and on academic staff perceptions of, and requirements from, it. The responses to the first ten of them are recorded in Table 12.1.

Two-thirds of the respondents believed that TAPin's impact had spread to other colleagues (Question 10). Comments included: 'We have all been fairly intensely involved in the development of the training strategy and materials used'; and 'This has been an informal teaching process and encouragement to develop their own skills'. This opinion was particularly prevalent in the new universities; only one such respondent gave a negative response, but added nevertheless, 'It has started'. Among other universities, one respondent noted that 'it is difficult to single out TAPin impact as such' and another the importance of the extra funding: 'a TAPin funded post helped training and support for all subject specialist librarians.'

Most respondents believed that their LIS had gained strategic or operational benefits from involvement with TAPin (Question 11). This was particularly true for respondents from the new universities. Some of the 'negative responses' were ambivalent:

> I don't think so in terms of strategic benefit in that the networked resources and the role of the librarians was already in place. Operational benefits – yes – [...] the post supporting training did help.

Table 12.1   Responses from LIS staff to questions about TAPin's effect on LIS

n=15	Total responses			'Yes' responses		'No' responses		'Don't know' responses	
	Yes	No	Don't Know	New	Old	New	Old	New	Old
Q10	10	5	0	8	2	1	4	0	0
Q11	9	4	0	7	2	0	4	0	0
Q12	*	*	2	*	*	*	*	2	*
Q13	2	3	9	1	1	2	1	6	3
Q14	6	3	6	3	3	2	1	4	2
Q15	9	2	4	7	2	0	2	2	2
Q16	9	5	0	7	2	1	4	0	0
Q17	9	4	2	6	3	1	3	2	0
Q18	*	*	5	*	*	*	*	3	2
Q19	2	10	3	1	1	6	4	1	2

* indicates a qualitative response.

The benefits varied: some were practical, such as the opportunity to develop Web-based services; others were in the nature of improved public relations: 'To some extent, the perception of the library as a place for networked support has increased'; 'Higher profile with academics'. Some reported general benefits: 'Strategic: increased status, increased involvement at strategic level. Operational: greater flexibility in staff skills, benefit to students, better liaison with computing staff.'

Generally, most respondents thought that TAPin had helped the participating institutions deal with recent developments either by enabling training or through support for development of Web services (Question 12). Some thought that, overall, TAPin had had little effect on the speed of changes:

TAPin helped to speed up training in some areas but in terms of availability and exploiting networked resources the infrastructure was already there.

Others felt that the project had had a major impact:

It would have been impossible to develop our Internet information skills to any comparable extent without involvement in this or a similar project. It was also useful to be able to compare and contrast our experience with those of colleagues from other HE institutions.

TAPin time was **very** important and cannot be undervalued. The training would have happened eventually as would resources, but time was crucial in giving librarians the unpressured space to practice and develop.

Most respondents were not aware of any change in academic staff perception of their own role (Question 13). Comments included:

Staff saw their role as essentially the same as before but with an increased awareness of resources which will continue to help them.

Possibly for some in that they perceive a need to ask for support. There is also a more general acceptance of having to take responsibility for their own IT training, although I don't think TAPin caused this change.

TAPin hasn't but roles are changing through other external and internal processes – curriculum, Dearing, electronic journals etc: TAPin helped find a way for some.

Perhaps very slightly. Some would espouse technological developments, others would ignore changes in delivery of information etc.

There was some uncertainty over the question of whether the TAPin work had altered academic staff perceptions of their own competence (Question 14): 'In some cases yes, but mostly no. They also have problems with time and practice.' The answers depended on the LIS staff perception of the academic staff competence before the delivery of the TAPin model:

No. Academics were already finding they had more and more on their plate, and were not gaining the skills needed in all relevant areas. Some appreciated our offer of training, which meant they got it from people, whom they had traditionally found to be friendly and positive. Other academics have since learnt about the training we could give them, and feel they would benefit from it.

Some felt the training had been welcomed:

Academic staff appreciated the effort of one on one training which helped increase the confidence of their use of IT etc. Their own competence was further increased when they began to use the resources previously trained on.

Most respondents thought that a positive change had occurred in perceptions of LIS roles on the part of academic staff (Question 15). The change was mainly one of degree, rather than perceiving the LIS staff in an entirely new light:

I think academic staff see me more as an IT provider and trainer than they did before.

I think I've always been associated with electronic information retrieval services.

Yes. It seems that their understanding of our role is now closer to our own. Our information retrieval skills are being acknowledged.

Some respondents reported a more significant alteration in academic staff attitudes:

> Dramatically, where TAPin has brought me into contact with them. They see that the training I have given them can be transferred with great benefits to groups of students. They view me now as a real contributor to the teaching and learning process.

> Status, recognized expertise, collaboration on projects, teaching role of librarians.

Most respondents (Question 16), particularly those at new universities, felt that the work done through TAPin had affected work with students:

> I have run many training sessions in the IT suite as a result of requests from academic staff and some sessions are embedded now in the modules.

> I have now introduced networked skills to all information skills teaching.

> Definitely. Academic staff have involved librarians in teaching on subject modules, not just information skills modules. This area is growing!

> The academic staff involved sought to ensure all their students were provided with information skills training. This has been enabled by the liaison role of my position as well as demonstrating to staff the effectiveness of a good clear training programme which sought to match skills with resources.

Some respondents had been doing this kind of work with students for some time:

> We have provided information handling skills sessions using a variety of electronic sourced material for about ten years.

Two-thirds of respondents thought that there had been an increase in demand for information skills work (Question 17), but most believed that it was part of a general trend, driven by a range of factors such as a higher number of students, the increasing emphasis on skills teaching and policy factors such as the impact of the Dearing Report (National Committee of Inquiry, 1997). TAPin helped by boosting the confidence of LIS staff in their network skills, which were then passed on to staff and students .

Comments on the effectiveness of the TAPin model were mixed (Question 18): one-third of respondents did not know whether the model provided a suitable methodology for providing support to academic staff. There were some negative comments:

> Too time consuming.

> It hasn't really. The one-to-one support was already in place. Cascading of information by academics is unlikely to be very effective or widespread. The tendency is for that academic to refer another one to us therefore increasing our workload.

However, others were positive:

> It has established a firm link between library and academic staff, The TAPin model involved one-to-one delivery, which clearly is not practicable for large numbers of students. It's the content of the training sessions which is the real basis for developing future collaboration with academic staff and the way it was delivered.

It is a good basis because it was based on our practical experience and should help to avoid the pitfalls that were evident.

Some felt that the basis was sound, but had reservations:

The model, I think, is principally wrong although the general idea is good. To target individual members of staff to make them core champions with skills that can be cascaded is fine. The problem with TAPin was the targeted staff were not necessarily the most appropriate individuals.

The model was applied with variations even within this university. Any librarian will negotiate with academic staff in own way [sic]. However basis of training, practice, delivery is sound.

Most respondents were unaware of any structural or operational changes to LIS as a direct result of the TAPin project (Question 19), although it coincided with a period of change in some institutions:

The university has recently restructured to take account of the changes in higher education and the support we provide for users. TAPin came in on the back of that.

Two-thirds of the respondents saw a growth in subject specialist support provided by librarians in the networked environment (Question 20): none saw it decreasing in the future. The perception of the reasons for growth were broadly similar, summarized as: 'Information resources are growing'; 'Growth in these resources and the need to filter and point in the right direction. Again academic staff do not always have the time or inclination.' One respondent, who foresaw growth in this area sounded a note of warning:

Selection of information from the 'information overload' together with good search skills will remain important. Despite being a promoter of technological products there will be a place for the printed word for a long time to come and the information trade should not forget this.

On the whole, respondents, particularly those from the new universities, were positive about the effect of the TAPin project on their LIS. Few reported structural and operational changes, but respondents did mention significant effects on attitudes and competencies. In the case of the former, a positive effect on users' perceptions of LIS was reported. In the case of the latter, TAPin-funded time and training gave the participants the opportunity to develop or enhance skills in networked information. Those who reported little effect worked in universities which had embraced networked information before the project began. A particular benefit of the project was the development of the TAPin model which was useful as a practical basis for structuring training, although some respondents expressed reservations.

THE USE OF NETWORKED RESOURCES BY LIS STAFF

As an integral part of the project, the librarians involved had been asked about their training needs and were offered training in the exploitation of networked resources (Flatten, 1996). The questionnaire sent out at the end of the project included questions about LIS staff use of these resources. The results are set out in Table 12.2.

All the respondents used e-mail daily. The use of discussion lists varied, but all users mentioned LIS discussion lists such as LIS-link, LIS-ukolug, LIS-medical and LIS-law. A few subject-specific lists – for example, CHMINF-L – were also mentioned. Most respondents used the Web on a daily basis: a wide range of 'favourite' URLs were cited, and some respondents made comments such as 'Depends what I need it for', 'Too many to list' and 'Impossible to list all'. Twelve respondents mentioned more than one 'favourite' search engine: AltaVista was mentioned by all but two; Yahoo was mentioned by six; Northern Light by three; a range of others such as Infoseek, Excite, Euroferret and others by one or two respondents. Database hosts were less used: the most popular were BIDS (mentioned by four); Datastar, Dialog and STN (two each); and a number of

Table 12.2   Frequency of use of networked resources by TAPin librarians

n=15 librarians	Daily	Weekly	Monthly	Termly	Do not use	No response
E-mail	15					
Discussion lists	11		1		3	
Web	12	2				1
Search engines	11	2	2			
Database hosts	1	4	3	2	4	1
OPACs	5	5	2		3	
CD-ROMs	8	3	1		2	1
BIDS	5	5	2		3	
NISS	1	4	6	1	3	
BUBL		3	2	4	6	
Current awareness	2	1		1	11	
E-journals	1	2	4	4	4	

others were mentioned once each. The most frequently mentioned OPACs (outside the respondents' own institution) were the BL OPAC 97 (mentioned by six respondents); Library of Congress and COPAC (by three each). As with the URLs, the CD-ROMs favoured varied greatly (although one respondent commented that there were 'Too many to list'), but a mixture of the general ones (such as newspapers, and TES Bookfind) and subject-specific were cited.

The BIDS databases mentioned included: ISI (five), specifically SSCI (three) and SCI (two); IBSS (three). British Education Index, Compendex and Uncover were cited once. Various uses of NISS were mentioned, but the most common was for access to OPACs (four). One respondent commented that it 'depends on the nature of enquiries'. Of the four respondents using current awareness document delivery services, two used Newsagent daily, one used BOPCAS weekly and one used an unspecified service termly. Electronic journals referred to included *Ariadne* (three); *Journal of Current Legal Issues* (two); *British Medical Journal*, *New Scientist* and *The Times Educational Supplement*.

THE FOCUS GROUP DISCUSSION

Opinions recorded in the focus group at the end of the project continued to show variations in assumptions on the role of LIS staff. The first proposition under discussion was that the increasing importance of the exploitation of networked information could be viewed as a threat or as an opportunity. Responses included:

> … the skills that are needed to find the best sources on the web are the same as those needed to use books. The web is like the chaos of books before librarians ordered them. The end user is not empowered without information skills.

> The role is changing, we are just custodians. We are there to empower the users through user education.

> … providing BIDS, IDEAL etc. over the web. Users don't know that they are paid for by the library, and the library becomes irrelevant in the process.

The participants were asked to reconsider the findings of the TAPin researcher during the earlier case study visits – in particular, the references to the promotion of networked resources to users, and the reliance on print for guides and for user instruction. Responses included:

> Printed guides … are intended as a backup. We rely on humans.

> TAPin has been important but two years is a short period. We will start seeing a telling impact in, for example, another two years. Things have started to change.

Others agreed:

> The time needed to organize a policy, and to train staff has not been there. I believe we

203

should be promoting the library and networks though, even up to providing a 24-hour library.

… Librarians are still in the position of guiding choices, particularly with reference to networked information.

[The library] has made some progress, providing printed materials and back-up with human support. The hybrid libraries project is about developing this mid-point between network and printed support.

The experience of assisting academics to assess the quality of networked resources varied:

Librarians can offer opinion on quality, but academics do not ask.

If sources are free and easily accessible, academics will take them whatever the quality.

It's not a question of print or electronic. It's hard to strike a balance. You have to consider the economic implications and the quality issues of sources.

One academic asked about having the librarians change the curriculum to favour use of IT. I said this is not the library's responsibility. Recent Total Quality Assessments (TQAs) have been asking about the use of electronic information.

Most of the responses to the suggestion that libraries might provide a roomful of machines dedicated to browsing the Web were negative. Some LIS provided everything on one workstation, others distinguished between PCs with software and PCs with browsers or had dedicated workstations for the individual services. Some commented further:

… number of users allowed simultaneous access [to software] at one time is controlled by the cost charged by suppliers. Also applications are spread [between machines] to avoid queues for PCs for word-processing while someone surfs the net.

I would like to stop buying PCs and lease them. Buying computers is a big capital expenditure.

On the subject of the different skill levels among LIS staff (those who have network skills and those who have not):

Shelvers would refer to subject librarian – training them is an inappropriate use of resources. Some will put up barriers – true in every profession. Some are only comfortable with print and must be got up to speed.

There was general agreement with this comment.

We are committed to our staff being multi-tasking.

[Managers] will find that a number of staff don't deal with the public and don't know about the collection outside their own area.

To the question 'Where did the TAPin model go wrong?' the general response was that it was too early to say but that it had provided a useful starting-point:

The Model is practical and manageable.

The project succeeded because it was embedded in institutions which were expecting to get something out of it. There were small benefits, but real ones.

We need time to see if it has worked first.

The value of TAPin has been that it stated the obvious, documented it and then passed it on well.

The overall view which emerged was that of a revolution in the exploitation of networked information only just beginning. The TAPin model of planned support had its place in the development of strategies to deal with the changes, but was only one of a number of influences. The project exit strategies of the partner institutions were continuing to tackle the issues at the heart of the project. Plans included: cascading the expertise and experience of participating staff to colleagues who had not participated in the original project; creating or revising Web-based guides to sources; continuing to provide targeted support to new and existing academic staff; reviewing user education; developing the role of support staff to enable subject specialists to deliver the TAPin model; increasing the support in networked resources for postgraduate and final-year students; and maintaining the strong links forged during the project through future training/awareness seminars to ensure the regular updating and sharing of ideas and skills (Flatten *et al.*, 1998).

CONCLUSION

A number of commentators have noted the relative lack of literature on the human aspects of electronic information handling, which is only now being addressed, particularly through the IMPEL projects. Some of the TAPin findings match those in the IMPEL project; these include a growing instructional role for LIS staff and closer links between LIS staff and academic departments due to the increasing impact of technology (Day, 1995). The greatest reported benefit of the TAPin project perceived by the LIS staff delivering the model was the boost to confidence which occurred through the training, professional contacts and experience-sharing. It is intended that these contacts will continue at the end of the project.

An increase in interinstitutional cooperation, alongside the increased use of networks and networked resources, has also been noted (Morgan, 1997; Mowat, 1993). Confidence increased particularly in technical and network skills but also in teaching and in interactions with academic staff. For some LIS there was the added benefit of a raised profile in the academic departments of their institution, achieved primarily through consultancy on networked information. However,

205

significant as these changes were, the survey evidence suggests they be seen not as ignoring or supplanting the importance of traditional librarian skills (locating information and evaluating information sources), but as emphasizing their new and expanding role in the networked environment.

REFERENCES

Day, J.M. (1995), 'Towards the electronic library: impact on librarians', in *Proceedings of the UK Office for Library and Networking (UKOLN) Conference, Networking and the future of libraries 2, Bath, 19–21 April 1995*, London: Library Association Publishing in association with UKOLN, Bath University, 23–36.

Flatten, K. (1996), *TAPin: Training & Awareness Programme in Networks: Interim Report*, University of Central England: Centre for Information Research & Training.

Flatten, K. *et al.* (1998), *TAPin: Training & Awareness Programme in Networks: The Impact Study*, University of Central England: Centre for Information Research & Training, http://www.uce.ac.uk/tapin/publications/impact.htm

Morgan, S. (1997), 'Future academic library skills: what will they be?', in P.L. Ward and D.E. Weingard (eds), *Human Development: Competencies for the Twenty-first Century*, Munich: Saur, 19–29.

Mowat, I. (1993), 'Introducing networked electronic information services', in M. Morley and H. Woodward (eds), *Taming the Electronic Jungle. Electronic Information: The Collection Management Issues*, Leeds: NAG/UK Serials Group, 14–28.

Mulvaney, T.K. (1997), 'The TAPin electronic libraries project and the experience at the University of Birmingham', paper presented at the 2nd International Symposium on Networked Learner Support, 23–24 June, Sheffield, UK, http://www.netskills.ac.uk/reports/netlinks/mulvaney.htm

National Committee Of Inquiry Into Higher Education (1997), *Report*, (Dearing Report), Chair: Sir Ron Dearing, London: HMSO.

Newall, L. *et al.* (1997), *TAPin: Training & Awareness Programme in Networks: Second Annual Report*, University of Central England: Centre for Information Research & Training, http://www.uce.ac.uk/tapin/publications/2annual.htm

Stant, P. (1997), 'The Electronic Libraries Programme: a law librarian's experience in the West Midlands', *The Law Librarian*, **28**(4), December, 221–23.

Wade, A. (1996), 'Training the end-user. Case study 1: academic libraries', in R. Biddiscombe (ed.), *The End-user Revolution: CD-ROM, Internet and the Changing Role of the Information Professional*, London: LAPL, 96–109.

13 Learning organization theory in the networked environment

Linda Newall

INTRODUCTION

Much has been said in earlier chapters about the role of the TAPin Electronic Libraries (eLib) project in facilitating the changes in culture afforded by new information technologies and networks. Essentially, TAPin worked with higher education (HE) librarians to develop and promote professionals confident in the exploitation of their skills in information provision and the opportunities that were provided to support their IT development. Although TAPin was working with individuals in the six university libraries involved, it needed to take into account the cultures that prevailed in each of the universities, libraries and subject departments. The threats and opportunities that were present for the librarians had to be managed within the context of these cultures, which could be radically different even within a single university.

In 1995 the project manager attended meetings at four of the universities. These meetings had a responsibility for shaping strategic plans for networked information within the partner universities. In order to consider how TAPin might work within each environment it was important to gain an understanding of the following issues:

- the move towards a networked environment at the university
- the culture change effects, seen or expected, at the university resulting from a fully networked campus
- the awareness of the advantages of a campus network including its value-adding potential
- the demand for networked information at the university
- the usefulness of a networked environment to the university's mission and aims
- any other issues surrounding the performance and sustainability of the university's information networks and future scenarios.

In 1995 the meetings demonstrated that the demand for networked services had not been great when universities originally made their strategic decisions to network campuses. However, while the networks were under development, demand increased dramatically. Nevertheless, strategic planners did recognize from the outset the need for a culture change that would allow the utilization of all the opportunities provided by the new networks.

In order to assess the changes that occurred in both the perception of, and action on, the issues at the strategic level a strategic audit questionnaire was devised. This was sent to managers, at each university and in each subject area, who were responsible for dealing with issues of networked information provision. They were asked to consider their universities in terms of *Learning Organization Theory* (Dakshinamurti, 1997).

LEARNING ORGANIZATION THEORY

For any organization to continue to be competitive in the changing world, and continue to fulfil its primary functions, it must 'adopt a new way of managing that is based on [its] capacity to learn and change – consciously, continually and quickly' (Bennett and O'Brien, 1994: 41). In essence, it should be a *learning organization* that continually monitors the changes that are happening outside itself and then seeks ways to deal with them, because constant and continual improvements require a commitment to learning how to manage change.

The concept of the learning organization was first proposed by Argyris and Schon in the late 1970s (Argyris and Schon, 1978). However, it was not generally accepted until Peter Senge redefined learning organization theory by developing it to consider organizations more holistically. Senge finally held that learning organizations exist

> … where people continually expand their capacity to create results they truly desire, where new and expansive patterns of thinking are nurtured, where collective aspiration is set free and where people are continually learning how to learn together. (Senge, 1990: 3).

He identified five disciplines that characterized the learning organization:

- **Personal mastery** – organizations learn as a result of encouraging the individual to learn.
- **Mental models** – for an organization to move forward, it needs to constantly reassess the organizational beliefs about the world and the way it works.
- **Shared vision** – encourages consonance in the way that individuals see the organization and its goals.
- **Team learning** – encourages the cross-fertilization of ideas across boundaries.

208

● **Systems thinking** – the discipline that holds the other four together and provides a holistic view of the organization.

As Worrall states:

> ... the core disciplines describe an organization culture in which individual development is a priority, outmoded and erroneous ways of thinking are actively identified and corrected, and the purpose and vision of the organization are clearly understood and supported by all its members. (Worrall, 1995: 352)

Alternatively, Ganga Dakshinamurti suggests that:

> ... anyone who wants to be a part of a learning organization must first go through personal change, put aside their old ways of thinking (mental models), learn to be open with others by having open dialogue (personal mastery), understand how their organization really works (systems thinking), form a plan everyone can agree (shared vision) and then work together to achieve that vision (team learning). (Dakshinamurti, 1997: 353)

By 1997 it had been recognized, within the TAPin research team, that an essential element of how staff respond to the threats and opportunities implied by the implementation of new information technologies was a culture that allowed for development both personally and globally across the organization. The eLib supporting studies project, IMPEL2, suggested that the process of disintermediation that took place within higher education as a consequence of new information technologies would result in two possible divergent roles for organizations. The first would be a technocracy; the second, a learning organization (Edwards *et al.*, 1996). Learning organization theory suggests that, for change to occur, an organization must find ways to 'continually learn, to assess the environment, absorb relevant changes important to its mission and to integrate adapting strategies' (Phipps, 1993: 19). This can only be achieved by listening to staff, by supporting their development and by giving them the opportunity to extend their abilities. These were the issues considered important by TAPin for the facilitation of rapid change within a networked environment – in short, by allowing staff to develop both personally and globally.

LEARNING ORGANIZATION THEORY AND ITS APPLICATION WITHIN LIBRARIES

Learning organization theory is essentially a management concept: it is currently being used in ways similar to those in which such theories as TQM (Total Quality Management) have been at earlier stages in the development of 'management' as a concept. The main difference between learning organization and other management theories is its emphasis on the power of the culture in which the organization operates. As Worrall states:

> The learning organisation concept calls for no less than a cultural realignment of any

organisation and may be an effective tool in breaking an organisation free from powerful inertial forces. (Worrall, 1995: 356)

The concept of organizations as learning organizations was one considered by TAPin as an essential ingredient to the culture changes inherent in the evolving global information networks. It would be normal for a university to see itself as a *teaching* organization, rather than as a *learning* organization, because that is its principal function: its primary mandates are to teach students and conduct research. New information networks offer considerable opportunities but require substantial investment to optimize them. Furthermore, the changes which they precipitate have a major effect on the way in which university staff work. They need to work with new systems and procedures for service delivery which, in turn, are often achieved by using new technologies. It has become essential that the university, at all levels, *learns* to manage the changes that affect both it and the services it provides.

In turn, the function of the library in higher education is to support the primary mandates of the organization by offering access to information and resources. It is also a service organization that has a commitment to its users to provide the best that is available and practicable. However, the parameters for what is best and practicable are changing on an almost daily basis because of the use of new technologies and a competitive global information industry. In order to support the staff who in turn support the users, the library has to look to a continuous improvement that can best be supported by a proactive approach to management of change.

THE TAPin STRATEGIC AUDIT

It was against this background of massive technological change that the strategic audit questionnaire was developed and sent to 60 strategic managers. The managers targeted included vice-chancellors, directors of information services, deans, heads of schools/departments, course directors and some staff who had a strategic responsibility or interest in this area. Each manager was asked to consider 16 questions, including 10 statements identified by Garvin (1996) and relate them to their organizations.

Section one of the questionnaire identified the sector for which the respondent was answering. They had a choice of: old or new universities; business studies, education, law or life sciences; library, computing or converged services.

Section two asked respondents to consider their own organization in terms of the importance of each learning organization theory and the effectiveness with which it was applied. They were asked to rank the statements as follows:

A – is important and it is done effectively.
B – is less important and it is done effectively.
C – is less important but it is **NOT** done effectively.
D – is important but it is **NOT** done effectively.

The statements used in the questionnaire were as follows:

1. My organization learns collaboratively, openly, and across [all] boundaries.
2. My organization values *how* it learns as well as *what* it learns.
3. My organization invests in staying ahead of the learning curve in its area.
4. My organization gains a competitive edge by learning and applying new areas more quickly/effectively than other HE organizations.
5. My organization turns management data into useful knowledge quickly and at the right time and place.
6. My organization enables every employee to feel that every experience provides him or her a chance to learn something potentially useful.
7. My organization exhibits little fear and defensiveness; rewards and learns from what goes wrong as well as right.
8. My organization allows groups and individuals to try out potential risk areas to achieve the objectives of the organization without being penalized for sharing information and conclusions across internal and external boundaries, as long as the basic security of the organization is maintained.
9. My organization invests in experimental and seemingly tangential learning.
10. My organization supports people and teams who want to pursue action-learning projects by allowing them to work through problems and devise solutions that are based upon their own understanding and experience, rather than that of the organization (adapted from Calvert *et al.*, 1994: 38–43).

Section three asked whether the organization's mission statements and IT strategies had changed since 1995. It also asked for examples and further comments.

RESULTS

Response

A total of 23 questionnaires were returned by strategic managers. This represented a 38 per cent response rate. In cases where respondents felt they were able to answer for more than one sector, these multiple responses were added as additional cases. There were, however, no responses from departments or schools of education.

The importance of collaborative learning across boundaries

Collaborative learning means that, for organizations to grow and improve, they need to learn across a variety of boundaries which can be both physical, in terms of distance, and cultural, in terms of the type of organization. Those organizations that believed cross-boundary learning was important for them encouraged staff to link with others to support their own work and development. The links commented on by respondents were both *internal* to the university, faculty or department and *external*. One respondent from an old university demonstrated how both worked, with the comment that their organization 'promotes a termly teaching forum to share ideas on cross campus or discipline issues. [and] Encourages staff attendance at external events and internal cascading of knowledge gained'. Another respondent, from a new university, said that their organization 'attempts to use cross-boundary meetings to address key issues to share experiences and learn mutually'.

Figure 13.1 shows that almost all sectors considered it important to encourage collaborative learning, and most also felt they were effective in managing it. Life sciences and computing services were the only groups to feel that it was not an important issue. This may have been due to their long experience of networked resources and information, which may have resulted in networks that supported these areas being in place very early on.

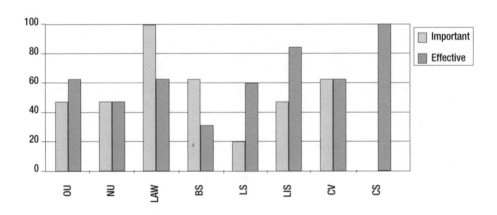

Key: OU = Old Universities, NU = New Universities, BS = Business Studies, LS = Life Sciences, LIS = Library and Information Service, CV = Converged Service, CS = Computing Service

Note: Missing columns indicate a nil response.

Figure 13.1   Percentage responses reporting the importance and effectiveness of collaborative learning across [all] boundaries

The value of how and what organizations learn

The value of what, as well as how, things were learnt was not considered important by most respondents. It was possible that the specialist nature of many of the sectors meant that the *what* was already defined by the role of educator and that the *how* became the main source of change. A business studies respondent said, 'As a management team we learn from our mistakes in dealing with sensitive issues and our approach is to try and take ownership of problems and the learning.'

One respondent from a new university said that the organization 'tries not to promulgate a blaming culture but one that genuinely reflects on mistakes and turns them into opportunities'. This theory demonstrated that, within a learning organization, there was a need to create an environment where staff feel comfortable with innovation that may go wrong as well as right.

Staying ahead of the learning curve

Investment in staying ahead of the learning curve generally refers to making a financial commitment and supporting the promulgation of a culture that encourages recognition of the way in which the world is moving. For instance, a respondent from an old university said that 'new research discoveries are incorporated into teaching programmes quickly', and that there was a 'fast move to develop [the] medical school in line with current political trends'. One respondent also indicated the need to 'invest in keeping on top of new methods of teaching and learning and research, eg in the use of the Internet'. The TAPin overall audit (Flatten, 1998) indicated that teaching and learning methods were changing in the light of new information technologies, and these often helped to attract students interested in new ways of studying.

Competitive edge

The drive to develop competitively was relatively new to higher education. With issues such as funding under discussion, greater competition amongst all universities has taken place. This has led to the development of other areas – for instance, using networks to support distance learning. For example, one respondent said that they had set up 'an educational technology group ... to experiment with use of advanced multimedia technologies'.

Respondents also indicated that there was pressure on the staff to secure funding from other sources. A member of staff from an old university commented that 'development funding harnessed from income generated by academic departments' was important to their organization and that they had a 'successful track record in [attracting] external funding to support innovation'.

This idea of developing competitively seemed to work in tandem with investing in 'staying ahead of the learning curve' (Statement 3). Figure 13.1 indicates that all sectors felt it was important that organizations recognized opportunities as early as possible so that these could then be turned into advantages, attracting new and additional business. For instance, Worrall (1995) cites the case of the AIMS (Advanced International Management Seminar) project between Digital Equipment and INSEAD (Institut Européen d'Administration des Affaires) which sought to redefine the relevance of the business school within current business practice. Digital Equipment managers were encouraged to use the expertise of the academic staff at INSEAD in developing new management strategies and then planning to implement them. The findings were then disseminated to identify any implications for future business initiatives.

However, in addition to the opportunities there are also threats associated with new information technologies. The Internet provides a vast resource that is easily tapped by anybody with even the most basic access and computing knowledge. This large market of, in many cases, easily satisfied inept end-users may well be exploited effectively by private business competitors unless information professionals assume their appropriate advisory and teaching roles within their organizations.

Respondents across all sectors showed that Statement 4 was generally important for their organizations (see Figure 13.2). There has always been competition between universities as a result of the (unofficial) ranking systems

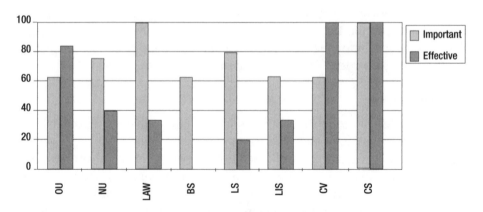

Key: OU = Old universities, NU = New Universities, BS = Business Studies, LS = Life Sciences, LIS = Library and Information Service, CV = Converged Service, CS = Computing Service

Note: Missing columns denote a nil response.

Figure 13.2   Percentage responses reporting the importance and effectiveness of gaining a competitive edge by applying new technologies quickly and effectively

that exist. This has resulted in a need to develop specialisms. New universities, which mostly grew out of local authority-funded institutions, are new to this and thus felt that they were not managing it effectively, whilst the competitive culture was embedded into the older universities which, consequently, perceived themselves as fairly successful. Similarly, the subject areas had started to tackle issues such as funding sources and, with the introduction of initiatives such as the Research Assessment Exercise, subject areas were able to compete for additional funding.

As a result of disintermediation, library services were beginning to reinvent themselves and were learning how to promote their services more effectively. Staff and students can now access the catalogues and services of many universities and data sources across the Internet. As a result of this explosion in information provision, the need to promote the library service to internal users may increase, but will also offer the opportunity to exploit additional markets from external users as well.

The very nature of new technologies in a fast-paced environment has always meant that computing support services have been competing, but usually internally. Now that students are evaluating the facilities which a university or faculty can provide in order to help decide where to study, this may also become a threat.

The use of management data

Effectively used management data supported many other strategies that were important for learning organizations. One respondent said that 'high priority [was] given to management data, particularly for student recruitment to improve [the] admissions process on [an] annual basis'. It was probably used to support the organization in its drive to attract more students and, therefore, additional funding.

This type of data also supported the increased competition within the HE sector. One Business Studies respondent said that they 'produce data, but not useful management information, but we are learning and changing this slowly'. The effective use of such data is dependent on the systems in place. This may explain why old universities and converged services felt that they were effective in their use of management data (Figure 13.3).

215

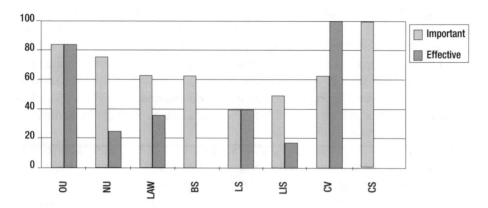

Key: OU = Old universities, NU = New Universities, BS = Business Studies, LS = Life Sciences, LIS = Library and Information Service, CV = Converged Service, CS = Computing Service

Note: Missing columns denote a nil response.

Figure 13.3   Percentage responses reporting the importance and effectiveness of converting management data into useful knowledge quickly and appropriately

Experiential Learning

Organizations rely on staff to perform jobs that are necessary for their continued functioning. Responses seem to suggest that changes and developments within organizations are often due to staff recognizing a need. Learning organizations allowed this process to happen fairly unhindered – for instance, a university may 'allow[s] course teams to deliver new modules, new methods of delivery and new methods of assessment. [and] Place[s] few constraints on the types of qualifications staff can study for'.

Respondents also recognized the need to allow staff to motivate themselves. One respondent said 'we invest heavily in encouraging staff to stay ahead by making them take ownership of their own personal and professional development'. This type of support benefited the employee in the short term, and the organization in the long term.

IT continued to be a major catalyst for change, and this probably explained why respondents frequently said that they provided relevant training. According to work by IMPEL2, staff training supported not only improvements in service provision, but also the management of change itself (Huntingford, 1998). However, despite being perceived as important by most sectors (Figure 13.4), it was not thought to be managed effectively by respondents from most sectors. This would indicate that training was still a new concept within higher education.

216

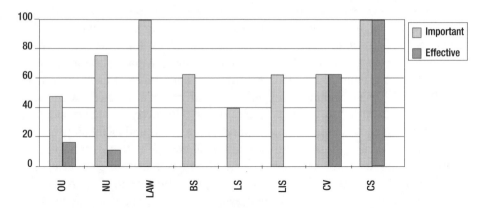

Key: OU = Old universities, NU = New Universities, BS = Business Studies, LS = Life Sciences, LIS = Library and Information Service, CV = Converged Service, CS = Computing Service

Note: Missing columns indicate a nil response.

Figure 13.4   Percentage responses reporting the importance and effectiveness of enabling every employee to feel that every experience provides him or her with a chance to learn something potentially useful

Fear and defensiveness

Organizations must foster an open atmosphere in order to grow and continue learning. This type of support needs to be driven by those at the highest institutional levels. In a competitive society where funding for higher education is tied to many different criteria, it is probably difficult to initiate – especially when 'doing it right' is essential to financial gain. This may explain why this statement was not considered important by most respondents. Those respondents that did feel it was of importance were probably those from organizations that had gone through restructuring as a result of creation (new universities), new technology (computing) or governmental change (law and business studies). The effectiveness that was measured by these respondents was concurrent with this. They were (mostly) applying the theory rigorously and had become adept in its use. This theory, however, can only be implemented effectively where staff do not feel threatened by a 'blaming culture'. Some respondents indicated that they had dealt with this issue by saying that they were not 'afraid of making mistakes'. Others felt that they learnt from mistakes and had encouraged staff to take 'ownership of problems'.

Risk and security

An organization's objectives change as it changes and, in order to support such

217

ongoing processes, staff members have to support innovation. Such innovation took place across many different boundaries as staff communicated with other people and organizations, and built upon new ideas that were generated. Respondents from old universities indicated that they enabled 'the formation of special interest groups ... to share information in an informal environment' or that they were 'very willing to experiment and to form alliances with other organisations in order to achieve [their] goals'. However, as one respondent recognized, this method of working required more 'focus and facilitation'.

Respondents from those same organizations that felt it was important to exhibit little fear and defensiveness also believed that a certain amount of risk-taking should be allowed. This may have been due to the need to allow individuals to develop in order to help move the organization forward. Many new universities and computing services that were still undergoing radical changes in the way they operated – and hence needed to define themselves – needed to tackle the issue. Law and Business Studies departments, for instance, are constantly updated in the light of external pressures, such as governmental changes.

Investment in experimental and tangential learning

The purpose of an organization is to grow its business. This can be done either by buying into new areas or by encouraging staff to consider alternatives and new approaches. In higher education this often referred to the way its business was conducted. For instance, one respondent said that they had an 'innovative teaching and learning strategy' and another that 'innovative ideas [were] encouraged from all staff [and] a degree of experimentation [was] allowed, commensurate with requirements to provide a service'.

Only respondents from two sectors, new universities and law, felt that it was important to support experimental learning of this type. However, new universities, together with a further three sets of respondents (computing services, library services and business studies) also felt that they had procedures in place that supported it.

Support for action learning projects

Innovation was seen to move organizations forward. In 1997 the higher education sector felt this often referred to changes in teaching and learning practices, provision of access to resources at the desktop, and access to networked materials by students.

In many ways this was at the heart of the learning and organization statements. Without innovation nothing else happened. Respondents indicated a number of ways in which they had managed this area. These included:

- supporting project groups
- use of different management approaches
- encouragement of innovative ideas from staff and allowing experimentation
- supporting groups changing methods of teaching
- experimenting with the use of networks.

Summary

The summary of results shown in Table 13.1 shows that respondents from old universities and life sciences indicated that the learning organization statements were, on the whole, of less importance in their organizations. This was possibly because they had already made changes and had embraced new technologies that were supported by the theories, so that the systems and procedures which the statements advocated were already in place. The fact that more than 50 per cent of respondents for old universities perceived themselves as successful in applying the statements also serves to support this assumption. However life sciences did not believe that the statements were applied effectively, suggesting that there was a rigidity of thinking within life science schools and departments that prevents the easy facilitation of change.

Conversely, respondents from all other sectors indicated that the learning organization theories were, on the whole, important to them. These sectors represented some of those areas in higher education that had faced significant changes, either in structure, funding or working practices. The learning organization statements were probably important to these respondents because

Table 13.1   The overall importance and effective application of all statements by organization

	Important	Effective
Old Universities	47%	55%
New Universities	61%	43%
Business Studies	50%	30%
Law	90%	37%
Life Sciences	36%	30%
Library Services	50%	40%
Converged Services	50%	70%
Computing Services	50%	80%

the changes and their implications had not yet been completed. However, only respondents for two sectors (computing and converged services) felt that they were successful. For the rest there was general feeling that the statements were not applied effectively. This again suggested that the change in Senge's 'Mental Models' had yet to take place.

CONCLUSIONS

CHANGES IN ORGANIZATIONAL MISSION STATEMENTS

In 1995 strategic planners at four of the six partner universities offered comments on the usefulness of a networked environment to their universities' missions and aims (see Figure 13.5). The networked environment was seen as a crucial factor in a university's ability to fulfil its mission – that is, to be excellent in research and teaching, and to provide services to the local and regional community. Comments were offered about how high-speed, high-bandwidth networks facilitate research – especially cooperative research – and will eventually transform teaching by permitting the combination of staff with mutual interests to teach modules, deliver courses, bid for contract research funds and engage in consulting work, which in turn will change both internal and external perceptions of the university (Flatten, 1996).

By 1997 respondents indicated that the mission statements of almost all sectors had experienced some degree of change since 1995. Some had changed more than others – probably reflecting the amount of change that had occurred in other areas of those subjects and services.

Once the networks were in place the emphasis changed to include other areas that reflected the increased need to look for new sources of funding and support.

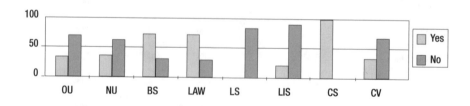

Key: OU = Old universities, NU = New Universities, BS = Business Studies, LS = Life Sciences, LIS = Library and Information Service, CV = Converged Service, CS = Computing Service

Note: Missing columns indicate a nil response.

Figure 13.5   Changes to mission statements since 1995 by percentage

The networks added an 'international dimension' and also cross-boundary 'research partnerships'. Respondents spoke of 'continuous improvement' and mentioned the need to actively seek out new business opportunities by becoming more market- and customer-focused. One university also changed from an external to an internal focus to provide more support in terms of teaching, learning and research.

CHANGES IN ORGANIZATIONAL IT STRATEGIES ON NETWORKED INFORMATION

In 1995 the importance of a networked campus to a university's mission and aims was well understood by strategic planners. Partner universities were in the early stages of formalizing this association (Flatten, 1996).

By 1997 respondents across most sectors reported a greater degree of change to their IT strategies than had been exhibited by their mission statements (see Figure 13.6). This probably reflected the fluid nature of IT strategies required to constantly respond to changes in technologies. Indeed, a number of respondents indicated that their strategies were being updated regularly.

There were also signs that demand was continuing to grow. Some respondents stated that, previously, no strategies had been in place. Others mentioned that their strategy reflected the changes in the types of use that the networks now supported. For instance, one respondent commented:

> We are moving towards using the network capabilities more fully by developing teaching and learning materials that can be accessed by our students and others from remote locations. We are also using it to improve internal communications.

Another said that they had:

> A university policy on web page design and content. ... Within learning resources a web editorial board is now active. [The] Planning framework for departments includes the creation of subject pages for each subject area and [a] move to contribute to staff development programmes.

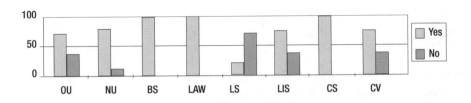

Key: OU = Old universities, NU = New Universities, BS = Business Studies, LS = Life Sciences, LIS = Library and Information Service, CV = Converged Service, CS = Computing Service

Note: Missing columns indicate a nil response.

Figure 13.6   Changes in IT strategies since 1995 by percentage

In 1997 IMPEL2 identified six factors crucial to institutional change (Huntingford, 1998):

- support at an institutional level
- access to technology
- comprehensive information strategies
- communication at and between all levels
- project management and teamwork
- commitment to learning and training together with on-going support.

Results from the TAPin strategic audit supported these statements, reflecting the changes that were taking place in higher education. The four learning organization statements that were seen as important by the majority of respondents in almost all sectors are those most concerned with the above issues. Respondents emphasized the importance of collaborative learning and using management data effectively. They also recognized that adopting a positive approach to competition and support of the employee would ultimately benefit the organization. However, one respondent did point out that:

> In a learning organization, by definition you never do anything effectively, because there is always ... room for improvement if only because the social reality which described the first situation of choice will never be replicated.

The effectiveness with which the various statements were executed in the different institutions probably reflected the relative starting-points of the organizations. Learning organization theory also represented some of the issues that face organizations when they confront change. Those groups that have already made changes have embraced new technologies and may already be using and adapting the statements. The statements therefore become less important because they are already in place. Those organizations that were just beginning to make changes found the statements challenging, possibly because they were still tackling the issue of supporting new cultures.

REFERENCES

Argyris, C. and Schon, D.A. (1978), *Organizational Learning: A Theory of Action Perspective*, Reading, MA: Addison Wesley.

Bennett, J.K. and O'Brien, M.J. (1994), 'The building blocks of the learning organisation', *Training*, **31**(6), 41

Calvert, G. *et al.* (1994), 'Grasping the learning organization' *Training*, **31**(6), 38–43.

Dakshinamurti, G.B. (1997), 'Libraries as learning organizations', in P.L. Ward and D.E. Weingard (eds), *Human Development: Competencies for the Twenty-first Century*, Munich: K.G. Saur, 350–57.

Edwards, C. *et al.* (1996), 'Disintermediation in the year 2010: using scenarios to identify key issues and relevance of IMPEL2 eLib Project', *Online 96 Proceedings*, London: Learned Information, 357–61.

Flatten, K. (1996), *TAPin First Annual Report*, Birmingham: University of Central England.

Flatten, K. (1998), *TAPin Impact Study*, Birmingham: University of Central England.

Garvin, D.A. (1996), 'Building a learning organization', *Business Credit*, **96**(1), 18–22.

Huntingford, J. (1998), 'The impact of IMPEL', *Ariadne*, (13), January, 3, http://www.ariadne.ac.uk/issue13/impel/

Phipps, S.E. (1993), 'Transforming libraries into learning organizations – the challenge for leadership' in G.M. von Dran and J. Cargill (eds), *Catalysts for Change: Managing Libraries in the 1990's*, New York: Haworth, 19–37.

Senge, P.M. (1990), *The Fifth Discipline: The Art and Practice of the Learning Organization*, New York: Doubleday.

Worrall, D. (1995), 'The learning organization: management theory for the information age or new age fad?', *Journal of Academic Librarianship*, September, 351–57.

Out of our past: understanding our communication environment

14

Matt Holland

BACKGROUND AND CONTEXT

This chapter is based on two assumptions: first that new technologies (computers, networked communication and networked information) are driving cultural change in academic libraries; and, second, that current organizational culture will influence responses to computerization.

The arguments that technology drives cultural change are widely accepted. In higher education, cultural change and adapting to new technologies are seen as both desirable and inevitable. It is desirable to exploit the new capabilities of new technologies and inevitable in order to keep pace with the world outside academia. This is evidenced in eLib and other digital library projects worldwide, which seek to encourage new thinking, new ways of working and the creation of innovative uses of new technologies.

CULTURE AND TECHNOLOGY

Digital library research, of which TAPin forms a part, has increased our understanding of networked information and its human contexts. This research has generated two new areas of study: social informatics and organizational informatics. These terms have emerged from discussions in workshops and seminars sponsored by the National Science Foundation (NSF) in connection with the Digital Libraries Initiative (DLI). Social informatics describes the wider context of computers and society. Kling and Star offer the following definition: 'the social aspects of computerization – including the roles of information technology in organizational and social change and the ways that social organization of information technologies influence social practices (and are influenced by them)' (Kling and Star, 1997: para 4, line 3).

In an extensive review of social informatics and digital libraries Bishop and Star (1996) examined what they termed 'the social informatics of digital library use'. A key theme of this review is the persistence of personal communication. Examples are: interaction and collaboration with friends in information-seeking; the role of 'social worlds' in providing a reference group within which discussion of information-seeking takes place; and a preference for communication between close colleagues where discussion in a wider forum is perceived to be risky.

The new area of organizational informatics has emerged to integrate research into computing and applications development on one side and, on the other, the impact of computing on organizations and their human context. Kling and Allen (1996) argue that organizational informatics gives us two key insights into the relationship between computerization and organizations.

> 1) *The behaviour of human organizations affects the design and implementation of computer systems.*
>
> 2) *The effective use of computerization systems in organizations does not depend on technology alone.* Many other aspects of organizations – including job design, reward and incentive schemes, political negotiation, and cultural understandings – combine with technology choices to affect how computing is used in practice. (Kling and Allen 1996: 265)

Identifying different levels of interaction enriches the discussion of organizational informatics. Between the level of the organization and that of the individual, groups described as *communities of practice* are identified. These are individuals who share a common task, are part of the same group or use the same tools. Communities of practice may form part of the formal organization or have an informal status. For example, subject librarians interact with colleagues who may share the same tasks, they may be part of a teaching team with academics from their school/department/faculty or communicate with colleagues who share a common interest.

New themes emerge from social/organizational informatics discussions, which have relevance to this research. These are: the persistence of interpersonal communication in seeking and using information; the need for appropriate responses to people's needs which are sensitive to the human context; and the requirement for appropriate forms of organization to manage technology and the human interface. The symbiotic relationship between organizations, the people who work in them and computers provides further support for the specific conclusion of the research reported here that the existing culture influences the organization's response to networked communication. Equally important is the recognition of the mechanisms by which culture influences computer use through people's values, attitudes and behaviours in their workplace. The complexity of this interaction is reflected in the possible levels of analysis that comprise the human context. The term that I propose to encompass this area is the *communication environment*.

UNDERSTANDING THE COMMUNICATION ENVIRONMENT: A TOOLKIT

Broadly, the TAPin project sought to create a process of change within academic libraries by providing subject librarians with training and support to introduce academics to networked information. The results of this process were recorded and analysed, and form the basis of this chapter.

The implication of the TAPin research is that an understanding of 'where we are now', in terms of culture, helps us to predict likely responses to networks. This determines the most appropriate choice of strategies to reach our desired future destination.

The aim of this chapter is to provide simple models and tools to visualize key areas that underpin academic library culture. These key areas are derived from the TAPin experience and focus on the implications of networked information and networked communication for academic libraries. As with all models, however, it is recognized that these are a stylized interpretation of the evidence, not a literal representation of the truth. While it is not proposed that the conclusions of the TAPin project be generalized to all academic libraries – although all libraries share key common relationships – it is suggested that considering the communication environment is a starting-point for understanding the implications of networked communication for individual organizations and the subject librarians who work in them.

INTERPRETING THE COMMUNICATION ENVIRONMENT

Understanding the communication environment is too complex a task to be represented by any single measure. The analysis proposed is at three levels:

1. the organization
2. within the organization
3. the individual.

Within these levels are measures which together form a picture of where our organization is now. These are:

1. a typology of possible organizational responses
2. interactions with groups outside the library
3. modes of communication – how we communicate with users
4. modes of use – the levels of network use and access in the departments and in the library
5. communication strength – the way we communicate with schools/ departments and faculties
6. values and perceptions – our personal perceptions of our role
7. personal orientation – how we think about our role.

ORGANIZATIONAL RESPONSES TO NETWORKED INFORMATION

The typology presented here is a synthesis of observed organizational response to networks. It comprises two elements. A verbal description of four cases and the cultural response matrix which provides a visual representation of possible cases along two key axes: compatibility with networks; and the strength of existing culture.

THE TYPOLOGY

The adaptive library

The adaptive library does not change culture to meet networked information and networked communication, but adapts its approach to fit them into existing cultural assumptions. The adaptive library focuses on its presence, and it has an established role within the institution. The library's role in relation to its users is passive. As users know and understand the value of the library, the library neither seeks, nor feels the need, to promote itself. Electronic resources are available for users to consult, but they are not differentiated from other forms of information, such as print. The adaptive library is likely to have some or all of these characteristics:

- a focus on physical access to resources
- a practice of placing the responsibility for acquiring skills and knowledge of resources with the user
- a strong expert culture, which places the subject expert at the centre of the resource provision
- weak communication links with the academic department
- a lack of experimentation with new modes of communication
- a passive exploitation of resources, the availability of which is not supported through such activities as end-user training
- weak internal links between subject experts and technical support services.

The transforming library

The transforming library has a weak cultural identity. Its role is less established within its home institution, and its development is likely to have been characterized by many reorganizations and rapid expansion. The transforming library is sensitive to changes in the external environment and is likely to have the following characteristics:

- a preference for informal communication over formal communication

- many advice and friendship groups within it
- evidence of experimenting with new forms of communication
- culture change activities, such as training
- initiation of changes to its organizational structure
- evidence of changing or adapting its librarians' roles
- some conflict within the library
- some conflict with organizations within the institution.

The learning library

The learning library has a strong and responsive management culture, which supports and encourages change. It is likely to have, within it, reservoirs, or access to reservoirs, of relevant technical expertise and is likely to be practised at responding to innovation. The learning library is likely to have the following characteristics:

- integrative approach to resources – likely to expend efforts communicating this to end-users
- proactive relationship with users – likely to routinely deliver information skills training to end-users
- innovative – will experiment with new modes of communication as part of a coordinated formal response
- a close formal and informal relationship with academic departments
- a high level of communication between subject experts and technical support
- an awareness of strategic issues on the part of librarians
- a focus on communication with users about physical resources or location.

The unresponsive library

The unresponsive library has a weak culture whose response to environmental pressures is to ignore them. It is likely to have autocratic management style, perhaps led by an older professional unable, or unwilling, to take on new technologies. The unresponsive library will have weak links with academic departments and with other groups within the institution.

THE CULTURAL RESPONSE MATRIX

The cultural response matrix measures responses on two key axes: the strength of existing culture in defining responses to forces which create cultural change; and the degree of compatibility of existing cultures with the force for cultural change – in this instance, networked technology and networked communication (see Figure 14.1)

Strength of existing culture Low	**Unresponsive** likely to experience conflict leading to radical organizational and cultural changes	**Transforming** likely to experience cultural and organizational changes
Strength of existing culture High	**Adaptive** adapted in the present, will experience conflict and change at a future date	**Learning** adjusts existing culture and organizations to absorb forces for change
	Compatibility with forces for change (networked information) Low	Compatibility with forces for change (networked information) High

Figure 14.1   The cultural response matrix

The matrix poses the question, 'What is our response to networked communication and networked technology?'. An instructive exercise is to place a library within this framework to test the implications of current culture against future expectations.

The unresponsive or adaptive library is unlikely to make planned responses to the forces for change, since both are reactive rather than proactive. Such libraries will encounter greater negative effects of conflict and disruption either now or in the future when the forces for change become overwhelming.

Positive effects

The transforming library is engaged in a process of change. The forces for change in the external environment are likely to be the catalyst for change and shape it in a compatible direction.

Planned responses

Learning libraries are likely to be making planned responses to networked communication and networked technology. They will encounter greater positive effects as they adjust to meet the forces for change, and are least likely to be overwhelmed as a result.

ORGANIZATIONAL AND INDIVIDUAL RESPONSES

RELATIONS WITH OTHER GROUPS WITHIN THE ORGANIZATION

The TAPin project reported relationships with outside groups as either positive or in conflict with the library. These comments represent some of the attitudes present in the research.

- 'The computer centre was slow to put in networked links.'
- 'People within the department said it was not our job to teach Internet skills to students.'
- 'Academics preferred advice from colleagues or technical support within the department.'

The exploitation of networked information builds on the creation of a network infrastructure to support desktop access within the academic departments. Positive relationships with mutual understanding of the technical issues and end-use are essential for effective and efficient implementation. Where positive relationships existed with technical support staff, outcomes tended to be positive as well.

Conflict existed between groups who felt they had exclusive claims to the same role – that of trainer/adviser/teacher. Confrontations were reported with staff who claimed to fill the same role as the subject librarians implementing the TAPin model or training students. These conflicts represented a process of establishing credibility in new roles and taking ownership of areas of knowledge. They represent evidence of a process of defining new roles or defending old roles.

Each of these conflicts requires a different response. Conflicts with technical personnel who are building the networks which libraries are seeking to exploit must be resolved. In this sense they are negative because they hinder the process of creating the networked infrastructure. Conflicts which seek to define roles, however, need to be engaged in because the outcomes will directly affect the library's position, its self-image and its relationship with its users. In this way they are the healthy manifestation of a process of change.

THE ACCESS LIBRARY

The concept of the access library culture was devised as a research instrument to give researchers a point of comparison. Two cultures were proposed; an access or network-friendly culture; and a holdings or network-averse culture. The observations of actual responses are reported as modes of communication in the next section.

The concept of the access library remains an ideal. The following description, however, represents some of the activities that might be present in an access library.

The access library allows end-user access to networked information and access to subject experts. Networked users can access information created for them, and consult subject experts electronically or in person if they need to. Networks provide choice in the medium of communication – for example, synchronous or asynchronous, face-to-face or electronic, one-to-one or one to many. Users and subject experts can manage their communication efficiently and effectively, choosing the medium that is most appropriate for their needs.

Networked activities might include:

● answering a student query about information for an assignment using a mailing list or electronic conference, distributing the same information to those on the same course/level who may also need it
● creating subject-based Web guides directing students to electronic and non-electronic resources in response to a request from a member of staff, perhaps in advance of an assignment being set
● designing customized pages from which to link to networked information resources such as BIDs, giving the user the information and guidance they need to use the resource effectively
● arranging a face-to-face meeting via e-mail with users who require expert advice.

The aim of the access library is to manage interactions with subject experts and to reduce both the need for physical presence and the importance of physical location. The purpose is not to eliminate the library's physical existence or face-to-face contact with the subject expert but to exploit the choices offered by networked communication and networked information.

MODES OF COMMUNICATION

Modes of communication describe the underlying assumptions observable in the library service at the point of use. Failures in communication were observed where:

1. the assumptions about what represents an access library culture were in conflict with the existing assumptions
2. where the implementation of networked solutions conflicted with existing modes of communication.

This typology is derived from the post-case analysis of the TAPin data. The modes of communication identified were visible to the researchers because they conflicted to some degree with the definition of an access culture.

degree of cultural change required to get there. Although the communication matrix is intended to inform an organizational approach, it is equally applicable to groups and individuals.

Modes of communication mark a point of departure rather than a plan of action. However, positioning academic library services within this matrix defines attitudes to: expert centredness; physical presence; control of resources; channels of communication to users; and the degree of users' assumed responsibility to operate the service. The TAPin evidence suggests that these are inherited assumptions embedded within the history of the organization. Planned change requires that these hidden assumptions are exposed and understood. They will become visible, in any case, at the point where they conflict with new areas of activity.

LEVELS OF USE

Levels of use refer to the ways in which networks are used to communicate with users. The use of networks is best measured as levels of development. A measure of 0–3 is offered here.

- **Level 0**. There is no use of networked communication or networked information.
- **Level 1**. The assumptions that underpin existing activities are directly transferred into new forms of communication. For example, e-mail can be used instead of a telephone.
- **Level 2**. Networks are used to locate new information created by other individuals or organizations, using tools that already exist. Examples might be electronic versions of government reports, statistics or databases.
- **Level 3**. Networked technologies are used to distribute information that is created specifically for distribution across networks. Within the context of this study this would include individual Web pages and library websites. Of course, with technical support, this process can be extended into the creation of new databases and interactive guides.

The relative position of the library and the academic department to each other at each level determines, to a significant degree, the nature of their dialogue about networked information. This dialogue is the focus of the TAPin model and the research that it has generated. The evidence of the TAPin research is that where the library is ahead or at the same level of development as their academic departments they have positive dialogues and move forward with least difficulty. Learning is a shared experience, with subject librarians and academics learning together, or in cases where subject librarians have skills they are responsive and sensitive to the information and training needs of their academic colleagues.

The levels of use matrix

The levels of use matrix gives a visual representation of the relative position of the library and the academic department (see Figure 14.3). In this diagram, the two axes represent increasing levels of network use for the LIS and academic department, level 3 being the highest attainable. The cases represent five different hypothetical cases with different pairings of levels of use, and the arrows show the distance to be travelled to reach the ideal situation where both the LIS and academic department are at level 3 and are therefore making the best use of networks in their relationship.

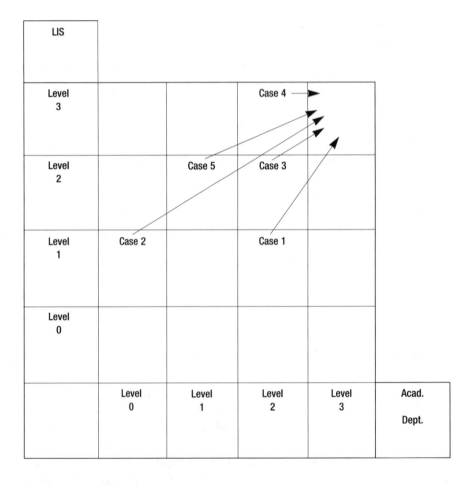

Figure 14.3   The levels of use matrix

236

It is an informative exercise to place the library in relationship to academic faculties/schools/departments. The implication of this research is that where the library leads, dialogue is positive and productive. However, a disparity of level implies managing the gap between library and academic department. Understanding the nature of the gap points to areas of concern. This will inevitably include the following:

- **Technology**. LIS does not have the capability to deliver over networks, or the academic department is not physically connected to access information through networks.
- **Shared vision**. Libraries and academic departments do not have a shared understanding of what is possible, desirable or achievable with networked information, because they have no (shared) experience of it.
- **Service fit**. Gaps in networked use/access create mismatches in service. A typical example might be library development of networked delivery for departments who have limited networked access. The gap between library and department has the potential to create a positive cycle of mutual development and support, or a negative cycle of mutual divergence.

COMMUNICATION STRENGTH

Communication strength or weakness is reflected in evidence by two factors: the subject librarians' degree of integration into the formal structures of committees, boards and meetings; and the nature of informal communication between academics and subject librarians.

Examples of integration might be routine attendance at school or faculty committees where the library and networked communication form part of the discussion. This represents communication at a strategic level where subject librarians are in a position to speak and influence the school in matters that are relevant to the library. Library committees represent a second tier of integration. In this case, both librarians and academics meet, but outside the principal forums of both the library and the academic department.

Informal communication takes place outside the formal structures of the organization. Examples might include visiting the library or meetings during the lunch hour. Such communication gives opportunities for using personal influence and persuasion. Generally, frequent informal contact is equated with strong powers of influence, while casual infrequent contacts are a powerful mechanism for disseminating information to colleagues, although they are unlikely to be a means of persuasion.

The degree of integration into the formal communication structure and the frequency and extent of informal communication between individuals and groups combines to give a picture of the relationship between library and faculty.

The communication strength matrix

Observed relationships are categorized in the communication strength matrix (see Figure 14.4).

In the diagram 'multiplex' represents the ideal with high integration and frequent communication, which combine to form a rich pattern of both information exchange and influence. 'Bureaucratic' describes situations in which subject librarians might be required to be present as routine practice but which are not underpinned by informal links. 'Low power' relationships will undermine initiatives such as TAPin. Here, the power to influence at a strategic or personal level is weak and support for library projects is difficult to generate. Libraries and subject librarians in this position need to create a stronger communication base before they can successfully embark on a proactive initiative such as the TAPin model. Networked libraries have strong influencing power. One of the outcomes reported from TAPin libraries was greater visibility and invitations to participate at a formal level, thereby moving towards a multiplex relationship.

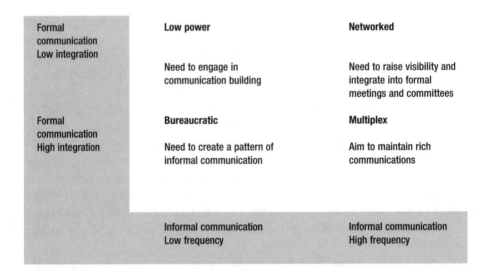

Figure 14.4   The communication strength matrix

INDIVIDUAL RESPONSES

VALUES AND PERCEPTIONS

This section describes end-users' levels of expertise or perceived expertise as assessed by subject librarians and the value which subject librarians place on their own expertise. Personal attitudes have an effect on both motivation and outcomes. The following statements, reported in the research, represent attitudes expressed by subject librarians about academics' use of networks:

- 'The technology is easy to use, academics can acquire skills themselves.'
- 'Academics can easily acquire the skills they need from colleagues.'
- 'Academics only need networked skills at a basic level.'
- 'They already have networks, therefore they are experts.'

Attitudes about the value of subject librarians' expertise to academics are also significant. These statements represent attitudes expressed in the research:

- 'Academics cannot *see* my expertise.'
- 'Academics need advice from technical experts, not librarians.'
- 'Academics do not need expertise themselves, they can ask colleagues for help.'

Attitudes about the expertise and the perceived value of subject librarians conveying expertise to academics combine to form a significant indicator of the relative success or failure of the TAPin model.

The concept of perceived value is informed by the theories of cognitive choice (Kanfer, 1990) – specifically, Vrooms Valance–Instrumentality–Expectancy (VIE) theory. VIE seeks to explain the motivational force behind individual actions. It comprises three elements: effort–performance expectancy; immediate or first-level outcomes; and instrumentalities or second-level outcomes which derive from first-level outcomes. Perceived values are high where all three elements are positive whereas low or negative expectancy creates perceived values resulting in low motivation. VIE theories have generated an extensive literature. Here, they are used solely to improve our understanding of the evidence, and an extensive explanation of or analysis of VIE is neither intended nor attempted.

Low perceived values may occur for subject librarians who believe that their skills are undervalued in their department and their influence is low. In these circumstances, subject librarians believe that effort in implementing the TAPin model will not be rewarded with significant positive first-level outcomes, in terms of gaining appointments, access to the faculty or positive training encounters. Second-level outcomes, such as improved communication, personal profile and personal satisfaction, are therefore unlikely.

High perceived values may occur for subject librarians who believe that they have valuable skills and have influence in the department which is likely to result in cooperation and positive responses. First-level outcomes will be positive and will lead to second-level outcomes.

Perceived difficulty describes subject librarians' views of how easy or difficult it is to use networked information. If it is believed to be easy to use, the subject librarian will consider that offering training is of limited value. If it is seen as difficult to use, the subject librarian will place a high value on offering training.

The perceived value matrix

The significance of the perceived value matrix (see Figure 14.5) is that it addresses the question of what individuals think about themselves and others and what they believe about the usefulness of what they are offering. Figure 14.5 does not represent an objective assessment of the situation, but a subjective analysis of what subject librarians believe.

In the matrix subject librarians in the low perceived value area need to address their relationship with their client community at a fundamental level. This issue contains within it a complex mix of personality, library culture and academic culture which is not addressed by the TAPin model. In fact, the outcomes of

Perceived Value Low	Leads to inaction – negative outcomes.	Action/inaction – mixed results.
	'Academics cannot see my expertise.'	'Academics cannot see my expertise.'
	'Networks are easy to use.'	'Academics are not interested in complicated resources. They only use them at a basic level anyway.'
	'Academics can find out for themselves.'	
Perceived Value High	Leads to action – positive outcomes – communication benefits.	Leads to action – positive outcomes – communication benefits – training benefits for academics.
	'Worthwhile, I made useful contacts.'	'I was able to give them useful skills in networked information retrieval – they value my expertise.'
	Perceived level of difficulty Low	Perceived level of difficulty High

Figure 14.5   The perceived value matrix

implementing the TAPin model are undermined if it is implemented in situations where attitudes equivalent to the low perceived value measure are held.

Subject librarians in the high perceived value area need to test their beliefs within the academic community and adjust their objectives to fit. This process is built into the TAPin model. In the case study libraries valued benefits, such as improved communication and building formal and informal relationships with academics, even if they were found to be relatively expert users, were gained.

PERSONAL ORIENTATION

Personal orientation describes the individual's perspective on their role and the way this determines their interaction with others.

Physical orientation describes a curatorial approach that focuses on maintaining collections, and being in physical proximity with the collection to offer guidance and advice to users who choose to visit. This is a reactive approach that emphasizes physical presence and physical place.

A communication orientation describes subject librarians who are proactive in communicating with users. Activities that evidence this approach are providing information skills training to students and staff, with an emphasis on global communicating skills over and above particular, local physical space/resources.

The degree of personal choice is limited by how much freedom of action is permitted within the institution. Resources limit choice. Activities in the communication mode may be incompatible with an excessive workload, such as cataloguing or service management duties.

In an uncertain, changing environment a communication orientation is preferable. It offers the opportunity for informal and formal face-to-face contact with users and allows the possibility of a two-way flow of information from the library to the academic department and vice versa.

Subject librarians experience dissonance when a communication orientation is constrained at a time of uncertainty, when users need a proactive advice network. Models such as TAPin need to be considered in the context of personal orientation. Both personal orientation and resource limitations can combine to create conflict.

CONCLUDING THOUGHTS

Reflecting on this chapter prompts some additional thoughts. Perspectives are different at each level within an organization – for example, the head of library services has a different perspective from the subject expert. A complete picture requires a cumulative assembly of views and opinions. Understanding the communication environment is a cumulative process that begins at an individual level and builds towards an understanding of the organizational response to networks. Reflecting on culture in the way proposed here is a starting-point – not an end in itself. It requires a desire to change, or an acceptance that an autonomous process of change has been initiated, and therefore a willingness to contemplate new ideas and less attractive current realities.

REFERENCES

Bishop, A.P. and Star, S.L. (1996), 'Social informatics of digital library use and infrastructure', in M.E.W. Williams (ed.), *Annual Review of Information Science and Technology*, Medford, NJ: Information Today.

Kanfer, R. (1990), 'Motivational theory and industrial and organizational psychology' in M.D. Dunnette and L.M. Hough (eds), *Handbook of Industrial and Organizational Psychology*, Palo Alto, CA: Consulting Psychologists Press.

Kling, R. and Allen, J.P. (1996), 'Can computer science solve organizational problems? The case for organizational informatics', in R. Kling (ed.), *Computerization and Controversy: Value Conflicts and Social Choices*, (2nd edn), London: Academic Press.

Kling, R. and Star, S.L. (1997), 'Human centered systems in the perspective of organizational and social informatics', http://www.ifp.uiuc.edu/nsfhcs/bog_reports/bog4.html

15 Change, research approaches and the future

Bruce Reid, William Foster and Matt Holland

INTRODUCTION

If being in a transitional period means that many people are looking very carefully at where we are now in relation to a major factor for change (information and communication technology) and thinking about how we get to where we want to be in that relationship, then information professionals (and perhaps most people) are in a transitional period.

Some view the transition in apocalyptic terms:

> A transition crisis lies ahead. The new information and communication technologies are more subversive of the modern state than any political threat to its predominance since Columbus sailed. This is important because those in power have seldom reacted peacefully to developments that undermined their authority. They are not likely to now.
>
> The clash between the new and the old will shape the early years of the new millennium. We expect it to be a time of great danger and great reward, and a time of much diminished civility in some realms and unprecedented scope in others. (Davidson and Rees-Mogg, 1998: 22)

Whatever degree of credence one gives to radical social, economic and geopolitical predictions of this kind, it is certain that, within our professional purview, designing the information future we want, rather than accepting the one that is thrust upon us, can only be achieved by a combination of proactive awareness-raising, accommodating stakeholder perspectives, cross-boundary cooperation, and the eliciting of refined end-user feedback.

The rapid technological development of the last ten years has provided academic libraries with an opportunity to radically enhance the range of services that they offer their users. Unfortunately, many library users are themselves well aware of the potential of IT, and this has led to some extremes of conflict. On the one hand, many users conversant with the technology expect libraries and their systems to respond immediately to the technological changes of the IT marketplace. On the other hand, there are still many academics from traditional

243

disciplines who have yet to come to grips with even basic IT functions or indeed refuse to have anything to do with them.

Where does this leave the library and its staff? Clearly, libraries can no longer afford to provide extensive 'just-in-case' materials. The rising cost of printed journal subscriptions, the demands from part-time and distance learners, the need to provide electronic resources in competition with the easy access to the Web all require libraries to take rapid drastic action, and most have done so. Migration to third-generation systems using industry standard components is now keeping library systems in line with other computer systems. Involvement in the eLib projects has reinvigorated the profession, providing substantial opportunities for young professionals to use newly acquired IT skills. Yet libraries have recognized that training of their own staff and especially of their customers has become paramount – training to use IT as well as training to search more effectively and evaluate the resource accessed more carefully are perhaps more important than anything else.

Libraries must continue to form the cornerstone of the electronic library despite the fact that a physical library building may become increasingly redundant as information and teaching and learning materials can be networked across the campus, the region or even the globe. This means that library staff must be given the opportunities to keep themselves up-to-date either through specific LIS current awareness services, continuing professional development or even studying for new degrees in aspects of the electronic library at departments of information studies. Without ongoing programmes of this sort the role of the librarian and the library could become marginalized in the future.

Two strategic issues of great importance to the future development of networked information are those of access to technical expertise (or development) and access to content (or resources) in what are often competing HE institutions.

Technical expertise and a developing infrastructure are key functional areas, and their absence or stagnation in an institution are often both symptom and cause of an inability to cope with new technology. However, the emergence of networking could be said to export the technical problems back to source (that is, the supplier), easing the situation for libraries and their institutions and re-empowering subject/information specialists as the technology simplifies and rationalizes.

However, access to content remains a problematic and contentious issue, and it is instructive, even chastening, to use it as a touchstone for particular developments. The National Electronic Site Licence Initiative (NESLI), for example, is undoubtedly a 'Good Thing', assuming that all academic libraries have the same digital needs, but it could be argued that its emphasis on hard science journals favours 'old' universities.

Taken together, these two issues allow us to envision a scenario in which the cultural legacy may overwhelm weaker institutions, as those with low tech struggle to wire up, whilst those who are high-tech, well resourced and prestigious tap into global content on the back of global networks, using nationally distributed resources. Might there be an argument for differential funding for the basics for smaller, newer institutions to permit them to compete?

As the impact of networked information widens and deepens a major responsibility of information professionals will be to remain clearsighted, sceptical and flexible in response to the sometimes self-serving and disingenuous political and social pressures that have accompanied, and will continue to accompany, that impact. In particular, the profession must ensure that provision and access improve, rather than degrade. Improvement is not inevitable. Ensuring it will often require effective research skills. An instructive, and sometimes chastening, spot test that one of the editors has occasionally used over the years, as a kind of progress index, is to reassess the present cost and feasibility of the SDI (selective dissemination of information) services offered manually at Aston University *circa* 1975 (Vincent and Seals, 1975). The reader is invited to try it.

COLLABORATION AND NETWORKED COMMUNICATION

To some extent, digital library research is directed at enabling change in library practice to fit the new networked environment, or at understanding the unplanned effects on professional practice of networked technology in the workplace. One significant, but subtle, change is the information professional's relationship with colleagues in other professional communities. An appropriate label to describe the basis of this new relationship might be 'collaborative working'.

Partners are a required element for funding in many digital library initiatives. The preparation of bids for European funding starts with a search for suitable partners. One service offered to potential European bidders is a partner-locating service. The requirement for partners reflects many different factors: the size of projects; the need to utilize a mix of expertise; and the political imperative of involving people from preferred locations or backgrounds. Many of these factors will be familiar to those who work on large projects in other areas of activity – for example, in scientific research. It could be argued that such partnerships are marriages of convenience undertaken to secure resources. Nevertheless, funding authorities still need to be convinced that the partnership is genuine.

A partnership describes individuals or a group joining together to achieve a common objective. Collaboration is the positive and creative outcome of sharing

245

within partnerships. Collaborative working is proposed as one of the benefits derived from the eLib experience. In the digital library context this nearly always includes information professionals and technical experts. This symbiotic collaboration (Ring, 1995) reflects a situation to which each partner brings a different element of the solution. User-centred philosophies that underpin digital library research will also include client communities as partners. Symbiotic collaboration has transformed the traditionally passive relationship between librarian, technician and user into a proactive, creative partnership that encourages sharing skills but erodes traditional roles. The question is not who you are but what you can contribute. The librarian remains the coordinator of the relationship but

> ... is perhaps more that of the entrepreneur, who sees a match between issues presented by the collections for which he or she is responsible and the technical possibilities whose range and potential increase daily. (Carpenter *et al.*, 1998: 27)

Anecdotal evidence suggests that this also describes the experience and practice of information professionals outside the framework of digital library projects, or even that this is the common experience of the transformation in working practice engendered by networked technologies. Examples may include: a lecturer in information science who participates in learning groups with students to learn about Web publishing, with the aim of creating a shared resource for teaching and learning; an academic librarian responsible for the task of digitizing an archive working with colleagues teaching in computing and media; or an academic librarian participating in projects to catalogue and preserve images on the theme of the history of science.

Collaborative working is initiating a process of change in the methodologies used both to understand others and our own professional practice. TAPin deployed the full continuum of research methods, statistical analysis, questionnaires, participant observation, case studies and qualitative analytical techniques – from a positivist to exploratory/inductive perspective. More interesting and potentially more significant are the knowledge areas reflected in the scholarly experience of each of the participants in the project. Different methodologies are the manifestation of a wider and more stimulating process of breaking down boundaries between library and information science and other disciplines.

REFERENCES

Carpenter, L., Shaw, S. and Prescott, A. (1998), *Towards the Digital Library: The British Library's Initiatives for the Access Programme*, London: The British Library.

Davidson, J.D. and Rees-Mogg, W. (1998), *The Sovereign Individual*, London: Pan Books.

Ring, P.S. (1995), 'Collaboration', in N. Nicholson, R.S. Schuler and A. Van de Ven (eds), *The Blackwell Encyclopedic Dictionary of Organizational Behavior*, London: Blackwell.

Vincent, I. and Seals, J. (1975), 'A manual current awareness service at the University of Aston', *Aslib Proceedings*, **27** (6), June, 247–61.

Glossary

AAU	Association of American Universities (USA). http://www.aacu-edu.org/
Access	A database software product produced by Microsoft™.
Acrobat Reader	Adobe Acrobat (qv).
AD	access and delivery.
ADAM	Art, Design Architecture and Media. An eLib project in the 'access to network resources' strand of the programme, involving the creation and maintenance of a subject gateway to HE information resources in art and design. http://adam.ac.uk/
Adobe Acrobat™	A suite of computer programs produced by Adobe Systems, used to create, enhance and read PDF (qv) documents. http://www.adobe.com/
ADONIS	A CD-ROM-based article delivery service using scanned images. Comprises nearly 700 international biomedical journals, from over 70 publishers, published since 1991, http://www.adonis.nl/
AIMS	Advanced International Management Seminar.
AIOPI	Association of Information Officers in the Pharmaceutical Industry (UK). http://www.aiopi.org.uk/
ALA	American Library Association (USA). http://ala1.ala.org/
ANR	The 'access to network resources' strand

	of projects under the auspices of the eLib Programme (qv).
Ariadne	An eLib project in the 'training and awareness' strand of the programme. *Ariadne* is a monthly newsletter produced in both print and electronic form. It provides information on Internet resources in general, and the eLib programme in particular. http://www.ariadne.ac.uk/
Aslib	Originally the Association of Special Libraries and Information Bureaux; now the Association for Information Management. http://www.aslib.co.uk/
ATHENS	Authentication Systems. A JISC (qv)-funded project, ATHENS is an access management system that prevents unregistered or unauthorized users gaining access to electronic resources. http://www.athens.ac.uk/
AT&T	American Telephone and Telegraph, Inc. One of the largest USA telecommunication providers. http://www.att.com/
AUT	Association of University Teachers (UK). http://www.ucl.ac.uk/unions/AUT/index.html
Battelle Memorial Institute	Independent US institute founded in 1925 which serves industry and government in the generation, application and commercialization of technology. The Institute supports research and development activities of clients in 30 countries. http://www.battelle.org/default.htm
BC	bibliographic control.
bibliographic database	An online file containing descriptions of books, journal articles, reports, conference proceedings, often including an abstract or even full text. Usually searchable by author, title, descriptors

	and, often, free text. A library's bibliographic catalogue made publicly available via a network is referred to as an OPAC (qv).
BIDS	Bath Information and Data Service. A JISC (qv)-funded service, BIDS acts as an information utility which offers fixed-cost access to a variety of online databases with licence agreements arranged through CHEST (qv). Databases include Compendex, ISI (qv) citation indexes, Embase (Excerpta Medica), Inspec. http://www.bids.ac.uk/
Biz/ed	Business Education on the Internet. An eLib project in the 'pre-prints' strand of the programme. This project provides a free information service about business studies held on computers around the world. http://www.bized.ac.uk/
BLCMP	Originally Birmingham Libraries Co-operative Mechanisation Project, an OSTI (qv)-funded cooperative cataloguing project; later BLCMP Library Services, now Talis Information Ltd – a provider of automated library management systems and a bibliographic database of 17 million MARC catalogue records (UK). http://www.blcmp.org.uk/
BLRIC	British Library Research and Innovation Centre
Boolean logic	The use of the operators 'AND', 'OR' and 'NOT' in information retrieval systems.
BOPCAS	British Official Publications Current Awareness Service. http://www.soton.ac.uk/~bopcas/
BP	British Petroleum plc. http://bp.com/
BPR	business process re-engineering. A corporate initiative designed to increase the effectiveness of information communication and dissemination.
browser	A computer program that enables users

to read World Wide Web (qv) pages encoded with HTML (qv).

BRP Boundary role person. An individual who acts as a link between an organization's or group's internal and external environment.

BT British Telecommunications plc. http://www.bt.co.uk

BUBL Bulletin Board for Libraries. A JISC (qv)-funded service, BUBL is a Web-based information service to the academic and research communities. Its hierarchical interface provides access to a classified list of preselected Web sites, reference section, directories, mailing lists, electronic journals, texts and other services, such as retrieval engines. http://www.bubl.ac.uk/

BUFVC British University Film and Video Council. http://www.bufvc.ac.uk/

BUILDER Birmingham University Integrated Library Development and Electronic Resource. An eLib project in the 'hybrid libraries ' strand of the programme aiming to develop a working model of the hybrid library within both a teaching and research context. http://builder.bham.ac.uk/

C&IT communications and information technology. Dearing's (qv) alternative term for ICT (qv).

cache In the context of this book, a locally or regionally held copy of a global electronic resource that improves access to it and helps reduce congestion on the network. Also used to describe a small, fast memory holding recently accessed data, designed to speed up access to the microprocessor.

CAIRNS Cooperative Academic Information Retrieval Network for Scotland. An eLib project funded under the 'large-scale resource discovery' strand of the programme, aiming to integrate the 25 Z39.50 (qv)-compliant catalogues or information services of CAIRNS sites across Scotland into a functional and user-adaptive testbed service. http://cairns.lib.gla.ac.uk

CAL   computer-assisted learning.

CALIM   Consortium of Academic Libraries in Manchester – a regional cooperative. http://rylibweb.man.ac.uk/calim/

CAS/IAS   Current Awareness Service/Individual Article Service. Current databases containing details of articles published in a very large number of journal titles. They are backed by document delivery services, and are accessible by various routes on subscription (costs vary). Services such as searching regularly to a user profile and tagging journals held by customer institutions are also available.

CATRIONA II   An eLib project in the 'access to network resources' strand of the programme. The project investigates the approaches to the management and creation of institutional and departmental electronic resources in Scottish universities. http://catriona2.lib.strath.ac.uk/catriona/

CATs   colleges of advanced technology.

CD-Rom   Compact Disk – Read Only Memory.

CERN   European Organization for Nuclear Research (formerly called Conseil Européen pour la Recherche Nucléaire). http://www.cern.ch/

CGI   common gateway interface. A method of communication between an HTTP server and gateway programs. Any data sent to the server from the client has to be processed by a gateway program. The CGI handles the transmission of the data between the Internet server and any other program that will use it.

CHEST Combined Higher Education Software Team. A JISC (qv)-funded service, the aim of CHEST is to obtain quality software, datasets, training materials and other IT products for the UK higher education and research community at low prices and on attractive terms. http://www.chest.ac.uk/

CI community information. Also refers to a module of an LMS (qv) that is used by libraries to provide basic information about library services.

CINE Cartoon Images for Network Education. An eLib project in the 'training and awareness' strand of the programme. The project aims to create animated materials to aid explanation and understanding of concepts in a networked information environment. http://www.kcl.ac.uk/projects/cine/

CIRT Centre for Information Research and Training. Part of the Faculty of Computing, Information and English, University of Central England.

CIS campus information systems. More commonly called CWIS (qv).

CITED Copyright in Transmitted Electronic Documents. A European research project concerning ECMS (qv). http://www.twente.research.ec.org/esp-syn/text/5469.html

CLIC The Consortium Electronic Journal Project. An eLib project in the 'electronic journals' strand of the programme. The project will establish a parallel electronic version of the Royal Society of Chemistry's journal, *Chemical*

	Communications. http://www.ch.ic.ac.uk/clic/
client/server networking	A computer network in which the workload of using applications is shared between the user's computer (client) and the network (server).
CLIR	Council on Library and Information Resources (USA).
CMC	computer-mediated communication.
community of practice	The name given to a group of individuals who share the same tasks, interests or tools.
compression utility	Software application designed to reduce the storage space needed for data in a computer by encoding information and reducing redundant information.
COPAC	CURL (qv) Online Public Access Catalogue. A JISC (qv)-funded service, COPAC provides a unified interface to the combined catalogues of the Consortium of University Research Libraries. http://copac.ac.uk/copac/
CSIRO	Commonwealth Scientific and Industrial Research Organization (Australia). http://www.dhn.csiro.au/
CURL	Consortium of University Research Libraries. A consortium of the major UK research libraries, CURL's aim is to develop solutions to the wide range of tasks faced in the provision of library material for research, http://www.curl.ac.uk/
CWIS	campus-wide information systems. A computer network that extends across an HE campus.
database host	An organization which provides shared access to a wide variety of databases on a timesharing basis (for example, Dialog, ESA/IRS, BRS).
Dearing Report	Report of the National Committee into Higher Education (1997) chaired by Lord

	Dearing, published as *Higher Education in the Learning Society*, 1998. The committee made 93 recommendations directed at preparing higher education for the next 20 years. The report was also made available at http://www.leeds.ac.uk/educol/ncihe/
DeLiberations	An eLib project in the 'electronic journals' strand of the programme. DeLiberations is an interactive, electronic magazine designed to support information professionals in the design and delivery of educational courses. http://www.deLiberations.ac.uk/
DES	Department of Education and Science; now the Department for Education and Employment (UK). http://www.dfee.gov.uk/
diffusion theories	Theories aimed at studying the diffusion of innovations in organizations and society. Diffusion theories developed from studies in the USA during the 1940s, which looked at the diffusion of agricultural innovations. These theories were subsequently used widely in marketing, communication and geography. Everett Rogers in his book, *Diffusion of Innovations* (1983), made a definitive statement of diffusion of innovation theory. The theory centres on three aspects: innovation–decision process; innovation characteristics; adopter characteristics and opinion leadership.
discussion list	Facility for several parties to communicate over a computer network on a topic of common interest. Discussion lists for the UK's academic community are maintained and supported by Mailbase (qv).
DLI	Digital Libraries Initiative (USA).

	http://www.nsf.gov/home/crss/prgm/ dli/dli2faq.htm
DMU	De Montfort University (UK). http://www.dmu.ac.uk/
DOC	Harrison's Diagnosing Organizational Culture.
DOS	disk operating system.
DSP	data service provider.
DTI	Department of Trade and Industry (UK). http://www.dti.gov.uk/
ECMS	electronic copyright management systems. Systems designed to monitor the use of electronically held copyright material in order to ensure royalty payments to intellectual property owners.
EDDIS	Electronic Document Delivery – the Integrated Solution. An eLib (qv) project in the 'electronic document delivery' strand of the programme. The project aims to establish a software infrastructure for a national electronic document delivery programme. http://www.ukoln.ac.uk/services/elib/ projects/eddis/
EDI	electronic data interchange. The exchange of standardized document forms between computer systems, used by libraries to exchange data with book suppliers.
EDINA	Edinburgh Data and Information Access. A JISC (qv)-funded service providing online data services for the HE and research community in the UK. http://edina.ed.ac.uk/
EDUCATE	End-user Courses in Information Access through Communication Technology. An EU-funded user education website hosted by Chalmers University of Technology in Sweden. http://educate.lib.chalmers.se/
EduLIB	An eLib project in the 'training and

awareness' strand of the programme. The project aims to identify and provide training for the skills needed by librarians to teach others in the use of networked information resources. http://www.hull.ac.uk/Hull/CTLS_Web/edulib/edulib.html

EEVL
Edinburgh Engineering Virtual Library. An eLib project in the 'access to networked resources' strand of the programme, involving the creation and maintenance of a subject gateway to HE information resources in engineering. http://www.eevl.ac.uk/

EIS
executive information system. A system or software product designed to improve the visual presentation of, and access to, management information.

Electronic Libraries Programme
Established as a direct response to the Follett Report (qv) and funded by the Joint Information Services Committee of the Higher Education Funding Council. The programme had a budget of £15 million over three years to fund projects in a variety of programme areas. The main aim of the eLib programme is to engage the higher education community in developing and shaping the implementation of the electronic library. http://ukoln.bath.ac.uk/elib/

eLib, eLib programme
Electronic Libraries Programme (qv), http://www.ukoln.ac.uk/services/elib/background/

ELINOR
The first project to build a working electronic library. The project was based at and partly funded by De Montfort University and ran from 1992 to 1996. http://iierl.dmu.ac.uk/Projects/ELINOR/

e-mail
electronic mail. The electronic transmission of messages or documents over a computer network or the Internet.

This is usually done using a store-and-forward-technique to an individual's e-mail address box.

end-user The person who uses a computer application (such as a library OPAC) as opposed to those who developed or support it. The end-user may or may not know anything about computers, how they work or what to do if something goes wrong.

eOn Project eOn (qv).

ER electronic reserve.

ERCOMS Electronic Reserve Copyright Management Systems. An eLib project in the 'electronic short loan' stand of the programme, ERCOMS will develop an electronic reserve copyright management system capable of working with different electronic reserve managements and providing full tracking facilities. http://www.iielr.dmu.ac.uk/Projects/ERCOMS/

ERIMS Electronic Readings in Management Studies. An eLib project in the 'on-demand publishing' strand of the programme. The project aims to provide reading material in an electronic form to a cross-section of users in management studies. http://www.templeton.ox.ac.uk/www/college/library/erims/intro.htm

Ethernet A local area network Web address protocol developed by Xerox PARC.

ethnography The aspect of cultural anthropology concerned with the descriptive documentation of living cultures. In this context the cultures under consideration are those of particular organizations.

EuroLIB An alliance of three European LMS (qv) suppliers. EuroLib's aim is to coordinate their system development. http://www.sisis.de/eurolib.html

Eurotext
An eLib project in the 'on-demand publishing' strand of the programme. The project seeks to provide a national electronic resource bank of learning materials relating to the European Union. http://eurotext.ulst.ac.uk/

Excel
A spreadsheet software product produced by Microsoft™.

Fachreferenten
German subject reference librarian.

FCA
Fletcher's Cultural Audit.

Fielden Report
A follow-up to the Follett Report, specifically addressing human resource issues. The report is available at http://www.niss.ac.uk/education/hefce/pub94/m3_93.htm

Follett Report
Report of the Joint Funding Council's Library Funding Review Group, reporting on the impact of IT on librarianship and its implication for costs and management. The eLib projects (qv) emerged as a direct response to this report. The report is available at http://ukoln.bath.ac.uk/follett/follett-report.html

front-end
The user interface to a computerized system. The software supporting the front-end may reside on the user's personal computer or on the network.

FTE
full-time equivalent.

FTP
file transfer protocol. A protocol that permits files to be transferred across a network between otherwise incompatible computers.

Future Search
A methodology involving focus groups representing various stakeholder communities, which aims to create agreed ways forward.

gateway
A computer system, or front-end (qv) which allows communication between different computer networks. See also SBIG.

gopher	A protocol (qv) which supports the use of interlinked menus across the Internet. Developed at the University of Minnesota in 1991.
graphics viewer	A type of software application that allows the viewing of graphical files and images.
GUI	Graphical User Interface.
HE	higher education.
HEFC	Higher Education Funding Council (UK). http://www.hefce.ac.uk/
HEFCE	Higher Education Funding Council for England. http://www.hefce.ac.uk/
HEI	higher education institution
host	database host (qv).
Hot-desking	The practice of individuals in the workplace using the same desk and/or computer at different times.
HTML	HyperText Markup Language. A set of tagging formats for the creation of World Wide Web (qv) pages.
HTML Assistant	A software package to facilitate writing files in HTML (qv).
hybrid	Of libraries. Those aspiring to present information resources (whether electronic or print, local or remote) to their users through a single integrated interface.
	Of LIS staff organization. Model in which senior members of staff tend to hold responsibility for both subject (for example, geology) and functional duties (for example, acquisitions).
HYLIFe	Hybrid Libraries of the Future. An eLib project in the 'hybrid libraries' strand of the programme. The project explores how best to deliver the mixture of print and electronic services likely to be required of HE libraries in the foreseeable future. http://www.unn.ac.uk/~xcu/hylife/
hypertext	A system of managing information that

allows apparently discrete elements of data to be connected using associative links. These links may be followed by a simple action such as a mouse click. Used within the World Wide Web (qv).

IBSS International Bibliography of the Social Sciences, available through BIDS (qv).

ICOLC International Coalition of Library Consortia. A body representing the combined membership of over 5000 libraries worldwide. http://Isounix.library.yale.edu/consortia/index.html

ICT Information and communication technologies.

IDEAL International Digital Electronic Access Library. A collection of almost 200 electronic journals published by Academic Press, and available through the Web. http://www.ideallibrary.com/

IIP Investors in People (UK). A national standard administered at a regional level designed to promote high standards in the care for, and training of, the workforce. http://www.iipuk.co.uk/

IIS Institute of Information Scientists (UK). http://www.iis.org.uk/

IMPEL2 Impact on People of Electronic Libraries. An eLib project in the 'supporting studies' strand of the programme. The project aims to monitor the organizational and cultural change during the implementation of eLib. There is an earlier project called IMPEL1. http:/ilm.unn.ac.uk/impel/

IMPRIMATUR Intellectual Multimedia Property Rights Model and Terminology for Universal Reference (Sometimes IMPRIMATEUR). A European research project concerning ECMS (qv). http://www.imprimatur.alcs.co.uk/

INFSWG	Information Services Working Group. A subgroup of the IUIC (qv), formed to investigate the contents of a CWIS (qv) (UK).
INSEAD	Institut Européen d'Administration des Affaires. http://www.insead.fr/
intelligent agents	A software program that uses intelligence to accomplish an assigned task – for example, searching through and filtering incoming mail and reserving items related to a specific subject.
Internet archaeology	An eLib project in the 'electronic journals' strand of the programme. The project aims to establish an international electronic journal for archaeology. http://intarch.ac.uk/
intranet	An information network that provides similar services within an organization to those provided by the Internet and which is not necessarily connected to the Internet. The most common example is the use by a company of one or more World Wide Web servers on an internal TCP/IP (qv) network for distribution of information within the company.
IPR	intellectual property rights.
IS	information system.
ISI	Institute for Scientific Information. Owner of the Science Citation Index, Social Science Citation Index and Art and Humanities Citation Index databases. http://www.isinet.com/
ISO	International Organization for Standardization. http://www.iso.ch/
ISWG	Information Systems Working Group. A forum in which information professionals can discuss issues relating to information systems. http://www.fas.org/pub/gen/iswg/
IUCC	Inter-University Committee on Computing (UK).

IUIC	Inter-University Information Committee (UK).
JANET	Joint Academic Network. The network that links higher education institutions and research establishments in the UK. http://www.ja.net/
Java™	A programming language developed by Sun Microsystems for the creation of dynamic, multimedia websites and Web pages.
Java™ Virtual Machine	An abstract computer on which *all* Java features run.
JFC	Joint Funding Councils of the UK (see also HEFCE). http://www.niss.ac.uk/education/hefc/
JILT	The Journal of Information, Law and Technology. An eLib project in the 'electronic journals' strand of the programme. The aim of the project is to promote through the development of an electronic Journal of Information, Law and Technology and other journals, a discursive electronic culture involving the academic community in the writing and reading of law journals. http://elj.warwick.ac.uk/
JISC	Joint Information Services Committee of the HEFC (qv). http://www.jisc.ac.uk/
knowledge management	A framework or system designed to help companies capture, analyse, apply and re-use knowledge.
LA	Library Association (UK). http://www.la-hq.org.uk
LAA	Library Association of Australia (now the LIAA (qv)).
LAMDA	London/Manchester Document Delivery. An eLib project in the 'electronic document delivery' strand of the programme. The project aims to provide a document delivery service to selected libraries in the London and Manchester

	areas. http://www.ucl.ac.uk/Library/lamda.htm
LAN	Local Area Network
learning organization	An organization that has embraced a new management system founded on the organization's ability to learn and change.
LIAA	Library and Information Association of Australia. http:www.alia.org.au
LIS	Library and Information Services.
LISA	Library and Information Science Abstracts. Published by Bowker Saur, information about LISA can be found at http://main.bib.uia.ac.be/UABASE/info/lisa_en.html
LMS	library management system.
London MAN	London MAN (qv). http://www.lonman.net.uk/
LVIEW Pro	A brand of graphics viewer (qv) software application.
Mailbase	A JISC (qv)-funded service, providing and maintaining discussion lists for the UK academic community. http://mailbase.ac.uk/
Malibu	Managing the hybrid Library for the Benefit of Users. An eLib project in the 'hybrid libraries' strand of the programme, MALIBU aims to develop examples of 'hybrid libraries' offering a range of electronic and traditional services. http://www.kcl.ac.uk/humanities/cch/malibu/
MAN	metropolitan area network.
MB	megabyte. A unit of measurement used to describe the size of computer files, equivalent to 1 million characters.
MCP	Microsoft Certified Professional.
metadata	A term used to describe information about a document or other resource – that is, data about data.

265

metadata tagging	The practice of providing information about an HTML document. This is done by using a piece of HTML code called a <META> tag. The information inserted into this tag is called metadata (qv). This metadata can be extracted by Web servers to identify and index the HTML document. In addition, keywords can be inserted into the tag and used by search engines to find the HTML document.
MIA	MODELS (qv) information architecture.
Microsoft Access™	An industry-standard database software product.
Microsoft Excel™	An industry-standard spreadsheet software product.
Microsoft Windows NT™	An industry-standard computer operating system package.
Microsoft Word™	An industry-standard wordprocessing software product.
MIDAS	Manchester Information, Datasets and Associated Services. A JISC (qv)-funded project, MIDAS provides access to and support for many large and complex datasets such as the UK Census of Population Statistics. http://midas.ac.uk/
MidMAN	Midlands Metropolitan Area Network (UK). A regional computer network.
Millennium bomb	A popular term for the Y2K (qv) problem.
Minstrel	Management Information Software Tool – for research in libraries http://www.dmu.ac.uk/~camile/Minstrel .htm
MIS	management information systems.
model	A graphical representation of relationships between elements of a structure or process.
MODELS	Moving to Distributed Environments for Library Services. An eLib project in the 'supporting studies' strand of the programme. The project aims to develop

	a blueprint for a distributed library service. http://www.ukoln.bath.ac.uk/models/
Music Libraries On-line	An eLib project in the 'large-scale resource discovery' strand of the programme. The Music Libraries On-line project aims to use the Z39.50 (qv) protocol to create a virtual catalogue of music on the WWW (qv) providing access to all the holdings of participating libraries with a single search. http://www.musiconline.uce.ac.uk/
NC	network computer (qv).
Netskills	Network Skills Training for users of the electronic library. An eLib project in the 'training and awareness' strand of the programme, Netskills is a UK-wide network training skills project based at Newcastle University. http://www.netskills.ac.uk/
network computer	A scaled down personal computer used to access the Internet, promoted by Oracle Corporation.
Newsagent	An eLib project in the 'electronic journals' strand of the programme, Newsagent is a personalized current awareness service for library and information staff. http://www.sbu.ac.uk/~litc/newsagent/
Newsgroup	A distributed bulletin board system about a particular topic.
NISS	National Information Services and Systems. A JISC (qv)-funded service, NISS is a major information gateway for the academic community. http://www.niss.ac.uk
NSF	National Science Foundation
NESLI	National Electronic Site Licence Initiative.
Novell Netware™	A local area network operating system.
OCI	Organizational Culture Inventory. A

	methodology for measuring an organization's culture.
OCLC	Online Computer Library Centre. Originally a shared bibliographic utility, it is now a provider of automated library management systems and an online host (USA), http://www.oclc.org/
ODP	on-demand publishing.
ODPH	On Demand Publishing in the Humanities. An eLib project in the 'on-demand publishing' strand of the programme. This is a pilot ODP (qv) project aimed at students in the School of Media, Critical and Creative Arts from Liverpool John Moores University. http://www.livjm.ac.uk/on_demand/
OMNI	Organizing Medical Networked Information. An eLib project in the 'access to network resources' strand of the programme involving the creation and maintenance of a subject gateway to HE information resources in medicine. http://omni.ac.uk
online	Connected to, or available from, a computer system.
OPAC	Online Public Access Catalogue.
OSI	Open Systems Interconnection
OSTI	Office for Scientific and Technical Information. Set up by the UK Department of Education and Science to handle funds for research and development into information and information science, subsequently absorbed into the Research and Development Department of the British Library, now BLRIC qv.
PC	personal computer.
PDF	portable document format. A file format that enables the online reading of documents with Adobe Acrobat (qv) software.

Project Acorn	Access to Course Readings via Networks. An eLib project in the 'Electronic Short Loans' strand of the programme. This project aims to develop a transferable model for the process of providing electronic access to course readings. http://acorn.lboro.ac.uk/
Project eON	An eLib project in the 'on-demand publishing' strand of the programme. The project investigates the issues concerned with the delivery of on-demand publishing to HE students and staff. http://eon.unn.ac.uk
Project PATRON	Performing Arts Teaching resources Online. An eLib project in the 'electronic short loans' strand of the programme. This project aims to develop a system to store and deliver multi-media short-loan material in music on demand to students over a broadband network. http://www.lib.surrey.ac.uk/Patron/Patron.htm
Project Phoenix	An eLib project in the 'on-demand publishing' strand of the programme. The project aims to investigate electronic delivery of course materials to HE students on demand. http://www.sbu.ac/~litc/phoenix
Protocol	A set of agreed rules enabling computer–computer communication.
QUIPS	Quick Information for Part-time Students. An eLib project in the 'electronic short loans' strand of the programme. The project sets out to examine both the benefits and potential pitfalls of digitizing substantial sections of the reserve collections at Merseyside's three university sector libraries. http://www.ukoln.ac.uk/services/elib/projects/quips/intro.html

RADAR	Resource Access Detection Acquisition and Retrieval.
RAE	Research Assessment Exercise. A four-yearly assessment of the published research of British Universities carried out on behalf of the HEFC (qv) in order to determine apportionment of research funding for the next four years.
RAPRA	Rubber and Plastics Research Association (UK). http://www.rapra.co.uk/
ResIDE	ReSearch Information Delivery. An eLib project in the 'electronic short loan' strand of the programme. The project aims to develop a pilot electronic reserve system for the students in the Faculty of the Built Environment at the University of the West of England. http://www.uwe.ac.uk/library/itdev/reside/
REVIEL	Resources for Visually Impaired Users of the Electronic Library. REVIEL aims to ensure that electronic library services are available to visually impaired users. http://www.mmu.ac.uk/h-ss/cerlim/projects/reviel.htm
RIDING	An eLib project in the 'large-scale resource discovery' strand of the programme, RIDING aims to support large-scale resource discovery across the Yorkshire and Humberside region by using the Z39.50 (qv) protocol to create a distributed union catalogue. http://www.shef.ac.uk/~riding/
Robbins Report	The report of the Committee on Higher Education of the University Grants Committee, chaired by Robbins and published by HMSO as Cmnd 2154.
SACA	Scenario-assisted Culture Audit.
SBIG	subject-based information gateway. A website that provides information about,

	and includes links to, other sites containing information regarding a particular subject area.
SBU	South Bank University (UK). http://sbu.ac.uk/
SCI	Science Citation Index. Published by the ISI (qv), this indexing service covers 5000 of the world's most important scientific, technical and medical journals from 1955 and allows cited reference searching.
SCONUL	Standing Committee of National and University Libraries (UK). http://www.sconul.ac.uk/
SCOPE	Scottish Collaborative On-demand Publishing Enterprise. An eLib project in the 'on-demand publishing' strand of the programme which aims to build an electronic resource bank of articles and book chapters in key areas to demonstrate copyright clearance and logistical issues of course reader publishing and online viewing. http://www.stir.ac.uk/infoserv/scope/
SDI	selective dissemination of information. A service provided by many LIS, data producers and commercial agencies to individuals or small groups in which bibliographic or news information matching a specific detailed profile of interest is regularly delivered. It may be manually or electronically executed.
search engine	A program that allows users to perform keyword searches for information on the Internet or an intranet (qv). There are several types of search engine which use a variety of ways to search for documents. Examples include Alta Vista, HotBot, Lycos.
SGML	Standard Generalized Mark-up Language. This provides a publishing

	standard for authors and means of generating electronic texts (BS 6868).
Showman™	A particular brand of combined PC (qv) and digital projection tablet.
SKIP	Skills for new Information Professionals. An eLib project in the 'training and awareness' strand of the programme which aims to discover the factors at work in the retraining of the information professional. http://www.plym.ac.uk/faculties/research/skip.htm/
SLC	short-loan collection. In academic libraries, a collection of heavily used course reading materials, often in multiple copies, shared between large numbers of students on the basis of short loan periods.
social informatics	Study of the way in which information users interact with networked information and with one another in the computer-mediated communications environment.
SOSIG	Social Science Information Gateway. An eLib (qv) project in the 'access to network resources' strand of the programme, involving the creation and maintenance of a subject gateway to HE information resources in the social sciences. http://www.sosig.ac.uk/
SSCI	Social Sciences Citation Index. Published by the ISI (qv), this multi-disciplinary indexing service covers the international journal literature of the social sciences and allows cited reference searching.
STN	A German online host (qv). http://www.fiz-karlsruhe.de/stn.html
Studium Generale	A medieval place of learning to which either teachers or students might and did come from anywhere; it differs from a Studium Particulare in which the members are recruited from the locality in which the institution is placed.

subject gateway	SBIG (qv).
SuperJANET	Updated version of JANET (qv), providing greater capacity (bandwidth) for transfer of data files, graphics, multimedia and so on.
TAPin	Training and Awareness Programme in Networks. An eLib project in the 'training and awareness' strand of the programme, which seeks to improve the quality of academic teaching and research by enhancing the expertise of academic staff in the appropriate exploitation of networked information resources. http://www.uce.ac.uk/tapin/tapin.htm
TCP/IP	Transfer Control Protocol/Internet Protocol. The protocol used for computer–computer communications on the Internet.
teleworking	The use of telecommunication systems, such as telephone lines and computer networks, to enable individuals to carry out their jobs from geographically diverse locations, especially the home.
telnet	A protocol for accessing remote databases or connecting to other Internet clients or networks.
TES	*Times Educational Supplement* (UK), http://www.thesis.co.uk/
TIFF	Tagged Image File Format. A file format used for images.
TOA	type of activity.
TOL	type of library.
TOLIMAC	Total Library Management Concept. A European research project, TOLIMAC seeks to manage access to, and use of, networked resources and services within an institutional or campus context. http://tolimac.ulb.ac.be/
TONIC	The Online Netskills Interactive Course. An outcome of the Netskills (qv) eLib project, TONIC is an online interactive

273

	course of instruction on using the Internet. http://www.netskills.ac.uk/TONIC/
TQA	teaching quality assessment.
TQM	total quality management.
TWI	The Welding Institute (UK). http://twi.co.uk/
UCCL	University Centre for Complementary Learning (Thames Valley University).
UCE	University of Central England. http://www.ucc.ac.uk/
UGC	University Grants Committee (the forerunner of the Higher Education Funding Council).
UH	University of Huddersfield (UK). http://www.hud.ac.uk/
UKOLN	UK Office for Library Networking. Funded by JISC and the British Library, UKOLN is the national centre for support in network information management in the library and information communities, and is based at the University of Bath (UK). http: //www.ukoln.ac.uk/
UNESCO	United Nations Educational, Scientific and Cultural Organization. http://www.unesco.org/
UNIX	A command-driven computer operating system.
URL	uniform resource locator. The standard means of locating Internet information by source name, site and file pathname. http://www.talis.com/
Venn diagram	A diagram using overlapping and intersecting circles to show relationships between mathematical sets. Commonly used to show the effect of Boolean operators (qv) in an online search.
VIE	Valance–Instrumentality–Expectancy. A theory of cognitive choice which seeks to explain the motivational force behind individual actions.

Web	World Wide Web (qv).
Web address	URL (qv).
Web browser	browser (qv).
WebCat	An LMS (qv) module which allows a library to provide a catalogue compliant with their users' standard browser.
WinZip	A particular brand of compression utility (qv).
World Wide Web	An Internet navigational tool, initially developed by Tim Berners Lee at CERN (qv) in an effort to organize both information on the Internet and locally held information by means of a series of hypertext links.
Word	A wordprocessing package produced by Microsoft™.
WWW	World Wide Web (qv).
W3C	World Wide Web Consortium. Responsible for the development of Web technologies. http://www/w3.org/
Y2K	Year 2000 problem. Refers to the fact that many computers have not been programmed to distinguish years by century.
Z39.50	A standard of the National Information Standards Organization (UK), Z39.50 is the standard of a tool that enables the searching of multiple compliant databases with a single interface.

Index

academic information 1, 19–24, 63
academic librarians *see* subject librarians
academic libraries
    automation 27–8, 30
    convergence 63–73, 77–102
    organizational models 19–22
    see also universities
access 16, 35
    attitudes 239–41
    CD-ROMs 30–2
    commercial databases 30–32
    communication media 108–10
    community information 32–5
    culture 11, 231–2
    desktop 13, 35, 46, 49, 51, 155, 166
    electronic teaching and learning
        materials 28, 35–8
    intranet 32–5
    journals 31
    network resources *see* ANR
    OPACs 34–5
    open access 35
    training 54–5
    tools 11
Access to Network Resources *see* ANR
ADONIS 31
Advanced International Management
    Seminar *see* AIMS
AIMS 214
AIOPI 13
ALA 4–5
American Library Association *see* ALA
ANR 47–9
archaeological information 50–51
Ariadne project 54–5
art information
    ADAM project 49
Aslib 5, 13
Association of Information Officers in the

Pharmaceutical Industry *see* AIOPI
Association of Special Libraries and
    Information Bureaux *see* Aslib
Aston University 31
ATHENS 38

Birmingham Libraries Co-operative
    Mechanisation Project *see* BLCMP
Birmingham University 56
Biz/ed project 51–2
blaming culture 213, 217
BLCMP 27
British Library Document Supply Centre
    11, 54

Campus-Wide Information System *see* CWIS
catalogues 36
    retrospective conversion 37
CATRIONA II project 51
CD-ROMs 30–32
change agents 105–15, 130–31
    boundary-spanning individuals 106–7
    change organizations 107–8
    communication media 108–10
    information sources 110–11
    network communities 111–14
    role 114–15
    uncertainty and information seeking
        108–12
change management 72–3
    strategy 158–62
CHEST 37
CINE project 54–5
civic universities 8–9
collaborative working 245–6
Colleges of Advanced Technology *see*
    Universities: exCATS
Combined Higher Education Software
    Team *see* CHEST

277

commercial library *see* special library
Commonwealth Scientific and Industrial
    Research Organization *see* CSIRO
communication 108–10
  modes 232–5
  networks 112–14, 235–7
  see also communication environment
communication environment 225–42
  access library 231–2
  adaptive library 228
  conflict 231
  cultural response matrix 229–30
  individual responses 239–41
  learning library 229
  social/organizational informatics 225–6
  strengths 237–8
  transforming library 228–9
  unresponsive library 229
  see also collaborative working
community information 32
competition 213–15
convergence *see* technical convergence
CSIRO 5
cultural diversity 7–13
cultural legacy 1–14, 21, 245
culture
  academic libraries 19–24
  assumptions 15
  collaborative 67
culture audit 139–51
  behaviour indicators 141–2
  Fletcher's 143–4
  Harrison's 144–6
  methodologies 142–8
  networked information 148–9
  scenario-assisted 146–8
  see also organizational culture
CWIS 32–5
  difficulties 34
  gopher software 33
  WWW software 33

data service providers 37
Dearing report 87
decision making 21
desktop access *see* access: desktop
digital library *see* electronic library
DOC *see* Harrison's Diagnosing
    Organizational Culture audit
document delivery 53–4
  LAMDA project 53
  EDDIS project 54

ECMS 38–9
EDI 166
Electronic Copyright Management
    Systems *see* ECMS
Electronic Data Interchange *see* EDI
electronic journals 31, 49–52, 73
  Biz/ed project 51–2
  delivery format 51
  multimedia 50
  storage format 51
  subscription 50
  see also eLib
Electronic Libraries Programme *see* eLib
electronic library 27, 29–30, 35–8, 46–7
  catalogues 36
  ELINOR 36
  environment 225–42
  evaluation 39, 46–7
  initiatives 245–6
  metadata 36–7
  see also Resources: electronic; Project
    Phoenix; eLib
Electronic Reserve *see* ER
eLib 36–7, 47–57, 73, 92
  ADAM project 49
  ANR 47–9
  Ariadne project 54–5
  Biz/ed project 51–2
  BUILDER project 56
  CATRIONA II project 51
  change agency 107
  CINE project 54–5
  document delivery 53–4
  EDDIS project 54
  EEVL project 49
  electronic journals 49–52
  electronic reserve projects 52–3
  ERIMS project 52
  hybrid libraries 55–6
  HYLIFe project 56
  IMPEL project 54–5, 148–9, 205
  IMPEL2 project 54–5, 83, 90, 149, 209,
    216, 222
  LAMDA project 53–4
  Malibu project 56
  Netskills project 54–5, 107
  newsagent project 49
  On-Demand Publishing 52–3, 119–20
  REVEIL project 35–6
  SKIP project 56–7, 93–4
  training and awareness 54–5
  see also Project Phoenix; TAPin project
ELINOR project 36

engineering information
  EEVL project 49
environments 1–2
  communication 225–42
  special library 153–70
ER 52–3
ERIMS project 52
ethnography 146–8
experiential learning 216–17

faculty librarians *see* subject librarians
FCA *see* Fletcher's Cultural audit
Fielden Report 21–2, 70–71, 79, 92–3
Fletcher, B.C. 143–4
Fletcher's cultural audit 143–4
focus groups 122–3, 203–5
  see also project Phoenix
Follett Report 70
future 243–6

gopher software 33

Harrison, R. 139, 144–6
Harrison's Diagnosing Organizational
  Culture audit 144–6
higher education libraries *see* academic
  libraries
hybrid libraries 19, 55–6, 66
  BUILDER project 56
  HYLIFe project 56
  Malibu project 56

ICOLC 37
IIS 5, 13
IMPEL 54–5, 148–9, 205
IMPEL2 54–5, 83, 90, 149, 209, 216, 222
implementation 161
informatics *see* organizational informatics;
  social informatics
information librarians *see* subject librarians
information management 164–5
information professional role 15–17
information specialists *see* subject
  librarians
Information Technology *see* IT
Institute of Information Scientists *see* IIS
integrated services 64
International Coalition of Library
  Consortia *see* ICOLC
Internet 47–9, 166
  Ariadne project 54–5
Inter-University Committee on Computing
  see IUCC

Inter-University Information Committee
  see IUIC
intranets 35
  see also CWIS
IT 6–7, 164–6, 216
  strategy 30, 221–2
  see also technical services
IUCC 70
IUIC 33

JANET 23, 37, 47
  SuperJANET 47
JISC 35, 37, 47
Joint Academic Network *see* JANET
Joint Information Systems Committee *see*
  JISC

knowledge management 163–4

LA 4–5, 13
LAMDA project 53–4
learning organization theory 207–22
  blaming culture 213, 217
  collaborative learning 212
  competition 213–15
  experiential learning 216–17
  experimental learning 218
  fear 217
  IT strategies 221–2
  learning curve 213–14
  library application 209–10
  management data 215–16
  mission statements 219–21
  risk-taking 217
  support 218–19
  see also TAPin
learning resource centres 64
LIAA 5
liaison librarians *see* subject librarians
liaison officers *see* subject librarians
Library and Information Association of
  Australia *see* LIAA
Library Association *see* LA
Library Association of Australia *see*
  LIAA
library automation *see* technical services
library management systems *see* LMSs
library schools 5–7, 46
link librarians *see* subject librarians
literature review
  change agents 106
  convergence 63–73
  organizational culture 137–51

LMSs 28–30, 38–9
  marketplace 28–9
  open systems 29
London University 8

management information 38–9, 215–16
marketing 161
Martin, J.V.
  five-category organizational model 18
  three-tier category organizational model
    20–21
merging services see technical
  convergence
metadata 36–7
mission statements see learning
  organization theory
modelling techniques 173–9
  see also TAPin
motivation 177–9, 239–41

National Information Service and Systems
  see NISS
Netskills project 54–5, 107
network communities 112–14
network computers 35
networked information
  CD-ROMs 30–32
  culture audit 148–9
  individual responses 239–41
  levels of use 235–7
  organizational responses 228–38
networked libraries
  cultural substrate 7, 24
  network oriented culture 149–51
newsagent project 49
NISS 35, 38
non-professionals 5
North London University 35

OCI 142
OCLC 27, 36, 138
ODP 52–3, 119–20
On-Demand Publishing see ODP
open access 35
organizational culture 137–51
  culture audit 139–40
  culture audit applications 140–42
  see also culture audit
Organizational Culture Inventory see OCI
organizational informatics 225–6
organizational models 15–24, 66
  academic libraries 19–22
  dual model 19, 21

five-category classification 18
function-oriented 18–19
information professional role 15–16, 19
Martin, J.V. 18, 20–21
  special libraries 22–4
  subject-oriented 18–19
  teamworking 21
  three-tier category 20–21
  types 16–19
  university libraries 19–22
Oxford University 8

Phoenix project see project Phoenix
planning 161
plate-glass universities 9–10
Plymouth University see Polytechnic South
  West
polytechnics 11–13
Polytechnic South West 68–9, 72
professional associations 4–7
  AIOPI 13
  ALA 4–5
  Aslib 5
  IIS 5
  LA 4–5
  LIAA 5
  trend analysis 5–7
professional development 168–9
professionalism 1–14, 17
  cultural diversity 7–13
  IT 6–7
  library schools 5–7
  professional associations 4–7
  scholar librarian 3–4
  special libraries 13
  trend analysis 5–7
  US context 2–3
project Phoenix 52, 119–34
  change agents 130–31
  focus group results 123–5
  focus group conclusions 125–6
  focus groups 121–30
  Future Search 132–3
  implications 126–31
  objectives 119–20
  problem solving 132
  stakeholders 121–34
publishing 52–3

RADAR 15
RAPRA 13, 22
readers' advisers see subject librarians
reference librarians see subject librarians

research approaches 243–6
research associations 13
research information 1
Resource Access Detection Acquisition
   and Retrieval *see* RADAR
resources
   catalogues 36
   CD-ROMS 30–32
   data service providers 37
   electronic 21–2, 31, 35–8, 46
   electronic journals 49–53
   management 38–9
   network 48–9, 202–3
   Resources for Visually Impaired Users
      of the Electronic Library *see*
      REVEIL
   subject specific 49
   see also technical services
REVEIL 35–6
Rogers, E.M. 107
roles
   change agents 105–15
   conflict 231
   information professional 15–16, 46
   special libraries 156–8
   subject librarians 19–21
   systems librarian 40
   see also staff
Rubber and Plastics Research Association
      see RAPRA

SACA *see* Culture audit: Scenario-assisted
Salford University 68
SBIGs 48–9
   ADAM project 49
   EEVL project 49
Scenario-assisted culture audit *see* Culture
   audit: scenario-assisted
scholar-librarian 3–4, 20
school librarians *see* subject librarians
SCONUL 20, 33, 70
Senge, P.M. 208–9
SKIP project 56–7, 93–4
social engineering model 173–5
social informatics 24, 225–6
special libraries 2, 5, 22–4, 153–70
   change management 158
   change management strategy 158–62
   corporate initiatives 167
   desktop access 13, 166
   Handbook of Special Librarianship and
      Information Work 23
   host environment 154–6

information management 164–5
IT 164–7
IT training 165
knowledge management 163–4
librarians 156–8
parent company resources 162–7
physical environment 167–8
professional development 168–9
research associations 13
special libraries committee 6
staff 90–96
   problems 90–92
   professional development 168–9
   requirements 92–5
   see also change agents; roles; SKIP
      project
Standing Committee of National and
   University Libraries *see* SCONUL
stress
   academic libraries 12
studium generale 7
subject assistants *see* subject librarians
subject based information gateways *see*
   SBIGs
subject consultants *see* subject librarians
subject expert culture 10
subject librarians 5, 10, 19–21
   attitudes towards 239–41
   see also special libraries
subject resources 49
subject responsibility *see* subject librarians
subject support officers *see* subject
   librarians
subscription 37, 50
SuperJANET 47
systems librarians 30, 39–40

Talis *see* BLCMP
TAPin project xvii-xviii, 13, 149–50, 173–89,
   191–222, 227, 238
   adapting the model 186–8
   change agency 107
   comments about the project 188–9
   evaluation 191–206
   finance 183–4
   focus group discussion 203–5
   impact on LIS 197–203
   impact on LIS staff 193–7
   information modelling 175–9
   LIS culture 191–3
   management 184–6
   motivation 177–9
   networked resource use 202–3

promotion 183
questionnaire 191–2, 210–11
social engineering model 173–5
strategic audit 210–11
strategic audit results 211–20
support 182–3
TAPin model 179–86
training 182
user information need analysis 181
Tavistock Institute *see* project Phoenix
teamworking 21
technical convergence 63–73, 77–102
  case study research 77–102
  change management 72–3
  co-existence 66–7
  Dearing report 87
  evaluation 96–7
  full merger 82–3, 93
  implications 63–4
  influences 88–90
  integrated services 64
  managerial and organizational merger 79
  merging services 79, 81–7, 93
  non-merged models 83–4
  organizational and operational merger 79
  operational merger 81
  physical merger 81–2
  Polytechnic South West 68–9, 72
  reasons for merger 84–7
  recommendations 98–102
  response of the academic institution 77–102
  Salford University 68
  staffing problems 90–92
  staffing requirements 92–6
  UK literature review 67–73
  US literature review 65–7
technical services 27–40
  bibliographic control 28
  CD-ROMs 30–32
  CWIS 32–5

electronic library 35–8
LMSs 28–30
management information 38–9
open systems 29
system development 29–30
systems librarian 39–40
see also intranets
Texas Tech University 66
Training and Awareness Programme in Networks *see* TAPin
TWI 13

UGC 10
uncertainty 108–12
UNESCO 2
universities
  ancient foundations 7
  civic 8–9
  cultural diversity 7–13
  ex-CATs 10–11
  ex-polytechnics 11–13
  organizational models 19–22
  plate-glass 9–10
University Funding Council 70
University Grants Committee *see* UGC
University of Aston in Birmingham 31
University of Birmingham 56
University of London 8
University of North London 35
University of Oxford 8
University of Plymouth *see* Polytechnic South West
University of Salford 68
users 1–2, 52, 54–5
  visually impaired 35–6
  see also social informatics

Woodhead, P.A.
  five-category organizational model 18
World Wide Web *see* WWW
WWW 33–4, 47, 126–9
  publishing 52